Job One

Experiences of New Professionals in Student Affairs

**Edited by Peter M. Magolda
and Jill Ellen Carnaghi**

University Press of America,® Inc.
Dallas · Lanham · Boulder · New York · Oxford

Copyright © 2004 by the
American College Personnel Association

4501 Forbes Boulevard
Suite 200
Lanham, Maryland 20706
UPA Acquisitions Department (301) 459-3366

PO Box 317
Oxford
OX2 9RU, UK

All rights reserved
Printed in the United States of America
British Library Cataloging in Publication Information Available

Copublished by arrangement with the American College Personnel Association

Library of Congress Control Number: 2003114938
ISBN 0-7618-2784-6 (paperback : alk. ppr.)

DEDICATION

To our colleague, Ann Bolger
(1957-2000)

As a great friend, colleague, and Director of Residence Life at Michigan State University, Ann began this book project with us during the spring of 2000. And, Ann is still with us as we conclude this journey and present the finished product to be read and tested by our colleagues.

We recruited new professionals, more senior professionals, and faculty who would share narratives about their worlds of work, introduce conceptual and theoretical frameworks, and enrich readers' understanding of the student affairs profession. Ann was one of our senior professional respondents, a descriptor that is not quite accurate. No doubt, Ann was the consummate professional but would take exception with the senior designation. Although only 43 at the time of her death, she was a wise, experienced, service-oriented, and valued colleague.

Ann's intelligence and enthusiasm for learning were contagious. Regardless of her work setting — Michigan State University, Macalaster College, Chapman University, University of California, Davis — whenever she read and digested a new theory or perspective, she had to discuss it with others. Through these interactions, Ann nurtured students and new professionals — especially those willing to engage, reflect, and improve. She had low tolerance for the comfortably entrenched. During the conceptualization phase of this book, Ann simultaneously challenged our comfortable thinking and encouraged us to take risks. She used her keen intellect, quick wit, sense of humor, and animated hand gestures to influence the book's focus and direction. For these interactions, we are thankful.

Ann knew how to set and act upon her priorities. She loved her son, Nicholas, her family, Boston, sailing, tennis, Tina Turner, reading, and cooking. We hope this book, a priority of all the book contributors, honors Ann and her love of life in some small way. Thank you, Ann.

Jill & Peter
June 2002

iii

iv

TABLE OF CONTENTS

vi

ACKNOWLEDGMENTS

Job One: Work Experiences of New Professionals in Student Affairs would have been impossible to edit without the encouragement and enthusiasm of many people. Chief among them are the new professionals who trusted us enough to say, *Yes, this sounds interesting and signed on to share their professional journeys in very personal ways.* These diverse narratives make a unique scholarly contribution to the profession. We are also indebted to the senior professionals and faculty members, who took time from their busy work schedules, to offer their insights and wisdom. Their theoretical perspectives model the multiple ways new professionals' stories can be interpreted. We invite readers to generate their own interpretations as well.

A theme that permeates nearly all of the new professionals' stories is the importance of colleagues and mentors who have provided invaluable support both professionally and personally. We would be remiss if we failed to mention those who have nurtured, supported, and tolerated us. For Jill, Patricia Kearney, Rosalind Andreas, Howard Mehlinger, and Jim McLeod have served as coaches, mentors, and supporters. For Peter, Marcia Baxter Magolda, Robert J. Silverman, Thomas A. Schwandt have provided decades of sage advice and support.

There are also colleagues at Washington University in St. Louis, Miami University, and The American College Personnel Association whose efforts made this endeavor possible. Celia Knight, Sandy Graham, Linda Marcus, Jan Clegg, Peggy Bower, Michael Cubberley, Stan Carpenter, and Donna Bourassa have made sustained and important contributions to this project. Other important contributors include the thousands of students with whom we have interacted over the past few decades. Their insights about student affairs in general and our effectiveness as educators in particular have motivated us to undertake the writing of this book.

Finally, on the home front, Paul, Sarah, and Michael Schimmele, have provided Jill continued emotional support and encouragement. Marcia Baxter Magolda and Charles and Ann Magolda have been lifelong supporters of Peter and his work. Without these individuals' contributions this text would not have evolved as it did.

NOTES ON CONTRIBUTORS

Rozana Carducci

Rozana Carducci is a first year doctoral student in Higher Education and Organizational Change at the University of California - Los Angeles. Prior to returning to school, she spent four years coordinating leadership development programs at a large state university in the Midwest. This was her first professional position in Student Affairs after completing a Master's in College Student Personnel from Miami University.

Jill Ellen Carnaghi

Jill E. Carnaghi has served as the Assistant Vice Chancellor for Students/Director of Campus Life at Washington University in St. Louis since 1997. Previously, she worked in residential life at the University of Vermont and University of California, Davis as well as in the Dean's Office in the School of Education at Indiana University. She served as ACPA President in 2001. Jill's Ph.D. is in Higher Education Administration from Indiana University. Her M.A. in College Student Personnel Administration is from Michigan State University, and her B.A. in Human Development and Recreation is from Purdue University.

Kathleen Gardner

Kathleen Gardner joined University Housing at Southern Illinois University Edwardsville as an Area Director in July 2002. She previously worked as a Residential College Director at Washington University in St. Louis and as a Resident Director at the Illinois Institute of Technology in Chicago. She received her M.Ed. in College Student Personnel and her B.A. in Journalism from the University of Maryland.

Michael G. Ignelzi

Michael Ignelzi is an Associate Professor and Program Coordinator of the Student Personnel Program at Slippery Rock University. He has been on the faculty since 1994 after working as a student affairs practitioner for ten years and completing his Ed.D. in Human Development and Psychology at Harvard University. His research interests center on professional development and supervision of student affairs staff, and moral/ethical reasoning, development and education of college students. His M.A. is in College Student Personnel from The Ohio State University and his B.A. in psychology is from the University of California, Riverside.

Job One: Experiences of New Professionals in Student Affairs

Diana Jaramillo

Diana L. Jaramillo is working at her undergraduate alma mater as Assistant Director for Campus Outreach at the Career Planning and Placement Center. After attaining her B.A. in Humanities with emphasis in music at the University of Southern California, Diana studied at Miami University where she earned her M.S. in College Student Personnel in1998.

Christana J. Johnson

Christana Johnson is the Assistant Dean of Students and Director of Intercultural Life at Cornell College in Mont Vernon, Iowa. She completed her M.S. in Educational Leadership and Policies Studies at Iowa State University and her B.A. in Psychology and Ethnic Studies at Cornell College.

Susan Jones

Susan R. Jones is an Assistant Professor and Director of the Student Personnel Assistantship program (SPA) at The Ohio State University. She joined the Higher Education and Student Affairs faculty in 1996 after completing her Ph.D. in College Student Personnel at the University of Maryland, College Park. Her teaching and research interests focus on psychosocial identity development of college students, service-learning in higher education, and contemporary issues in student affairs administration. Susan's M.Ed. is in Higher Education and Student Affairs from the University of Vermont, and her B.A. in Sociology is from Saint Lawrence University.

Stephanie Kurtzman

Stephanie N. Kurtzman is the Coordinator for Community Service and Women's Programs at Washington University (WU) in St. Louis. She began working at WU after completing her M.Ed. in Higher Education and Student Affairs Administration at The University of Vermont. Stephanie completed her undergraduate degree in Psychology at Occidental College in Los Angeles.

Peter Magolda

Peter Magolda joined the Miami University College Student Personnel faculty in 1994, after completing a Ph.D. in Higher Education Administration from Indiana University. He teaches research and educational anthropology seminars. His research interests include ethnographic studies of college students and qualitative program evaluation. His M.A. is in College Student Personnel from The Ohio State University, and his B.A. is in Psychology from LaSalle College.

Deborah McCarthy

Deborah McCarthy is currently an Academic Services and Disability Services Coordinator at Southwestern University. Deborah also possesses a variety of experiences in Student Affairs ranging from residence life management to conference planning to marketing and admissions responsibilities. She has an M.S. in College Student Personnel from Miami University and a B.A. in English from William Jewell College in Missouri. She was born with cerebral palsy and works to present disability issues to staff and students in a non-threatening and engaging manner.

Anna Ortiz

Anna Ortiz is on the faculty at California State University, Long Beach. Prior to this appointment she coordinated the Student Affairs Administration master's degree program at Michigan State University. She teaches courses in student development theory, multicultural issues, and administration courses. Her research interests revolve around multicultural education topics and ethnic identity in college students. She holds degrees from UCLA (Ph.D., 1997), The Ohio State University (M.A., 1987), and the University of California, Davis (B.S., 1985).

Kevin Piskadlo

Kevin Piskadlo works as an Academic Advisor in the Mendoza College of Business at the University of Notre Dame. Prior to arriving in South Bend, Kevin was a graduate student at Miami University where he earned an M.S. in College Student Personnel. He received his undergraduate degree in Politics from Catholic University in Washington, D.C.

Molly Reas

Molly Reas joined the staff of KnowledgeWorks Foundation, an educational foundation that works to improve public education in Ohio, in June 2002. She previously worked for the Office of Admissions at Radford University in Radford, Virginia. She received her M.S. in College Student Personnel from Miami University and her B.A. in Psychology and Sociology from Indiana University.

Job One: Experiences of New Professionals in Student Affairs

J. Michael Segawa

Michael Segawa has been the Director of Housing at The Evergreen State College for the past seven years. Prior to that he served as Assistant Director of Housing at the University of Washington. He has been an active participant in a number of professional associations including NASPA, ACPA, and ACUHO-I. His most recent involvement has included NASPA V Regional Vice President-Elect and Chair of the 2001 NASPA National Conference in Seattle. He has a Master's Degree in Student Personnel Administration from Colorado State University.

Rich Shintaku

Rich Shintaku is the Dean of Students at Oregon State University and Assistant Professor in the OSU School of Education's College Student Services Administration and Community College Leadership programs. His teaching and research interests focus on multicultural issues in higher education as well as the contemporary issues of Asian and Pacific Americans. He holds a Ph.D. in Higher Education from UCLA, a M.A. in Higher Education Administration from Michigan State University, and a B.S. in Development, Resource and Consumer Economics from the University of California, Davis.

William D. Simpkins

Will Simpkins is the Program Coordinator in the College Activities Office of Barnard College. He received his M.Ed. in College Student Personnel from the University of Maryland, College Park with an emphasis on student leadership development; his B.A. in English with a concentration in cultural studies is from Virginia Polytechnic Institute and State University.

Patricia A. Whitely

Patricia Whitely has served as Vice President for Student Affairs at the University of Miami since 1997. Previously, she was Director of Student Life at Miami and earlier in her career was very instrumental in the development and implementation of their residential college system. Her Ed.D. is in Higher Education from the University of Miami. Her M. Ed. is in Student Personnel Services from the University of South Carolina, and her B.S. is in Management from St. John's University in New York.

Craig Woodsmall

Craig Woodsmall has served as a Psychological Resident and the

Coordinator for Outreach in the Student Health and Counseling Services at Washington University in St. Louis since August of 2000. He graduated from William Jewell College with degrees in psychology and communication, received his Master's degree in Counseling from the University of Missouri at Kansas City, and is currently working to complete his dissertation for a Ph.D. in Clinical Psychology from Illinois School of Professional Psychology - Chicago.

INTRODUCTION

Peter M. Magolda and Jill Ellen Carnaghi

I have been doing a lot of reflecting this past week about my job and working in general. It is strange, while you are in school, you can't wait to get out and get a job; yet, when we begin working we come to understand that it consumes the majority of our time. I am enjoying my job; however, I feel like I am living for my job. I also have been evaluating Creed University and how it does and does not match up with my values. One major concept I learned in grad school was how to embrace difference and how a diversified group of people can make a stronger bond than people who are all the same. Creed is ethnically diverse, but in other areas of diversity they are very homogeneous.

Christianity is a HUGE thing in people's lives here. Of course there is no room for anyone that is gay on this campus. I find myself being very careful here because people are so strong in their faith that it leaves little room for discussion on certain topics. For example, the only CDs I have at work are instrumental because I do not know if it would offend some people if I listen to secular music. Also, movies…I can't really talk with my co-workers about an "R" rated movie that I enjoyed. In some ways I should have known this coming into this job; I guess I was so excited that I did not think deeply enough about the negatives.

I am not writing this to portray that I am unhappy. I am actually very happy. I just find it interesting that I am working for a school that I would not want my own kids to attend because people are too much

1

the same. This is my first challenge with my job.
 — *Ned, email correspondence*

> I need to talk with you about my job. I have been trying to
> change my attitude/perceptions about it, but I am realizing
> that my attitude is only part of the issue. I just don't like what
> I am doing and would like to look for another job, maybe out
> of higher education. I don't want to be a job hopper, but I also
> have noticed weird patterns in my behavior. I have a hard
> time getting up in the morning to go to work which is VERY
> unlike me. Coming here really zaps my energy, which has
> never been the case with me. I love to work, but I don't think
> this job is right for me. I am fine on the weekends, and I am
> so happy with all other parts of my life, except my job. I have
> been feeling sick lately and I can feel my stomach turn as I
> get in the car to drive to work.
> — *Ramona, email correspondence*

Ned and Ramona are two recent graduates of a student affairs
Master's program. Their respective email messages convey to their former professor initial impressions of their first full-time student affairs
positions. Although these email messages do not generalize to all new
professionals, they do illuminate struggles that new professionals
encounter as they make the transition from graduate school to, what
they affectionately refer to as, the *real world*.

As Ned and Ramona suggest, the process of becoming a new professional is filled with unanticipated challenges. Kevin Ryan's (1970)
observations about new high school teachers in the 1960s are relevant
to new professionals in student affairs thirty years later. Ryan notes:

> The process of becoming a teacher is complicated because the
> new teacher is not simply entering a profession. He [sic] is also
> starting another phase of his life. He is entering the adult world.
> He has to negotiate a new role within the larger society. He
> becomes a taxpayer and a voter. Normally, he leaves home and
> must establish himself in a strange community. He must find a
> place to live, to bank, to buy groceries. He begins to think about
> things like buying a car and life insurance. He must make new
> friends... For some, the process is exhilarating; for others,
> painful. For all, it is new and demanding. (Ryan, 1970, xi)

Becoming a new student affairs professional is life changing — a complicated rite of passage that, as Ryan notes, is often painful, strange, demanding and exhilarating. The new professional must simultaneously juggle concrete and mundane tasks such as registering an automobile with more abstract and intellectual questions such as "What are my core professional values and beliefs?" New professionals cope with mixed feelings of loving their work and believing they are underpaid, overworked, and under appreciated (Woodard & Komives, 1990).

The American College Personnel Association (2001) identified critical issues currently facing undergraduates that influence the daily activities of new professionals. These issues include: multicultural competence (i.e., dealing with difference), academic learning, social justice (including political, economic and social issues), budgeting, career planning, character (i.e., focusing on the individual and addressing issues such as citizenship), spirituality (i.e., meaning of life, faith, religion), technology, health and well-being, consumerism, personal safety, relationships, community, and personal identity.

The current issues facing college students are also some of the same issues that new professionals encounter on a daily basis. Ned, in his email message, struggles with Creed University's narrow conceptualization of multiculturalism and social justice. This has prompted Ned to question his career planning and personal identity. Many of ACPA's critical issues are rooted in Ramona's email message as she attempts to bring into harmony her career aspirations, health and well-being needs, and community expectations. The proliferation of complex and thorny issues bombarding new professionals at warp speed can easily dampen the spirits of competent, energetic and idealistic new professionals.

Barr (1990) identified six issues that if addressed would ease one's transition into student affairs. They are: [1] obtain and use needed information; [2] establish expectations for performance (e.g., soliciting feedback from supervisors); [3] translate theory to practice (i.e., reconciling the dissonance between theory and actual practice); [4] map the environment (i.e., getting the lay of the land, ascertaining the gap between espoused and enacted procedures); [5] establish positive relationships with students; and [6] continue professional growth (i.e., remaining intellectually and professionally active). To address these issues, new professionals should establish expectations, seek mentoring relationships, develop new interests, maintain a sense of humor, and be true to themselves.

Ned heeds Barr's advice. He is gradually obtaining a wealth of new information about Creed University and its students. As he maps this unique environment, gaps between his espoused theory of diversity (i.e., "diversified group of people can make a stronger bond than people who are all the same.") and Creed's lack of diversity surface. Hope and fear collide (Levine & Cureton, 1998) as Ned struggles to be true to his own beliefs and to the university that hired him. Ramona's tensions, left unattended, lead to a humorless metaphorical crossroads as she ponders whether to stay or leave her institution. Student affairs must, as Barr recommends, provide continuing growth opportunities to assist new professionals in navigating their uncharted reflective expeditions. This book is aimed at charting a reflective expedition for new professionals and colleagues with whom they interact on a daily basis.

Purpose and Scope

For new professionals in student affairs, crafting a quality experience for themselves, their colleagues, and students is job one. *Job One: Experiences of New Professionals in Student Affairs* is about the many transitions and questions new professionals encounter as they reconcile their personal and professional beliefs with new job expectations (Toma, Clark, & Jacobs, 1998). Kirby (1984) noted that, "leaving the security of graduate school and entering the job market can be a tense and very anxious time for some. It can also be an exciting and challenging time, as the recent graduate seeks that very important first position" (p. 24). Kirby's scenario is formidable given the evolving and multi-dimensional roles of student affairs professionals, who are expected to be educators, integrators, conflict mediators, disciplinarians, administrators, ethicists, advocates, and loyal community members. Reconciling and assuming these roles is an arduous task as new professionals learn to interact with more diverse student populations in more technologically sophisticated, global, and increasingly conflict-ridden campus environments.

At the heart of this book are the nine narratives written by new professionals. These stories, about their transitions to first full-time work in student affairs, document the joys and angst as they learn the campus environment, meet and develop professional relationships with supervisors and colleagues, explore the limits of their capabilities, formulate professional identities, satisfy supervisors' expectations, assimilate campus and cultural norms, establish credibility, earn respect, encounter dissonance, manage stress, mediate cultural conflicts, build networks, while remaining true to their values and beliefs.

Job One: Work Experiences of New Professionals in Student Affairs also includes three chapters co-written by senior student affairs professionals and student affairs preparation program faculty. These theory-oriented chapters synthesize, integrate, and interpret the new professionals' case studies. The final chapter, written by the editors, provides a cross-case analysis of the preceding chapters, offers recommendations to improve the experiences of new professionals, and discusses implications for practice. In total, the book illuminates issues that warrant the serious consideration of aspiring and new professionals, their supervisors, and faculty in graduate preparation programs in student affairs and higher education.

Narrative Inquiry

This book differs from existing scholarship about new professionals' transitions into the student affairs profession (Barr, 1990; Coleman & Johnson, 1990; Cooper, Miller, Saunders, Chernow & Kulic, 1999; Trimble, Allen, Vidoni, 1991). The most common approaches to assisting new professionals have been for scholars to report findings based on research or for senior practitioners to offer sage advice based on their experiences (Amey & Reesor, 1998). Absent from this body of literature are the perspectives of new professionals, written by new professionals.

Making one's own experiences a topic of investigation in its own right is a unique aspect of this book, new professionals embraced a personal, intimate, and passionate writing style and made themselves the central characters in their stories. This reflexive process and product (i.e., the written story) makes public "multiple layers of consciousness... [where] concrete action, dialogue, emotion, embodiment, spirituality, and self-consciousness are featured"(Ellis & Bochner, 2000, p.739). The nine different stories, written by new professionals (who attended six different graduate preparation programs and accepted jobs in student affairs at eight different higher education institutions), fill this void. These job one journeys offer insights into how graduate school and early professional development opportunities can steer crucial transformations.

People naturally lead storied lives (Clandinin & Connelly, 1994). Yet, the value of storytelling is sometimes misunderstood in higher education. William Foote Whyte (1943) concluded that there is no better way of enriching readers' understandings of what is happening than by telling stories. The narrative inquiry process— generating data in the form of stories, interpreting stories, and writing representations in storied form (Schwandt, 1977) — is part of student affairs professionals' daily lives. Yet too often, scholars and practitioners ignore, bracket, or append disclaimers to life stories, labeling such information as anecdotal. The nine new professional narratives are anything but anecdotal. They bring to life characters:

> embedded in the complexities of lived moments of struggle, resisting the intrusions of chaos, disconnection, fragmentation, marginalization, and incoherence, trying to preserve or restore the continuity and coherence of life's unity in the face of unexpected blows of fate that call one's meanings and values into question. (Ellis & Bochner, p. 744)

Readers vicariously experience the complexities, struggles, chaos, and questioning of new professionals as well as their labors to preserve or restore continuity and coherence. Ellis and Bochner (2000) discuss the benefit of the narrative inquiry process for both authors and their audiences:

> The stories we write put us into conversation with ourselves as well as with our readers. In conversations with ourselves, we expose our vulnerabilities, conflicts, choices, and values. We take measure of our uncertainties, our mixed emotions, and the multiple layers of our experience. Our accounts seek to express the complexities and difficulties of coping and feeling resolved, showing how we changed over time as we struggled to make sense of our experience. Often our accounts of ourselves are unflattering and imperfect, but human and believable. (p. 748)

Writing critical self-reflective stories invites new professionals to better understand their worlds and communicate new ideas to others (McEwan & Egan, 1995). Narratives enable new professionals to articulate what they think and what they affectively experience and ground their thinking in their practice (Kramp, 1995). The lesson learned from these stories challenge conventional wisdom about "what matters" for new professionals in student affairs and offer invaluable insights for graduate faculty and supervisors to alter their practices to be more responsive to new professionals.

Witherell and Noddings (1991) suggest that narratives challenge our ways of knowing and connect the events, actors, storyteller, and readers to each other. Using narratives as a method of collecting data encourages the researchers and respondents to engage in dialogue. Narratives teach and foster learning, making them a springboard for action. Witherell and Noddings (1991) argue: ...

> we live and grow in interpretive, or meaning-making, com-
> munities; that stories help us find our place in the world; and
> that caring, respectful dialogue among all engaged in educa-
> tional settings — students, teachers, administrators — serves
> as the crucible for our coming to understand ourselves, oth-
> ers, and the possibilities life holds for us. (p. 10)

In the chapters that follow, the new professional authors embrace
Whyte's (1943), Ellis and Bochner (2000), and Witherell and
Noddings's (1991) storytelling conventions. Embedded in these narratives are lessons for further discussion rather than non-negotiable and
settled conclusions readers should automatically implement. A careful
analysis of the narratives will enrich readers' understanding of the complexities, paradoxes, contradictions, and intellectual and emotional
struggles associated with becoming new professionals - an important
contribution to the profession.

Audiences

Job One: Experiences of New Professionals in Student Affairs has
four primary audiences. The first audience is graduate students enrolled
in student affairs and higher education preparation programs as they
prepare for the transition from school to work. Bryan (1977) found that
new professionals often fall into student affairs rather than making a
long-term career decision when accepting an entry-level position. The
narratives can assist those in the career exploration process to hear first-
hand from new professionals about their experiences. The second audience is new professionals in student affairs. The theoretical analysis chapters will assist new professionals to make meaning of their complex work
experiences. A third audience is supervisors of new professionals. Burns'
(1982) research found a significant difference between men and women
staying in and leaving student affairs; women depart more often then
men. The stories offer new professionals' perspectives of what makes
them satisfied and successful. This is useful information for their supervisors who benefit from new staff who make a long-term commitment to
the profession. The fourth audience is student affairs and higher education faculty. The book would be a useful text for capstone seminars aimed
at students preparing for life after graduate school.

Genesis and Organization of the Book

Richardson (1975) stated: "There is nothing as sterile as a college where the process of growth and change is confined to the students" (p. 306). This book grew out of a desire to better understand the messy growth process of dedicated, thoughtful, and hardworking new full-time professionals in student affairs — whose growth and development is often overlooked in favor of tending to the growth and development of students.

Barr (1990) argues that:

> Acceptance of a first professional position in student affairs brings with it many questions, concerns, and emotions. Among the questions are those related to competence, achievement, relationships with new colleagues, satisfaction, and enjoyment. Each professional new to student affairs encounters a range of problems and concerns about the future. The process of transition and change brings with it both doubt and anxiety. (p. 17)

In each chapter, questions such as these are posed and explored. Of particular interest are new professionals' *survival* strategies related to: forming new relationships with students, colleagues, supervisors and mentors; identifying professional aspirations and passions; balancing idealism with pragmatism; budgeting time; balancing independence with inter-dependence; tolerating ambiguity, negative feedback, and the unknown; developing savvy political and social skills; and reflecting on everyday practice.

The first three chapters discuss the job search process. In Chapter One, Kevin Piskadlo describes how he used his graduate school knowledge to secure his first position in academic advising. Kevin also discusses the kinds of practical and theoretical knowledge that were assets as he began his full-time career.

In Chapter Two, Christana Johnson describes her job search process highlighting the dilemmas she encountered as a woman of color attending a professional conference, going through placement, visiting campuses, and accepting a job offer in student activities at a small liberal arts college in the Midwest.

In Chapter Three, Kathleen Gardner and Craig Woodsmall discuss complex issues they faced as a dual-career couple trying to balance one another's personal and professional goals as they searched for meaningful career opportunities within student affairs.

In Chapter Four, Susan R. Jones, Assistant Professor of Higher Education at the Ohio State University and Mike Segawa, Director of Housing, Evergreen State College offer their interpretations of these first three case studies.

The next three chapters center on new professionals' early days on the job. In Chapter Five, Molly Reas discusses transition issues from the *ideal world* of graduate school to the *real world* of work and the role of supervisors in this transition.

In Chapter Six, Stephanie Kurtzman vividly describes her early days on the job, trying not to feel like a fraud, balancing her professional needs with job demands, and focusing on the importance of knowing oneself and knowing one's supervisor.

In Chapter Seven, Diana Jaramillo discusses a supervisor-supervisee relationship that went bad. Diana's reflections remind readers of the need for clear and frequent communication, self-reflection, and patience on the part of new professionals.

In Chapter Eight, Michael Ignelzi, Assistant Professor, Slippery Rock University and Patricia Whitely, Vice President of Student Affairs, University of Miami, analyze the three case studies about early days on the job and theoretically interpret these stories focusing on the supervisor-supervisee relationship.

Chapters Nine and Ten focus on identity issues. In Chapter Nine, Deborah McCarthy explores her identity as a full-time residence life professional. This narrative focuses on the ups and downs of balancing a physical disability with her professional identity in relationship to the institution and with her colleagues, student staff, and students.

In Chapter Ten, William Simpkins discusses his first student affairs position. William reflects on his experiences as a gay man exploring the coming out process during the job search process and his first year at an all women's institution.

In Chapter Eleven, Rich Shintaku, Associate Dean of Students at Oregon State University and Anna Ortiz, a faculty member at California State University, Long Beach, synthesize, theoretically interpret, and critique the last three case studies.

In Chapter Twelve, Rozana Carducci explores the decision to leave her first professional job and return to school as a doctoral student in higher education. In addition to the challenges associated with making the transition from student affairs professional to student, Rozana's search for greener pastures also includes an examination of core professional values, the struggle to connect theory and practice, and the emotions that accompany the realization that it is time to leave job one.

In Chapter Thirteen, Peter Magolda and Jill E. Carnaghi use Rozana Carducci's *greener pastures* framework to synthesize the central themes of the new professionals' accounts and the respondents' analyses. This chapter provides specific recommendations for re-conceptualizing staff development opportunities for new professionals. Ways to alter the campus/office ethos to be more supportive of new professionals are also discussed.

In total, *Job One: Experiences of New Professionals in Student Affairs* reveals the multiple ways student affairs professionals choose their careers (Hunter, 1992); offers in-depth profiles of new professionals — focusing on characteristics, attitudes and learning styles (Forney, 1994); reveals core values that guide new professionals' practices (Young & Elfrink, 1991); examines this elusive notion of career fit (Trimble, Allen, & Vidoni, 1991), clarifies successful work strategies that lead to job satisfaction (Bender, 1980; Cooper et al., 1999); illuminates mutually beneficial professional development opportunities for the new professional and supervisors (Carpenter & Miller, 1980); enriches understanding of reasons why new professionals leave the field (Burns, 1982); and explores the multiple ways new professionals forge a professional identity (Young, 1985).

It is our hope that this book will lead to a well-educated and highly satisfied new professional workforce. Carpenter (1990) notes new professionals' unique contributions to higher education in general and student affairs in particular cannot be overstated:

> Student affairs needs a continuing supply of new professionals for many reasons. Changes in theory and research are most quickly communicated to the field and to practice by the most recently educated practitioners. New professionals bring vitality to student affairs organizations and to college and university administrations generally. (pp. 63-64)

Section One Introduction

Chapters One through Three provide readers with insights into how four new professionals pursued their first full-time positions within student affairs. Each story is unique, and as Ryan and Canfield (1970) noted, a complicated rite of passage. Kevin Piskadlo reflects on his graduate preparation and assesses how well it prepared him for a new job, new campus and new home. Christana Johnson highlights her experiences as a woman of color, discussing how she manages the placement process at a national conference and subsequent on-campus interviews. Kathleen Gardner and Craig Woodsmall enter the job search in tandem as they attempt to balance each other's personal and professional goals as each searches individually, and jointly, for meaningful dual-career opportunities within student affairs.

Susan R. Jones and Mike Segawa theoretically interpret this anxiety producing time as graduate students *morph* into new professionals. Securing a dream job is what every graduate student fanaticizes about, yet when this time approaches, the questions, the self-doubts, the *what ifs* can consume the new professional. Susan and Mike, utilizing the work of Robert Kegan (1994) and Marcia Baxter Magolda (2001), provide a conceptual framework from which to interpret the job search processes of Kevin, Christana, Kathleen, and Craig.

1

STARTING OVER—AGAIN:
THE MANY CROSSROADS OF A
NEW PROFESSIONAL

Kevin Piskadlo

When the editors approached me about contributing to this book, I was on the verge of completing my first year as a new professional. To put it simply, what a year it had been. In looking back at my experience, I could not help but feel amazed at how quickly time had passed. My first year at work was a fantastic whirlwind of activity and new experiences, and I never really took the time to reflect on all that had happened. Since accepting the invitation to write this chapter, I have spent considerable time reflecting on my professional and educational experiences and have identified two important themes: being at a crossroads and valuing my formal education.

Constantly being at professional and personal crossroads and having to continuously *start over* since first arriving at college is an ongoing theme for me. Starting over involves saying goodbye to established relationships and being open to saying hello to new ones. The crossroads involves leaving a community and a job with which I am comfortable and adjusting to new environments, cultures, and people. It also includes transcending the rites of passage that comes with each new experience. The crossroads includes the doubt about whether or not I am doing the right thing and making the right decision. Crossroads are often unavoidable: graduation from college, starting a new job, moving to a new city. Other crossroads are optional, brought about by decisions we freely make: deciding on a graduate school, getting married, or purchasing a home. Regardless of how crossroads come about, they are special circumstances where we are required to re-evaluate our lives. Many times crossroads are the trajectories that are needed for both personal and professional development.

The second reoccurring theme centers on my curiosity regarding the optimal use of my formal education: first as a new college student, then as a new graduate student, as a new professional, and now as a more experienced educator. How important is formal education in the real world? The crossroads and my utilization of graduate school education themes are hard for me to ignore and I present them here.

***

I glance at the clock and notice only three minutes have passed since I last opened my eyes. Unlike most mornings when I want time to stand still, today, I am urging time to move a little faster. I start playing little mind games with the clock. I start by attempting to ignore it, pretending not to really care what time it is. Maybe if I do not look at it so often, time will go by faster. In my effort to snub the clock, I re-evaluate what I am going to wear, make a mental checklist of what I need to take, and even daydream about how the day will unfold. I wonder if the renovation of my new office is complete and count the days until my first paycheck, 30 to be exact. I start to worry about whether or not my colleagues, all significantly older and more experienced than I, will welcome me and if my lack of business school knowledge will be obvious to the students. Pushing these fears aside, I look at the clock after what seemed like a good half-hour. The clock's bright red numbers taunt me by showing only four minutes have passed.

Today is not like any other day in my life; I am starting my first professional job. No alarm clock was needed to awaken me for my first day of work. I was only 24 years old, fresh out of graduate school, and on the verge of becoming an academic advisor in the business school at the University of Notre Dame. As I continued to urge the passing of time, I reflected on the many events and the numerous crossroads that led me to this place. Leaving home for the first time and starting college, my undergraduate internships, my resident advisor experience, and my decision to attend graduate school all flashed through my mind.

***

My path to the Mendoza College of Business at the University of

Notre Dame was not one that I would have ever predicted. In 1993 when I left my small suburban hometown outside of Boston to head to Catholic University in Washington, DC, I was looking forward to this new chapter in my life. Excited and nervous, young and idealistic, I held vivid visions of someday working in the hallowed halls of Congress. Unlike many of my friends who looked at picking a major as a confusing and horrible ordeal that would somehow pigeon-hole them into some undesirable career, I knew from the day I applied that I wanted to study political science. I had been captivated by the study of government in high school and interned with my State Representative and later my Congressman, spent four summers as a tour guide in the Massachusetts State House, and volunteered for numerous political campaigns. Like many who enter public service, I thought this would be a great way to help people and to make a real difference in our society.

During college, my interests, thoughts, and goals started to change. My internships, while extremely interesting, were not as satisfying as some of my campus activities. I found myself becoming captivated by the college campus community. From the people to the culture, the intellectual climate, the sights, and the sounds, I felt completely comfortable in collegiate surroundings. Much to my surprise, I started to think of the college campus as more than just a four-year stop on the way to my government career. Instead, it was a place that was made for me and where my future career might be located.

While an undergraduate student, I was extremely active in campus organizations. With a four-year, work-study position in the Career Services Office and two years as a resident assistant, I was becoming more curious about a career in student affairs. I quickly discovered a new passion, albeit an unfamiliar one, that was in striking contrast to my long-standing government plans. Something was drawing me to student affairs, and my work with students seemed to be fulfilling in ways that my previous political positions were not. My interactions with students created real change and affected people more directly than my government internship experiences. Although government can create substantial change, the results I saw in my daily interactions with students were more tangible and satisfying. It was rewarding to discover how my support could encourage a student to seek help for a personal problem or to feel comfortable being away from home when she never thought she would be. Thus, I knew that my interest in student affairs was something I needed to pursue.

After talking with my mentors at Catholic University, I explored the possibility of attending a graduate school program in student affairs and higher education. I found myself at another crossroad in my life. Similar to how I felt when I left my small town for DC, I was again anxious and uncertain about what the future would hold if and when I pursued graduate education. Would I be academically prepared? Was I ready to experience a whole new campus culture? Was I ready to start over again: new friends, new school, new city?

***

As I left Catholic University for a graduate school interview in the winter of 1997, I had no idea what lay ahead. Although I knew I wanted to work with students and thought I needed a Master's degree to do so, I was hesitant to leave behind what was so comfortable for me. I enjoyed school, had many friends, had made progress in politics, and loved living in Washington, DC. Still, I had a nagging feeling that my lifetime dream of a career in politics would be unsatisfying; instead, I decided to explore the college student personnel profession and various graduate school programs.

It was about seven in the morning when I began the ten-hour drive to Miami University in Oxford, Ohio. The air was still fresh, unblemished by engine exhaust, and my car had a very thin layer of frost on the windshield. I had a lot on my mind as I slowly scraped the ice off, feeling the now familiar mixture of excitement and anxiety, the same feelings I had when I visited Catholic University for the first time five years earlier. The previous evening, my friends kept mentioning how I was going to hate it in Ohio and how they could never envision me living in a rural area. Did I really want to spend the rest of my life babysitting students? How could I give up all that I had worked for in government? Friends reminded me that walking the halls of a residence hall would not be as exciting nor as prestigious as walking the halls of our government.

Despite the advice of my friends I continued on, knowing that I was at an important crossroads in my life. Although graduation was just around the corner and I would have to address my future anyway, I could have ignored the feelings I had about student affairs and maintained my initial plans to pursue a career in government. However, I needed to satisfy my curiosity about this field and about Miami University, an institution that I had heard so much about from some of my mentors in the Catholic University Career Services

Office. Since my first year of college, Career Services staff were my surrogate family; and when they found out that I was interested in student affairs, they immediately recommended graduate school.

After what was probably several hours, but seemed like minutes, I crossed over the Pennsylvania border into Ohio. The entire ride was a blur as my mind raced with worries about the future, which upset my stomach. I never would have entertained the possibility of living in the Midwest. Looking around and confirming my uninformed belief that Ohio was filled with farms, I saw miles of pastures, cornfields, and cows. I found this scenery surprisingly comfortable and very Americana.

Miles and miles of farms and cornfields began to make way for signs recognizing fraternities who sponsored particular sections of the highway. Ten hours of driving was beginning to take its toll, but I forgot my minor aches and pains when I saw the first sign that officially announced Miami University. Instinctively pressing on the gas pedal, I sped up a bit, knowing that my journey was coming to an end. I laughed to myself as I passed another green John Deere tractor and drove the rest of the way with a pit in my stomach, continuing to take in the surroundings — cornfields... cows... combines. Despite how odd this seemed at the time, it was then that I became comfortable with my decision to pursue graduate school. This feeling did not preclude me from later pursuing a career in politics, just that there was something important awaiting me at the moment. Something was calling me to Miami University and to this profession and I had to listen.

***

My Miami campus visit was perfect. The beauty of the campus, the residence life practica, the teaching opportunities, the students, and the faculty all impressed me, and I left Oxford knowing that Miami University was where I wanted to pursue my graduate education. There was no doubt in my mind. I immediately withdrew all of my other applications and enthusiastically accepted Miami's offer a few weeks later.

When I first began graduate school, I was unsure about what I was getting myself into. I confronted my newest crossroads, which were numerous and reflected all the uncertainties I was feeling about myself personally, professionally, and academically. Was I ready to live so far from friends and family? Would I make new friends? Would living in a rural town after living in a city be challenging? Was

I prepared to run my own residence hall? Was I even qualified to do so? What kind of supervisor would I be to the resident advisors in my hall? Would it be obvious that I had never done this before? Was I academically ready for graduate work? What exactly was a career in the field of student affairs going to be like? Was a Master's degree even necessary?

I decided to pursue graduate education with few academic expectations in mind. Originally, I viewed my time in graduate school as a rite of passage that one needed to go through to enter the field, a necessary evil. I believed that if I wanted to work in student affairs, I had to get a Master's degree. I was more excited about my assistantship than I was about the academic curriculum. The classes were almost secondary. Sure, I was expecting to learn *how to* be a student affairs professional and figured that I would learn how to run a successful student affairs office. What I found after arriving was my program was going to be more than a student affairs boot camp. In fact, academic expectations were very high and the coursework rigorous. This was not a mere rite of passage, but an important component to becoming an effective professional.

***

During the first couple of weeks at Miami, I concentrated on learning about myself in relation to the university and my residence life assistantship. Staff training, the arrival of residence hall staff, and the eventual arrival of the first-year students were some of the best days since coming to Oxford. I relished the opportunity to work with the men in my hall and to be a graduate assistant, now supervising resident advisors who were doing the same job that I was doing only a few months earlier. However, when classes finally got underway, I was unprepared for what I encountered. I halfway expected classes to be *how to* sessions. Faculty immediately made clear that the college student personnel (CSP) program was anything but practical. Instead, we devoted the first few informal gatherings to discussing learning community expectations and how this new academic community fostered a mutually beneficial educational environment for students and faculty. Although I was certainly curious about an atmosphere of teachers as learners and learners as teachers, the process of mutually developing this community was totally foreign to me. There was a great emphasis on working closely with peers and discussing various issues posed in the classroom.

For the first couple of weeks, I remember that the Introduction to College Student Personnel class was one of my least favorite courses and symbolized some of the issues I was having at the time. It was my first class each week and I would ride my bike to the class feeling a bit testy that this course took me away from my enjoyable residence hall work. Instead of the traditional undergraduate classroom settings where the professor stood in the front of the room and lectured to the class, we sat around a seminar table and talked with each other, judiciously examining various student affairs-related issues. Likewise, instead of writing down copious pages of notes, we analytically examined pertinent topics and critically processed our opinions and assumptions, eventually forming our own beliefs, opinions, and philosophies. During the first couple of weeks, I would take my notebook to class thinking to myself that today was going to be the day when the professor would lecture and the *real* coursework would commence. I soon discovered that the class, notebook aside, had definitely started and that this was going to be a very different learning experience.

It was not easy to give up my strongly held assumptions about what constitutes an academic course. We tended to debate issues without ever coming to clear-cut conclusions, and I would quietly plead for the instructor to end discussion and give us *the* answer. The opinions that I shared seemed to rarely be in the majority. Many of my views, ones that were considered liberal at a school like Catholic University, were often perceived by my classmates as being staunchly conservative. Debate of a case study revolving around a student-proposed Filthy Film Festival is one that I will never forget. It seemed as if no one agreed with my position that a student group activity revolving around the viewing of pornographic films was inappropriate. I was quite dumbfounded and felt alienated from my classmates.

When the honeymoon period of both my residence hall and classes came to an end, a wide range of feelings and emotions engulfed me. I found myself at an unexpected crossroads. Unlike any earlier ones, brought about by grand events such as graduation, this crossroads was quite unexpected. I began to seriously doubt my role in the field and regularly questioned the necessity of a Master's level education for my career aspirations. Some topics we covered seemed unimportant and others seemed down right obvious. As I do when I find myself at a crossroads, I sought the advice of my friends, family, and mentors. They unanimously agreed that I must give graduate school a chance.

Although it took well over a semester, I soon learned the purpose of a graduate education and why it was important for new professionals to be formally educated. I found that the CSP curriculum went beyond the basics to not only teach me the skills that I would need to succeed in student affairs, but also to challenge me to be a leader in higher education. Faculty and assistantship supervisors encouraged me to explore my professional identity and my professional roles. I was soon initiated into a new community of educators whose mission was to provide the right amount of challenge and support to the young men and women with whom we work. Together faculty and students were going to critically examine higher education and the roles student affairs plays in the academy. We looked at the origins of the profession and where it is going. We took time to learn about student development and examine issues students face. From there, we determined how to facilitate a student's journey in the most safe and supportive environment.

My peers were an important aspect of my graduate school experience. They were always willing to take a moment to talk about a project or critique a paper. I had heard horror stories from friends at different universities about their competitive graduate environments. I quickly noticed that the CSP program was anything but competitive. By immediately establishing community norms that favored collaboration over competition, we were able to collectively think about and examine different topics together. Whether it was forming a study group, getting a colleague to proofread my papers, or studying with friends, a community of scholars was more than an ideal; it was a reality.

For me, graduate school served two different purposes. It was a time to critically examine issues facing higher education and student affairs, while simultaneously gaining practical experience through structured assistantships and practica. As I reflect about my classes, whether they were in student development theory, organizational development theory, or educational anthropology, each course addressed the many complexities of student affairs. Graduate school also afforded me the opportunity to grow interpersonally, intrapersonally, as well as cognitively. Faculty and peers constantly challenged me to examine topics more critically, to write well, and to apply what I learned in class to my assistantships. Congruent with the values that we discussed as important for undergraduate students, I was receiving an education that addressed my own growth and development.

My time as a graduate student was extremely fulfilling and I graduated feeling prepared to begin my career. Leaving Miami University was another crossroads; it was not an easy task. I had fallen in love with the community, and the school represented many of my own values and beliefs. I also grew to enjoy the academic component of student affairs and was going to miss the classroom interactions. Similar to my experiences at Catholic University, I was happy at Miami, had made a lot of friends, had made important contributions in my assistantship, and was enjoying Oxford. Graduation, however, brought me to yet another crossroads. Leaving Miami would once again subject me to the task of establishing a new identity in a new city and at a new school. I again had the worries and fears that the unknown typically evokes.

***

As I am shaken from my daydream about my first trip to Miami and my experience there, I again find myself on the morning of my first day on the job. With a quick look at the clock, I get up and prepare for the first day of my professional career. For the first time in several months, there was little else on my mind. After years of schooling, countless papers and exams, and self-reflection *ad nauseum*, I had finally arrived. It was July 1, 1999 and with my new Master's degree in hand, I officially became a new professional.

As I drove toward work that day, leaving early of course, I recall that a wide range of emotions overcame me. On one end of the spectrum was extreme exhilaration, excitement to have completed graduate school with a lot of knowledge. I was ready to practice all of the things that I had learned and experienced. Yet, I was also very nervous, uneasy to be leaving the friendly, comfortable, and nurturing confines of school. For the first time in my life, I was no longer a student.

***

From atop the dome, the Blessed Virgin Mary overlooks the campus that is named in her honor, and the beauty of the surroundings engulfed me. I was well aware of the school's reputation and the legends that preceded me, catching even myself being mesmerized by the beautiful golden dome, the peaceful grotto, the legendary football stadium, and the immense library. The university's values and mission statement were congruent with my beliefs about education and about the Catholic ethic of care, which I sometimes felt conflicted with the *Miami Way* and the limitations of a public university. The fact that the University classified advisors as members of the faculty left me with the impression that I was an educator, something I believe all student affairs professionals are. My supervisor assured me that there would be an opportunity to teach after I settled into my new position. Since I had fallen in love with teaching at Miami, I knew that a professional position where teaching was one of my responsibilities was a very important component for me.

***

I entered my new work environment thinking *Notre Dame is a great fit*. As I exited my car, I tried diligently to remain cool, calm and collected, reminding myself that I was well prepared for what lay ahead. I was entering a field that I felt passionately about and was excited at the prospect of working with students. Besides, I was confident my graduate education had prepared me well. I knew my Chickering vectors and could *layer* my developmental theories when applying them to practice. There were D'Augelli, Kegan, and a number of other theorists whom I could draw upon in my work to help students. I had studied various management theories and looked forward to being part of an *open system* where colleagues shared ideas and I would be an important team member. I had examined various student cultures and was looking forward to observing the Notre Dame student subcultures.

As I confidently walked to the main entrance, I gazed up at the golden dome, brilliantly shining in the sunlight. At that moment I felt a chill go up and down my body. "Let's get started," I thought as I entered the large foyer.

Over the past couple of years, as I have delved deeper into my career at Notre Dame, my graduate school-inspired idealism has met the harsh realities of professional life and I barely have had time to notice. Starting a new position meant that I had a number of crossroads that dominated most of my attention during my first year on the job. I had moved to a new part of the country, starting over in a place where I did not know anyone. I was living off campus for the first time, no longer benefiting from the cozy and supportive campus environment. I also needed to adjust to a new office, new co-workers and an unfamiliar campus culture while trying to create my own professional identity.

When I graduated, degree in hand, I was filled with immense excitement. Like a new athletic recruit prior to the first days of practice, I envisioned myself on the cusp of becoming a star in the field of student affairs. I had lofty plans of being a change agent; but after two years, I feel like I have been merely a facilitator of the status quo. I knew my student development theories and was prepared to apply them; however, I quickly discovered that I was the only person in my office who knew them. In fact, decisions, of which I was rarely a part, were never made with these theories in mind. I was an opponent of in loco parentis and am almost ashamed to admit that our system at times embraces the concept. During graduate school, I studied the division between academic affairs and student affairs and hoped to bridge this gap. Instead, I note with much embarrassment, I know few members of the Notre Dame student affairs staff as there is little collaboration between them and the business school. I could not but wonder if my two years in graduate school were in vain. To be an academic advisor, does someone really need to earn a graduate degree?

While things are not necessarily the same as I envisioned them, still I would never trade my graduate experience. When I left school I expected to be a major player on my new campus. I examined all of the pertinent issues and formed my own ideas, theories, and philosophies that I was excited to try in my first job. I left graduate school with the idea that I was not only supposed to be an agent of change but that I had made a commitment to be one.

What I soon realized at Notre Dame was that I was merely one person within a system that has been in existence for a very long time. No new philosophy or theory, despite how cutting edge and exciting I believed them to be, was going to easily infiltrate the long-held paradigms of my more seasoned colleagues. Basically, my entry-level job is often just that: entry level. As such, I am often at the mercy of the organization. I soon found myself being the cog in the machine that I vowed never to be.

Where does this all lead me? Despite how negative some of my observations may be, not all is lost and writing this paper helped me to realize that. It is hard to come to terms with the idea that I am not going to immediately become the mover and shaker that I had envisioned when I first went to school and that I dreamed about when I left. I realize that I must relax and take advantage of all the experiences that I have been afforded thus far.

I still believe strongly in what we do as student affairs professionals and believe that our graduate programs are the best way to prepare to do them. When you are in the trenches of the everyday job, you lose perspective on the things that you do. Although the Chickering vectors may not be discussed in staff meetings, the knowledge of student development theory is so ingrained in my psyche that it does inform my practice. I reviewed the syllabus I use in the undergraduate course I teach and see theory informing how I structure my class. I look at the peer-tutoring program I helped coordinate and I see theories there. I also see it most importantly in my advising and daily interaction with students. Whether it is working with a student who has not developed purpose or working with a student who is still struggling with his or her sexual identity, the theories I learned are always being referenced. Although I may no longer cite the theorists and scholars, it is impossible for me to go a day without using them to inform my work with students. Undoubtedly, the knowledge and use of theory make me more effective in being a student advocate.

My graduate education has helped me develop into the professional that I am today and the one that I will be in the future. However, I needed more from my graduate program to help me make a better transition between school and work. While my graduate program prepared me to think of myself as an educational leader, I needed to learn how to better navigate my first professional job. While programs should not ignore some of the more practical aspects of preparation, I also share the responsibility to become more patient with my first position and to slowly encourage change while gaining more experience.

Now that I have been working for a couple of years, I am once again at a crossroads. As I have alluded to, I am extremely grateful for my experience in student affairs thus far and am confident that I have become part of a profession that I truly value. I am still trying to figure out where it is that I may fit within this whole field, and I look forward to gaining more work experience. Over the past several years, I have been able to be involved in some incredible experiences. Since my years as an undergraduate student, I have had the opportunity to work with an amazing group of inspiring mentors in the field, individuals who have provided me with ambitious goals. From my assistantships and practica to my job now, I have been able to apply the things that I have learned in class to my various work responsibilities. My graduate education has greatly influenced my practice as an academic advisor and has allowed me to create seamless learning environments not only for the students with whom I worked, but also myself.

Three years into my job I am admittedly getting restless, ready for some new challenges. A crossroads lies ahead as I try to decipher where I want to go from here. As I look forward to greater responsibilities, I am preparing to start all over – again.

2

ARE THEY HIRING ME BECAUSE OF THE COLOR OF MY SKIN? THE JOB SEARCH AND ETHNIC FIT

Christana Johnson

"You will only do one job search of this magnitude during your career." This remark was made by a student affairs staff member at Iowa State University during the winter term in my second year of my Master's program. While this was meant to be comforting and reassuring, I thought if this is my only major job search, then I better get it right. I realized my opportunities were limited by the parameters I had already placed on my search. Due to individualized attention during my undergraduate studies at Cornell College, I preferred to work at a small private liberal arts institution. Working at a mid-sized public institution during a summer internship and attending a large public institution to complete my Master's degree, I knew how easy it was for students to slip through the bureaucratic cracks. I wanted to be certain that consistent, daily, and meaningful student contact would be a staple of my professional life. The second criterion, although not as crucial, was to experience life on a coast, since I had lived in the Midwest most of my life.

Keeping these parameters in mind, I also had several worries. First, I had neither a resume nor cover letter. I asked two of my mentors for their resumes to use as examples to construct my own. These mentors, in addition to my faculty advisor, reviewed and critiqued my resume until it was just right. I remember consulting with other graduate students about the type of paper we were going to use; a few of us even went shopping for paper together. Knowing employers would base their first impressions of us from how we looked on paper, we took pains to make the best first impression possible.

In retrospect, I cannot say whether all the energy I put into selecting just the right resume paper had an impact on employers. When the tables turned and I became the employer, I was more concerned what the resumes said about the candidates than the paper on which they were printed. However, at the time, my resume paper was just as important to me as what my resume said about me.

For me, a critical concern centered on being a woman of color. I did not want to be labeled or pigeonholed into only being able to work with students of color. I had a strong desire to work with this particular student population, but not exclusively. I wanted no limitation placed on my career before it even began. To prevent this, I did not apply for positions in multicultural or minority student affairs. Since my long-term career goal is to be a senior student affairs officer, I applied to generalist positions in residence life and student activities in order to build a solid foundation.

Another concern, and perhaps my greatest fear, was appearing to be *too ethnic* during the interview process. Most of the people who know me, especially African Americans, would never say that about me. However, growing up black in predominant white neighborhoods and attending predominant white schools all my life has made me very sensitive to the negative stereotypes that are commonly associated with my race. I was raised always to try my hardest to succeed. Sometimes that meant trying twice as hard as my white schoolmates. I also learned at a very early age how to adapt to my surroundings. I knew I would have to employ self-preservation defense mechanisms to remain true to myself and my heritage in the face of what I felt mainstream society said I should look and act like in my job search. I knew the majority of those interviewing me would be white. Of course, I had encountered other black female professionals who dressed and styled their hair as they chose, but they were all at the mid-management level and, in my view, already had job security.

Would a black woman with braided hair and no previous professional experience, who attended graduate school directly after completing her undergraduate degree, put off potential employers? I did not want to take the risk. Thus, I purchased more conservative interview attire. I even considered changing my hairstyle from the way I usually wore it, in braids, to a contemporary look, whether that be natural or straightened. Looking back, these issues and my actions seem silly, maybe even extreme in some way. However, comments I had heard from my white colleagues and an African American male mentor, who placed strong emphasis on appearances during interviews, created a great deal of stress at the time. Fortunately, I confided in another mentor of mine (an African American woman) who assured me that my hairstyle would be the last thing most employers would be thinking about, if they thought about it at all. And if they judged me unacceptable based upon my hairstyle, I probably would not want to work for them anyway.

My mentors reminded me of something important: I have never been one to change myself simply to be more acceptable to others. A long time ago I learned to accept and to be proud of myself and my race in the educational arena. To me, the job search process was really no different. I did not want to change my appearance, because then I would not have been presenting my true self to employers. "To be myself," was one of the most important pieces of advice I received during my job search. From then on, I made a conscious decision to not let my race and the reactions of others prohibit me from conducting a successful job search. I would not allow myself to become trapped in a situation where I could potentially be limited in any way.

With those fears put to rest and my resume completed, I began the next phase of my job search. As a graduate student on a limited budget, I could only afford to attend one national conference. Since most of my graduate program faculty and mentors were involved in the National Association of Student Personnel Administrators (NASPA), I decided to attend the NASPA conference in Philadelphia.

My NASPA conference experience went well. I loved the online resume program. I was able to create a resume by inputting my information into a database and selecting the headings I wanted to use. I even had control over the type and size of the font. The entire process was easy to understand and very user-friendly. It also did not take very long to finish, and I was happy with the final product. I was astounded to learn that the online version of my resume looked identical to the hard copy version I submitted. The fact that potential employers could easily get a copy of my resume without having to wait for me to mail them one was exciting.

After posting my resume online, I began to search NASPA's job listings. I targeted residence life and student activities positions at small (3000 or less full-time student enrollment), private liberal arts institutions on either coast. Although I refrained from applying to multicultural/minority affairs positions, I did consider the percentage of students of color at institutions. I was attracted to institutions with lower percentages of students of color, because I wanted to fill a void for students that was not filled for me when I attended college. Being one of the few

African Americans at a small predominant white campus, I knew what it was like to want and need to see myself reflected in the staff and faculty.

The desire to fill this void was a major reason I decided to become a student affairs professional. What was lacking for me during the first two years of my undergraduate experience was someone to go to for issues related to being a woman of color. My issues ranged from learning to respond to professors who expected me to be a spokesperson for all members of my race, to being a learning experience for white students who had never encountered a person of color before, let alone lived on the same residence hall floor with one. I derived a certain amount of comfort from knowing that there was a person of color who had already lived through those experiences and worked on campus for me to go to for help. I knew that because I had now lived through those experiences, I could help other students of color by ensuring they did not face that void.

While some of my colleagues applied to over twenty different positions, I remained selective and applied to approximately ten postings. Knowing that many private institutions are religiously affiliated, I questioned the strength and active involvement of religion in staff members' daily lives during my interviews. I wanted to ensure I would have the ability and the latitude to be as effective a professional and student advocate as possible. To assess the strength of the religious affiliation, I studied the institutions' mission statements and asked staff members if they had ever felt like the affiliation caused them to compromise their beliefs or values.

Interview preparation was a serious topic for both graduate students and our faculty. Faculty and student affairs professionals were supportive and provided seminars on successful interviewing. They answered all kinds of questions. At what point is it safe to ask about job benefits? How does one tactfully negotiate a salary? When and how does one know if a stated salary is competitive? Is it typical for employers to offer moving expenses? In addition to answering endless questions about the interview process, both the faculty and student affairs professionals regularly offered words of support and continually asked how we were doing and if we had any new job leads. Knowing that the faculty, student affairs professionals and my mentors had the confidence that I would be able to successfully complete my job search gave me faith that I would find an institution that *fit*.

Telephone Interviews

I received good advice about interviewing from a mentor. Telephone interviews concerned me, since this was unfamiliar territory. She said, "The key is to put as much energy into your voice as you can. A telephone interview is harder than a face-to-face one, because the person on the other end of the telephone will not be able to read your body language or tell if you are really excited about the position." She told me to make myself as comfortable as possible to reduce my nervousness, even if it meant doing the interview in my pajamas. And I did! For all my telephone interviews, I sat at my kitchen table with my feet propped up on a chair, my notes on the college and their position spread out before me, wearing the most comfortable pair of pajamas I owned. The first hurdle of the interview process was an easy one for me, thanks to my mentor's advice. I continue to share her advice with students.

Input and advice from my mentors was one of the most important keys to my job search. If I had not been able to draw on the lessons they had learned from their own searches, I do not think I would have had the success I did. Often my mentors did not wait for me to come to them, but instead checked in with me frequently. I could ask them any question. Sometimes they checked in daily and asked me how my search was going and if I needed any help. To this day, I still draw on their expertise for whatever professional challenges I face.

Conference Interviews

The next hurdle, navigating the NASPA conference career center, started out as a tricky one. NASPA's career center is typically divided into several areas. There are areas where interviews are conducted, and there are designated areas where candidates wait for the institutional representative to meet them. For some reason that I still do not understand and cannot really explain, I did not quite grasp the concept of the waiting areas and nearly missed my first interview. I was reviewing my notes while waiting for the school representative of my first interview. When I looked at my watch I realized fifteen minutes of my thirty-minute interview time slot had already passed and no one had come for me. I stood up and walked around, looking for someone, anyone, who seemed to be waiting for a candidate. I wandered into a different waiting area and ran into an employer. I asked her if she could clarify which seating areas were for which institutions, and it turned out I was the candidate she was trying to locate. Fortunately, we were able to make the most of our shortened time together; we hit it off and scheduled two more follow-up interviews at the conference. I have no idea how I got myself so mixed up, but I was able to recover and my interviews from that point on went fairly smoothly.

It was often distracting for me to focus on the interview with so much traffic passing by and seeing familiar faces. My most unforgettable interview location was next to an escalator with the dean of students at my current institution. Most who passed by did not realize that an interview was in progress.

Eventually, I learned to relax and to actually enjoy conference interviews. My goal was to get as much information as possible about the details of the position and about the interviewers themselves. I tried to read their body language (another skill taught to me by one of my mentors) to gauge their interest in my candidacy. I specifically noted if their arms were crossed, indicating possible disinterest; if they nodded after I said something, indicating that they were actively listening; and if they made eye contact with me, indicating they were engaged and interested in our conversation. Regardless of the interviewer's body language, I always tried to convey my sincerity and interest in the position.

There was only one incident with respect to my race that emerged during the conference. An institution invited me for an interview for a residence life position. Although the institution was located outside of my geographic search, I accepted the invitation to interview. I knew nothing about this institution and I wondered why this school was pursuing me. Since I was not sure if it was appropriate to question their interest, I asked a faculty member her opinion. She said I should feel comfortable asking why an employer was interested in me. So I did. The employers were very up-front with me; the institution wanted to diversify its staff and have professionals of color to better serve all students. This institution's deliberate hiring process impressed me, since they were taking the needs of their multicultural students into consideration. I eventually turned down their offer for an on-campus interview. I did not want to be considered for this position because the only thing the employers knew about me was that I was African American. Once again I was concerned about being pigeonholed.

Peer Competition

Many issues I faced during the early stages of my job search (such as creating my resume, how to present myself, which positions to apply for) were easily and quickly resolved. However, I did not expect the intense competition between some of my graduate peers and myself. I was not fully prepared to deal with the impact it had on my search. Two graduate colleagues were also conducting their first job search at NASPA. There was a bit of overlap in the positions for which we applied, but we thought we could handle whatever awkwardness might occur. We even made arrangements to share a room at one of the conference hotels. We kept an eye out for each other's interests while perusing position postings on the NASPA and *The Chronicle of Higher Education* websites. Things began to get intense once we started scheduling interviews prior to our arrival in Philadelphia. One woman in particular, *Heather*, made it a contest to see who could get the most interviews. "Well, I'm in the double digits," she would report to us whenever we mentioned a new interview.

I was becoming increasingly uncomfortable with Heather's comments and being around her for long periods of time. I found I could no longer share my job search successes or disappointments with Heather. In fact, I went to great length to keep the details of my search confidential and only shared them with one or two friends. While I wanted to support and offer Heather encouragement, she did not reciprocate. I was the first person from my graduating class to accept a job offer. It was announced in a class that both Heather and I attended and I really dreaded her reaction. It was not until the following year that we were able to rekindle our friendship at NASPA in New Orleans.

I would like to say that the only reason Heather was so competitive was because there was a shortage of desirable positions and we were in direct competition with each other; however, that was not the case. There were a lot of great positions available that year. It was just Heather's nature to be competitive, and she did not realize she was putting our friendship in jeopardy. I learned to be sensitive to the feelings of my friends who were conducting job searches, and I tried to be sensitive to their successes and disappointments.

On-Campus Interviews

As a result of my participation in the NASPA conference career center, I received three invitations for on-campus interviews. I believed that visiting a campus would help me determine the best campus *fit*. I interviewed the colleges' staff and students just as much as they interviewed me. I learned a lot about the campus culture at each of the institutions I visited. In addition to surfing the institutions' web sites and reviewing their mission statements, I read the student newspapers to see what was on the minds of students. I also asked students and staff to talk about what college traditions were their favorites and why. For example, at the third institution I visited, one student spoke about using cafeteria trays to go "sledding" with friends. She specifically enjoyed the bond she and her friends developed while sledding. Another student spoke about the sense of community she felt when she saw all the student mailboxes stuffed with flowers on Fridays.

The first campus I visited was a Catholic college on the East coast. The senior leaders of the college were priests, conveying for me a strong tie to the church. Being raised Catholic and being familiar with the Church's policies, specifically their position on homosexuality, I expected the members of this campus to be conservative, but they were not. The staff members appeared to support all students, including lesbian, gay, bisexual and transgendered (LGBT) students. The student staff members who interviewed me were the toughest audience. They were direct and critical. They definitely knew the qualities and level of experience they desired, and they wasted no time assessing my qualifications. They asked questions I considered technical in nature. For example, they asked how would I deal with a fire alarm. I answered in terms of ensuring students had evacuated the building safely, making sure no one was hurt, and working with the proper safety officials; they wanted to know how I would actually turn the alarm off. The best I could do was to be honest and tell them that while I did not have any direct experience with their fire alarm system, I was certain I could learn the technical skills required of a good hall director. I also indicated I would rely on the professional and student staff members for help if need be. I left that interview feeling like I had not fulfilled their expectations of what a hall director should be.

My time with the students of color was different from the time I spent with the student staff. I felt a certain amount of neediness from the multicultural students with whom I interacted. I could tell not so much by their words, but by their demeanor, that they were really excited by the prospect of having another person of color on campus. The admissions counselor who took me on a campus tour was a staff member of color as well. He articulated how he felt the students of color needed more role models and mentors of color to support them. This would not be the only time I heard this during a campus interview, and it did not surprise me to hear comments like this from the students and staff. After all, this was part of the reason I was in student affairs. However, the difference between hearing these comments from students and staff during a campus interview and hearing them from potential employers at the

NASPA conference was significant. The employers at the conference were the ones making the hiring decision and thus would have the power to structure my professional responsibilities once I was working for them. Students and staff with whom I interacted on campus did not have this power. In fact, they were helping me obtain a fuller picture of campus life.

My second campus visit was also on the East coast, but this time the college was not religiously affiliated. Instead, this institution was known for its fine arts programs. I even attended a student theater production while on campus. Unlike my first campus interview, it was the professional staff members who were more critical and direct in their questioning; yet they were more supportive and reaffirming than the students from my first campus interview had been. One of the staff members even said he did not intend to trap me with his questions (again, it was a technical question about crisis response), he just wanted to be sure I could be honest about the level of my experience, and that I had answered his questions perfectly. After interviewing with this group, I did not feel like I had been through the ringer with them as I did with the students from the first campus. In fact, I could see myself working very well with them. The students from this campus were rather informal. I met with the students over lunch and we spent our time getting to know each other. We spent more time talking about their campus traditions than interviewing each other. I definitely felt more comfortable on this second campus than the first. Staff and students were more welcoming and approachable at this campus, which made it easier to envision myself working at this institution.

Although I did not formally meet with students of color, when we crossed paths in their residence hall (where I stayed during the interview process) they were curious and approached me. We spent a few minutes chatting; once they learned I was interviewing for a position, they told me they hoped I would be hired because they really wanted more staff of color. The vice president of student affairs said the same. He told me in no uncertain terms that I was his first choice of the candidates they had brought to campus (but not only because I was a black woman). I left feeling that I had found my *fit*. The institution met my geographic criterion. I really liked the staff with whom I would be working, and I felt like I had formed a connection with them. I really enjoyed the students there, and I knew there were students of color with whom I would work and serve as a resource. I concluded I would be able to grow as a professional and person at this institution and not be judged or limited simply because of my skin color. However, I still had one more campus to visit before making my final decision.

The last college I visited was in the Midwest. I was hesitant to even apply because it did not meet my geographical criterion, but a faculty mentor had encouraged me. The invitation to campus surprised me. I did not think my initial interview at NASPA had gone well. The Director of Student Activities had not seemed excited about my candidacy. He did not smile once throughout the whole interview and he always had his arms crossed against his body, thus I thought he did not like me as a candidate. I later found out that he was, in fact, very excited. My NASPA interview with the Dean of Students went better than the first one with the Director, although that was the one conducted in a high traffic area next to an escalator. At this point, I still wanted to get an up-close look at their campus; hence I accepted their invitation.

The visit was by far the most intriguing of the three. I arrived on campus during a student protest. The college administration had recently announced a reduction of faculty and staff in several areas, including key academic and athletic programs. There were anti-administration chalkings all over campus sidewalks and ribbons tied around trees. Students were extremely upset and mistrustful of the administration. Almost all of the questions they asked me were loaded questions designed to reveal the nature of my loyalty to them as students or to the college administration as my employer. I told them I had to be able to look myself in the mirror everyday, thus my loyalties were to myself and to my professional ethics. They accepted my response. The Director of Student Activities and the Dean of Students worried that I would view the unrest negatively, but I was thrilled to see it. I had been studying campus culture and a protest spoke volumes about student involvement in and commitment to an equitable campus community. In addition, the college had just begun construction of a new student commons that would be approximately three times the size of the current student center. Clearly there was evidence of commitment to student and community development by the college administration.

I did not meet with students of color separately during this campus interview; they were included in the one large student group interview. I also do not recall any questions or comments specifically about my experiences working with students of color or their needs on campus. I never did find out why students of color did not talk to me about their needs, probably because I did not ask. With the other students, the topic came up naturally in the course of our discussion, or staff of color raised the issue. Meeting with students of color and white students in one large group provided me an opportunity to see how they interacted together, which gave me a more complete understanding of student life on campus.

I left this third campus interview feeling very torn. I really liked both my second and third campus visits; if offered both positions, I would not know which one to accept. On the one hand, the East Coast college was a residence life/student activities position that would fulfill my professional aspirations, and I could see myself working with and being supported by the college's staff. It also met my geographic criterion. The third campus, while not initially having residence life responsibilities included in the position, agreed to provide me with opportunities to be involved with the residence life staff. Each campus had its own elements that attracted me. I really enjoyed the students and staff at the first college. However, I liked that the third college was already demonstrating a commitment to professional development by offering me opportunities to grow in areas in which I was interested.

The third campus, St. Olaf, was further along in their hiring process than the second campus and they offered me the position. I did stall for a few days so I could hear from the second campus. Just as I was going to call them to see where they were in their process, they called me. They were just beginning to check references of the three finalists, and it would be at least a week before they would be ready to make an offer. At this point, I still was not sure what I wanted to do. I knew I could not ask St. Olaf to wait any longer. I talked with a friend of mine about what I liked about each campus. She helped me to see that the only reason I was hesitating was because I did not want to accept the first offer for the sake of being employed. She told me if I were to accept St. Olaf's offer, it would be because it was where I really wanted to be. I later learned that the second campus had completely restructured the student affairs division, and the position I had applied for no longer existed. Thus, it was divine intervention that I ended up at St. Olaf.

As I reflect on my experiences at each of the three campuses, my third campus interview was the only one where I was not told how much my presence was needed for the benefit of the students of color. What was surprising was that the needs of students of color did not weigh as heavily into my decision to accept a job offer as I thought when I began my job search. I could easily see myself in the students of color I met on all three campuses. I could see the surprise and happiness at finding a new face that looked like them. And I could see their desire to make that face a permanent fixture on their campus, but I could also see them trying to reign in their excitement and be reserved so to not overwhelm that new face and scare me away.

Instead of trying to find a balance between the needs of the students of color and my own, or trying to weigh which campus' students needed my presence the most (which would have been impossible for so many reasons and in so many ways), I allowed my own wants and needs to play a critical role in my final decision. I was able to fulfill my desire to be a source of support for students of color on my new campus by seeking out and accepting invitations to work directly with them during my first two years at St. Olaf. While I continue to be a resource for students of color, I also encourage them to take a more active role in the student government organizations with which I work closely. I challenge all student programmers, regardless of their ethnic backgrounds, to bring more diverse events to campus.

When I consider the fact that I am entering my fourth year at St. Olaf, I definitely got my job search right on the first try. When I first starting working, I was still somewhat concerned about the strength of St. Olaf's affiliation with the Evangelical Lutheran Church of America (ELCA) and how that affiliation would play out in my professional life. After all, St. Olaf is considered to be the flagship of the ELCA institutions, and I did not know much about the doctrines of this church. By the end of my first year, I learned that one of the most important doctrines is to seek out new experiences and knowledge. I have never once felt that St. Olaf's affiliation with the Lutheran Church has inhibited my ability to carry out my job responsibilities. I have the quantity and quality of student contact I wanted and then some. The end of the year is a hard time for me emotionally as I say goodbye to the seniors; opening day, while exhausting due to the amount of energy it takes to welcome a new class and their families into the college community, is one of my favorite days of the year.

Lessons Learned

If I were to give advice to new professionals based on my experiences, I would recommend: that you assess and articulate what you want from your first professional experience and do not take a job simply to be employed. In determining long-term career goals, the first professional position acts as a foundation for the future. Also, be honest about your intentions. Do not waste your and the employer's time by applying for a position you have no intention of pursuing or accepting, if offered to you. Do not be afraid to ask questions of your mentors and draw on the lessons they learned from their job searches to guide you. Be prepared to encounter some competition from your colleagues and friends. Think about how you will handle competition and what is needed to keep the friendship intact.

For new professionals of color, I would specifically suggest being true to yourself, and be proud of yourself. Do not let someone else's expectations convince you to present yourself as someone you are not. Do not apply for positions due to outside pressure from someone who thinks they know what is best for you or your career.

I would say the following to mentors. Be supportive and encouraging by being available for questions. Regularly check in with your protégés during their job search process. Often, it was just knowing that my mentors were interested enough to ask how things were going with me that provided the most support. The job search process can be confusing and uncertain. With support from mentors, faculty, staff, and colleagues, you can get your job search right the first time. Remember, "you will only do one job search of this magnitude during your career."

3

THE ART OF COMPROMISE AND
OTHER SECRETS OF THE
DUAL-CAREER JOB SEARCH

Kathleen Gardner and Craig Woodsmall

Kathleen

When describing my early relationship with Craig to friends within higher education, I often describe it as student affairs love at first sight. We met in the fall of 1997 during a National Collegiate Alcohol Awareness Week committee meeting at the Illinois Institute of Technology (IIT) in Chicago. I was a resident director at IIT, and Craig was completing an externship with the counseling center for his doctoral program at the Illinois School of Professional Psychology. Craig asserts that our first date was the IIT student formal at the Drake Hotel. This did not seem like much of a date to me, since we dined with other student affairs colleagues eager to support this student event. The evening did not call much attention to our relationship because we were technically at this event with a group of colleagues. I maintain that our first *real* date occurred weeks later when we went to dinner and a movie—without an audience of college students or colleagues from IIT. However, Craig is quick to remind me that we had a student audience for that date as well. Even in a city as large as Chicago, we ran into a group of student leaders from IIT at a coffee bar miles from campus after the movie. I was horrified as these students continuously walked by our table attempting to inconspicuously investigate Craig and the nature of our outing. They were obviously surprised to see their resident director out on a date and excited to report back to others on campus what they had seen. I had a small group of resident advisors with inquiring minds outside my office the following Monday morning demanding to know who this mystery person was in my company over the weekend. This experience gave a whole new meaning to living in a fishbowl, a phenomenon commonly experienced by live-in professional staff. To borrow a phrase from pop culture, worlds were colliding—the line between my personal life and my professional life became much too blurred for my liking.

I never expected to meet my life partner during my time in Chicago, especially a doctoral student five years my senior. I moved to Chicago as a single person during the summer of 1996 to take a bachelor's level resident director position at IIT. When I arrived in Chicago, I had a five-year plan: work for two years at IIT to gain full-time experience in student affairs, obtain a Master's degree in higher education/college student personnel from Indiana University or the University of Maryland, move to a large city with a job in residential life at a medium to large size public institution. The first five years (post-bachelor's degree) was going to be completely about my educational and career goals. It never occurred to me that I would meet someone for whom I would be willing to alter my life plan.

Attending a well-known and well-respected graduate program was incredibly important to me because I had attended my state school for my undergraduate degree. Coincidentally, my state school was the University of Maryland. Although I fell in love with the university within the first three days of my arrival on campus, I struggled to feel proud of my choice of schools as most of my high school friends were attending top-tier institutions like Swarthmore, Johns Hopkins, and Brown. I chose Maryland for financial reasons and, in my mind, it paled in comparison to the schools that my friends were attending. I remember a dramatic episode with my mother during the summer before college when I sobbed about the horrors of attending a state school. My mother, knowing that Maryland was a fine school, did not feed into my drama. She said, "You can go to Harvard for graduate school if that's what is important to you." This seemed like a pointless aspiration as neither of my parents graduated from college. But when I was accepted into Maryland's college student personnel graduate program in 1998, I called my mother and said, "I got into my Harvard."

Craig and I lived apart during my first year in graduate school. After completing his internship at Purdue University, he moved to Maryland to be with me and to work on his dissertation. Craig and I both took jobs at Washington University in St. Louis after I completed graduate school in May of 2000. We moved to St. Louis in July of 2000 where I took a position as a residential college director with the office of residential life and Craig started as a staff psychologist in the counseling center. We married in October 2000.

Craig

It would seem logical that the threads of this story begins in January 2000, when we started revising resumes and polishing interview skills and concludes with a successful dual career job search, two great job offers at the same university, and our first year of work together. However, life has not been so logical. Despite knowing since high school that I wanted a doctoral degree in psychology to become a psychotherapist, I found myself in 1991 at my graduation from William Jewell College, a small liberal arts college in Missouri, without any offers from graduate schools and unemployed. It took me two attempts to gain admittance to a Master's degree program in 1992 for counseling psychology, including two tries at the Graduate Record Exam, and two more rounds of graduate school applications to gain admittance into a doctoral program in 1995 for clinical psychology.

The hard work and struggle did not end with the completion of my course work in the spring of 1998. In the fields of counseling and clinical psychology, students are required to demonstrate that they are able to apply the knowledge learned in the classroom by working with patients or clients through a series of nine-month field placements called practica or externships. Typically, these are unpaid positions that are the responsibility of the student to secure through a process that resembles a cross between a traditional job search and a placement exchange like the one held at the American College Personnel Association (ACPA) convention. As often as possible, I sought externships in college or university counseling centers since that became my career objective in 1994.

Although Kathleen claims that we met during my practicum with the counseling center at the Illinois Institute of Technology, we really met at a holiday party the year before at a mutual friend's house. She just does not remember meeting me that night. We had the chance to work together the following year, in 1997, after I had started my practicum at IIT. We were both members of the National Collegiate Alcohol Awareness Week committee on campus. It was not long after that when other staff from the counseling center began to hint that I should ask Kathleen out on a date. I politely declined their advice, although I had intentions of doing just that when the right opportunity revealed itself. Being a doctoral student kept me busy, but I was determined to not let my graduate school responsibilities deter me from having as full a life as possible, including seeking out relationships. I had recently passed my comprehensive examination and was about to successfully complete my fourth different practicum in five years; however, I was still not finished with my training. The capstone training experience at the doctoral level is a full-time, twelve-month internship designed to launch a new professional psychologist into the field.

The application process for the internship year is similar to what medical school students complete to begin their resident programs. On a predetermined day, following the completion of all the interviews and paper shuffling, internship sites call applicants across the country to make internship offers. After the initial log-jam at the top where it seems like everyone puts offers on hold in hopes that they hear back from their first choice, all chaos breaks loose as students and employers scramble to fill positions before the allotted time runs out at 2 p.m., Central Standard Time. After I endured two painfully close alerts that I was a first or second alternate at two sites - Indiana University and Illinois State University, 2 p.m. rolled around and I had no internship.

I gave myself approximately thirty minutes to be irrational as I watched nine years of higher education and hard work seemingly amount to nothing. Not obtaining an internship leads to an extra year of graduate school. In other words, it meant repeating the past year until the next application cycle. I am not ashamed to say that I cried, yelled, screamed, pleaded with the forces beyond my control, and cursed my luck. Slowly, I began to compose myself and I started to make phone calls to former and current supervisors in the field for help, advice and support. Next, I applied to be a part of a clearinghouse process for applicants and employers who were still in the search process. Within about twelve hours I had faxed out nearly twenty new applications and within twenty-four hours I had three telephone interview offers. Two days after initially falling apart, I had two internship offers. I was very pleased to accept a position at Purdue University.

The story of my dual job search with Kathleen really begins in August of 1998 when my twelve-month internship with Counseling and Psychological Services Center of Purdue University was quickly coming to an end. I began an aggressive job search during the winter in hopes of finding an entry-level position with a college or university counseling center near the University of Maryland, where Kathleen was then pursuing her Master's degree. Having learned from my previous experiences, I did not limit myself geographically and applied to openings from coast to coast. My efforts paid off with an offer from a small Jesuit men's college in the Midwest. I have no doubt that this position would have presented me with great experience and many opportunities for professional growth. It was not the perfect job, but the position possessed many of the qualities and needs that I wanted in a first job, such as the opportunity to develop and implement innovative programs, support from key administrators, and a clearly defined role and mission within the campus community. However, as I considered my options, I felt a growing concern for my personal growth and happiness.

As confident as I was in my relationship with Kathleen and the way we had negotiated the burdens of a long-distance romance for more than a year, neither of us felt comfortable extending this arrangement. It became increasingly difficult for our relationship to grow given the distance. I had one of the most difficult decisions to make in my life. I was about to begin the career that I had envisioned for myself since high school. The cost of obtaining the dream appeared to be sacrificing my relationship with Kathleen, the person I considered to be my life partner. I relied on a lesson I learned from my mentors. My personal and professional lives are intertwined, not separate. I drew confidence from this lesson and from their years of experience; I turned down the job offer and decided to move to Maryland.

Moving to Maryland was not an easy decision to make. My mentors and supervisors raised many questions, concerns, and issues that I, too, had considered. What would I do for income? How difficult would it be to get back into the counseling field? How would I explain this *missing year* when I returned to the field in my next job search? I had made my decision. I moved to Maryland without a job and one year to recover from five years of graduate school and to finish my dissertation. Taking full advantage of the benefit of hindsight, I know that my decision was the correct one. At the time, it was a difficult and challenging process as Kathleen and I lived through it. She empowered me to decide on my own, out of respect for me and a desire not to complicate my decision any further. It took me a while to recover from these events as I spent some time after my move to Maryland unemployed. I unsuccessfully tried to find work at colleges in the area, and eventually took a part-time job with the Virginia Department of Health as a HIV counselor. As Kathleen's graduate school program neared completion, I soon discovered that even more problems and factors come into consideration when juggling two professional job searches.

Kathleen

My first job search took place during my senior year at the University of Maryland in 1996. I decided that I needed full-time experience in student affairs before pursuing a Master's degree in college student personnel. With the encouragement of my resident director, I attended the Oshkosh Placement Exchange (OPE) in March 1996. OPE is an annual placement conference primarily for entry level and mid-level residence life positions held at the University of Wisconsin at Oshkosh. I interviewed with a number of higher education institutions, visited and interviewed on three campuses, and then chose the position at the Illinois Institute of Technology that felt best given my needs, abilities, and values. As a soon-to-be college graduate I had very few limitations pertaining to my first job search, and I felt as though I had a thousand opportunities at my feet given the strong market. The job search excited me because I knew that I could seek a job in almost any of the fifty states. Often, I daydreamed during this job search. For a 21-year-old who had never lived outside of Maryland, every metropolitan region and rural setting outside of the Mid-Atlantic region seemed glamorous and exciting. I toyed with the idea of working at a small college located in a farming community deep in Missouri, a Catholic institution on the West Coast, and a variety of small schools in major cities. In the end, I accepted a position at the Illinois Institute of Technology, a small, private, technological university in Chicago.

As a resident director, I regularly attended meetings or programs until 9 or 10 p.m. and rarely socialized outside of work. I never dreamed that I would meet someone with whom I would even consider spending my life. My parents did not go to college, so getting into graduate school became my first priority. I wanted to enroll in a nationally-ranked and recognized graduate program. Despite all the time and energy that I devoted to developing professionally and preparing for graduate school, I somehow found *the one*. Since our relationship was so new, I never thought about altering my graduate school ambitions to remain geographically close to Craig.

Kathleen and Craig

When Craig completed his internship at Purdue, we decided that he would move to Maryland for a year until it was time for the two of us to job search together. We decided that if we combined households, we could save on expenses as we were faced with the challenge of saving and planning for our wedding that was to take place the following year.

Some of our family had a difficult time dealing with the fact that we would be living together before we were married. With the added stress from our family, Kathleen being in school full-time, and Craig working part-time, we began experiencing more problems in our relationship. Under these myriad worries and fears, we continued with our plans for the wedding, the job search, and the start of our careers as best we could. One factor in our favor was that we were not starting from scratch.

Some of the experiences and skills we both learned while conducting our previous job searches served to inform the dual search which began in earnest in early 1999. Yet, we soon realized that it was an entirely different process with a life partner. Most significantly, internal thoughts, feelings, and decisions have to be identified and communicated to the other and constantly re-evaluated. The greatest transition in going from a one-career job search to a dual-career job search was recognizing that we replaced the freedom to follow individual needs and values with finding a place that would support the shared needs and values of both of us.

One of the first issues we confronted as a couple, both seeking careers, was selecting a geographic location. We came to understand that since the odds were more difficult in finding two jobs in the same area, we had to cast a wider net. The amount of snow a city received or the summer temperatures no longer seemed as important as both of us being employed and living together. Discussions came to focus on what geographic regions were completely out of the question and this was only based on distance from family or proximity to an airport. Kathleen's family lives just outside of Baltimore, and Craig's family is in the St. Louis area.

Prior to our dual search, preferences for large state universities or small liberal arts colleges played a more significant role in our individual searches. The environment surrounding an institution was also considered in light of shared preferences. We both hoped to move back to Chicago but would have been happy staying in the Washington, D.C. area. In short, we had to decide early on what we as a couple were willing to negotiate to be successful and what was less important than both of us getting a start in our careers. Kathleen was willing to take a job at a small, liberal arts school. Craig was willing to live in a city again and not just the suburbs. We were both unwilling to give up our cat so we had to find a residence life program that allowed pets for live-in professional staff. We both were unwilling to live in separate cities again.

It took much individual reflection and values clarification to determine negotiable and non-negotiable issues. At the same time, new job search issues emerged. If we were to work at different institutions, commuting time would be a critical factor to consider. We were not willing to add an extensive commute on top of two new, and most likely demanding, positions.

Many factors typically important in a job search were altered as a part of this dual-career process. One example would be salary requirements. Individuals who choose to enter service-oriented, helping professions, such as psychology and student affairs, tend not to place income as highly in their value systems as persons in the business world. Despite having educational loans to repay and living expenses to meet, salary ranges were not a major factor in this search. However, we knew that salary would become a significant issue if one of us ended up unemployed.

Good communication skills were essential throughout the search processes. Not only did we talk openly about our frustrations and disappointments with having to change our job search strategies, we also had to develop a willingness to explain our parameters or limitations to each other. Kathleen was blessed to be doing a job search in residential life during an employee's market. There were more jobs than candidates at each of the major conventions in 2000. Craig had a more difficult time because there were fewer jobs available in his field; moreover, he wanted to work in an office that had more than one or two colleagues in order to reduce the risk of job burnout and provide more opportunities for professional development. We had worked so hard to get to where we were in our careers that we wanted and expected jobs that would excite and challenge us. We had to continuously communicate with each other, or risk letting anger, frustration, or defeat come between us. We managed to effectively communicate with each other for the duration of our search. This was accomplished mostly through the strength of how we already communicated as a couple, but was helped further by identifying what factors comprised our dream jobs and sharing that information in ways that brought about an understanding of how we reached those decisions.

Kathleen

I knew from the start of my job search that I wanted to work for a residential life office at a state school with a nationally respected division of student affairs. I fell in love with the idea of working at a school that would provide me with a similar experience as Maryland, such as The Ohio State University or Indiana University. I was young and naïve professionally, so I thought that I had to work at a large state school to have the opportunity to work with and learn from well-known and respected student affairs professionals. I was, however, willing to go to a smaller state school for the opportunity to work in a position similar to my graduate school assistantship where I worked specifically with enhancing the academic environment in the residence halls. My dream job consisted of the opportunity to create, implement, and evaluate residence halls programs and interventions in the areas of community formation, curricular support, and educational enhancement. I also wanted the opportunity to work with involving faculty in the residence halls through a residential life office.

Craig

My undergraduate experience at a small liberal arts college left a deep impression on me that influenced my professional identity. I find great appeal in the ideals of a community unified through a common purpose – the development of young adults through the pursuit of knowledge. However, my internship year at Purdue taught me that the environment of a large state institution could be just as rewarding in terms of my work life. This allowed me to be more flexible about the size and type of institutions that we investigated. I enjoyed my year living outside of the Midwest and was hoping to find more opportunities to explore living in new regions but was not opposed to returning to my roots. More central to the image of my ideal first job was the ability to be involved in a number of different activities and not just spend the day providing therapy. I envisioned providing educational and prevention programs to students, staff, and faculty on a variety of topics relevant to mental health issues. In addition, I hoped to develop my consultation skills through working with faculty and administrators. Specifically, I looked for opportunities to build relationships with students and staff in the areas of athletics and Greek life. Most of all, I wanted to be a valued member of a competent team of professionals.

Kathleen and Craig

Communication about our future did not always come easily for us. There were many dinners eaten in silence as we struggled to clarify and communicate to each other our needs and values. At first, this process plummeted us into a sea of *what ifs*. What if neither of us gets a job?

What if both of us get jobs but in different states? And most worrisome, what if both of us landed our dream jobs in different parts of the country? Living in separate households, let alone different cities was not an option for us after being apart for a year.

At the same time, our financial situation somewhat dictated what we as a couple defined as absolutes. We were continuously aware of the possibility that Craig would be unable to find any job given the low number of vacancies for entry-level counseling center positions and the high number of qualified applicants. Since Kathleen hoped to find a live-in position in residential life, we at least knew that we could afford housing even if Craig could not immediately find a job. It was disheartening at times to have to focus on the worst-case scenario during a time that should be exciting and optimistic. Plan B involved one of us taking a job, at least temporarily, out of the field to help pay the bills. We revisited Plan B on a number of occasions when we found that a position had been filled or when job opportunities did not match up geographically.

We eventually realized that Kathleen needed to find work at a university that would allow unmarried partners to live-in, since we did not plan to be married until October of 2000. It became one of our nonnegotiable factors; we could not make ends meet if we were unable to live under one roof. We naively assumed early in our search processes that housing would not be a concern, since we were engaged and planning a wedding in just a few short months. However, Kathleen turned down two job offers because the residential life department was not in a position to allow two unmarried adults to share an on-campus apartment.

It was almost as if we were conducting multiple searches simultaneously. Each of us was searching for our ideal job independently, but then also searching for jobs in the geographic region where the other partner had a job lead. As one of us would find a job that matched our skills and abilities that interested us, the other would then begin to look for any possible opportunities in that specific region. For example, Craig was offered a post-doctoral position in the counseling center at The Ohio State University. Kathleen assertively pursued resident director positions at OSU and similar positions at nearby schools. It was both heartbreaking and humbling when Kathleen received a letter from OSU saying that they would not be pursuing her candidacy and when other leads turned up empty. This involved using multiple resources and contacts, not just the traditional placement exchanges at national conferences such as the American College Personnel Association and the National Association of Student Personnel Administrators. We could not afford to be shy about networking. We reached out to faculty members, mentors, colleagues, and previous supervisors—anyone who might know someone who might know someone who had a job opening.

Often our job search felt like a roller coaster ride. There were many ups and downs. Craig finally got his first job offer in May; unfortunately it was in Ohio, a part of the country where Kathleen had no job leads. In addition, the offer was a 12-month post-doctoral internship. To accept this offer meant that in less than one year, we could be back at square one. Ultimately, Craig declined that offer. Fortunately, we had many friends and family who cared about us as individuals and as a couple; it was difficult for them to understand how challenging a dual-career search can be or why we declined good offers. The situation became even more difficult, considering that our friends and family already struggled to understand our professions, especially college student personnel.

Colleagues, supervisors, and faculty members provided us our greatest comfort and support, since many of them had experienced equally challenging dual-career job searches. Reaching out to these individuals provided us comfort because it helped normalize our experience, and they offered the best advice given their experience. It was a mutual friend who had been through a similarly challenging search with her partner that reminded us that our timeline would probably be very different from our unattached or single colleagues who were job searching. This helped us stay strong and optimistic when April rolled around and many of our classmates and colleagues had already accepted job offers and we were still seeking job leads. We constantly had to remind ourselves to stop comparing our experiences to those of our single colleagues.

Once we were heavy into the job search, we quickly began to realize that this business of timelines would cause us the most anxiety and even panic. We learned early on that residential life search and screening processes moved more quickly than counseling center processes. In 1999, it was an employee's market and there were easily five entry-level residential life positions for every candidate, so housing and residential life employers were moving quickly to fill vacancies. Kathleen had three campus interviews set up the week following a week-long job placement convention, while Craig's potential employers were still collecting résumés. We struggled to be honest and appropriately assertive with potential employers when one partner had to make a decision about a position. Occasionally, we were put in the position of having to ask for more time to consider a job offer or to ask to have campus interviews scheduled later in the search process.

Kathleen

Working together briefly at IIT in 1998, I was wary about doing so again. I was never comfortable mixing my personal and professional life, and it was uncomfortable for me when colleagues knew about my relationship with Craig. Word travels quickly at a small school! New relationships are difficult enough without the scrutiny (no matter how loving) of colleagues. If Craig and I were to work together again at the same institution, I was determined that it be a large public institution because size would somehow guarantee a professional identity separate from my personal life. My decision to keep my maiden name reflected my need to keep these two aspects of my life separate. I hesitated to bring up my anxiety about keeping our professional identities separate from our personal life with Craig, because I knew that it could be hurtful to him. I did not want him to read my desire to be known for my professional accomplishments and not as Craig's partner at work as my embarrassment of being his partner. Rather, I was not as secure in my professional identity as Craig.

Craig

Although I did not always feel comfortable having the eyes of colleagues, students, and administrators on me during those early days of our relationship, I managed to find some peace with the curiosities and minor intrusions of others into our new relationship. One factor that might have assisted me in this process was the sheer length of experience I had in my field. The year I spent working on the same campus with Kathleen in Chicago was my fifth year as a graduate student working at a practicum site. I was secure in my professional identity and had reached a point where my anxiety about being productive and a contributor had subsided. Furthermore, the previous year, I had grown weary of "living and breathing my work 24 hours a day." In short, I took the steps necessary to develop activities and friendships unrelated to my graduate school or work roles, and, in turn, this alleviated the pressure to secure a stronger work identity for myself. So when it came time for our dual-job search two years later, the idea of working on the same campus again as my partner did not worry me; rather, I found the prospect exciting. As an undergraduate at William Jewell College, I envied the Associate Dean of Students because he walked home every day to have lunch with his family. When I would try sharing this story with Kathleen as a selling point for working at the same school, she would roll her eyes and groan. However the idea of having my work life and my personal life in close synchrony appealed to me.

There was one very unexpected reality I had not considered – the impact of our potential housing arrangements on my professional role in regard to the ethical considerations that need to be given to students seeking counseling services. How comfortable would a student feel seeking services from me, if Kathleen sanctioned them judicially following an incident in the residence hall where I live? The number of potential dual-role conflicts began to multiply. We came to this realization at the time when offers for campus interviews started and the realities of such an arrangement were before us. As a result, I became concerned with what my future colleagues' reactions would be when they discovered this situation.

Kathleen and Craig

When Craig heard about an opening in the counseling center at Washington University, Kathleen immediately started looking for residential life positions in the greater St. Louis area. We sought out everyone who might know someone in residential life at Washington University or at a nearby institution. Kathleen is now embarrassed to admit that one administrator who did not even work in residential life received at least three phone calls on her behalf. Kathleen had turned down at least two job offers and a handful of campus interviews because there were not job possibilities for Craig, so she was now open to working at the same institution as her partner—it was late May and we both needed a job. We decided to put Craig's job search in front of Kathleen's needs to separate our professional identities.

Another parameter was soon thrown out the window. Early in our job search we agreed to seek neutral territory to begin our marriage—someplace that was not directly home to either of our immediate families. We did not want to hurt either family by choosing to live closer to one than the other. And since Craig's family is from just outside of St. Louis, we initially deleted the city from our search. There is much to be said for having a strong belief in providence or luck, as well as faith in the search process itself. How likely was it that Kathleen's former supervisor went to graduate school with the director of a counseling center that Craig was seeking to interview with at ACPA? This connection, as well as a good number more to follow, started the process by which we ended up in our positions as a residential college director and a staff psychologist at Washington University in St. Louis.

As we both progressed in our separate interview processes with Washington University, we were forced to revisit and redefine our needs related to our professional identities. We discussed all the ways that our paths could potentially cross in our professional lives if we worked at the same institution: at campus events, on university committees, etc. Without even having jobs in hand, we tried to anticipate and address potential concerns about the dual role that Kathleen's live-in position could put Craig in and vice-versa.

No matter how much Washington University was not what Kathleen wanted (geographical location, size of institution, private affiliation, etc.) we could not ignore the unique professional opportunities it offered the two of us. Ultimately, it was the way in which the university and staff treated us during our campus interviews and afterward that lessened Kathleen's fears about working at the same institution. What stood out in our minds most was the fact that this institution's policies regarding domestic partners extended to on-campus housing staff. Also, our potential employers collaborated in organizing our campus interviews so that we could visit the institution at the same time. One office coordinated both of our travel arrangements so there were no questions about logistics. Although we arrived together at the airport in St. Louis, there were representatives from both residential life and the counseling center to meet us and to take us to separate dinners. Although the counseling center was concerned about how Kathleen's job would affect Craig's ability to ethically serve students seeking services, they were certainly open to recognizing the advantages of both of us working for the same university: faster integration into the campus, probability that we would stay longer, and of course the value of having a broader grasp of the institution's mission and vision. However, we were realistic and understood that both departments had an obligation to choose the best candidate...despite this package deal.

Kathleen

I received a job-offer in mid-May from Washington University. I should have celebrated, but the offer added greater stress. No matter how much time the residential life department could give me to make my decision, it would not be enough time for the counseling center to finish their process. If I accepted the position, I would have to do so without knowing if Craig had a job. Although I was excited about this opportunity, I still had to wrestle with my feelings about living in St. Louis and potentially working for the same university as Craig. I knew that I would be devastated if I accepted this job and the counseling center declined to offer Craig a job. There are just not the same number of colleges and universities in St. Louis as in Chicago or Washington, D.C, and we wondered if accepting this job offer would jeopardize Craig's ability to find work in a university setting.

We made the decision to accept the residence life job offer together — only after much soul searching, list making, reflecting, and thinking. We decided that at the very least, my benefits would allow us to make ends meet for a few months if a job offer was not extended to Craig. In the meantime, Craig could find some other work. There really was not any leeway in negotiating a higher salary, as the offer in-hand was already very generous. We both recognized the value in moving closer to Craig's family and friends who could help support him during another job search. Craig also continued to express his interest in the counseling center position by following up with phone calls and letters.

Craig

Kathleen's Washington University offer pleased me. While I knew that it was not her *dream job*, we both were nearing the end of our personal limits as well as the number of potential jobs still available. As for my own prospects, I became more worried since I had not heard back in four weeks from the counseling center. In fact, I had resigned myself to the idea of moving to St. Louis without a job. Around this time, Kathleen graduated from Maryland with her Master's degree. Looking back, I should have started looking for other leads outside of the college or university setting, but I could not bring myself to do it. Instead, I focused all my energies on this positive and well-deserved life event for Kathleen and forgot about the search for a weekend.

Needless to say, I assumed the worst after listening to a voice mail from the director of the counseling center. My first thought was that if I returned his call, I would be informed, "While you were a strong candidate, we decided to hire someone else." I could not have been more wrong in my assumptions. We had really done it! Joy does not even come close to the feelings experienced that day. I soon learned the reasons for the delayed decision. As predicted, there was concern about dual roles and other ethical conflicts stemming from my potential residence hall living arrangements and Kathleen's job responsibilities. My future supervisor decided to solve the problem by limiting my work to students who lived off-campus. As a result, it took a while longer before I felt confident that I was *pulling my weight* as the new staff member in the office.

Craig and Kathleen

The most difficult part of the relocation was getting acclimated to our numerous new environments—new city, new departments, new institution, living together in a residence hall, etc. Both of us navigated this process at different rates and in different ways. Craig had the advantage of returning to his hometown where old friends and familiar places were waiting for him. At first, Kathleen resisted acclimating to the new environment since St. Louis and Washington University were not her top choices. This put added pressure on our relationship when feelings of resentment and disappointment surfaced at various times during our transition. We attempted to promote our acclimation as a couple into St. Louis by finding opportunities to connect with the community at large and with people not associated with the university. We invested time in visiting new churches, social clubs, and community service groups. This alleviated some of the more challenging aspects of the new location, such as living so close to Craig's family and trying to establish adult relationships with his parents.

Once our start dates rolled around, there was no longer time to focus on the transition or any regrets about the job search process. It was time for us to demonstrate that the institution made wise choices in hiring us as individuals and as a couple. Our orientations overlapped at times with us attending the same Student Services events. This made establishing our roles and professional identities on campus awkward for us both. We faced various issues such as what would be the perceptions of others if we attended work-related events together? Craig had no cohort in the counseling center, while Kathleen was oriented to the institution with four other young professional colleagues. Did supervisors worry about Kathleen not bonding well with her co-workers if Craig attended events with her?

Both of our new departments scheduled social events as part of our orientation process where partners were invited to attend. For example, both of our supervisors hosted potluck dinners in their homes that included all of the office staff. There was some initial unease during this time, until we could gauge each other's and our new colleagues' level of comfort with the dual-role issue. In general, these events served as positive experiences that smoothed the transition and satisfied our colleagues' and supervisors' curiosities. Craig's colleagues' questions revolved around how he was settling into residence hall living, and Kathleen's colleagues often asked about the inner-workings of the counseling center.

The opportunity to explore this new environment together as well as the comfort that comes with not having to face a new environment alone helped us overcome our initial discomfort about working on the same campus. We learned much more about the campus culture and institutional policies than our peers, because we shared and discussed what we learned from our respective orientation experiences. On the flip side, since we work with each other's offices, we made a commitment to keep work separate from our personal lives; otherwise, we could become consumed by work issues. More importantly, we limited *work talk* at home to respect the confidential nature of our positions and ethical obligations of our professions.

Keeping a balance between our personal and professional lives was significantly different for each of us. For example, it was an adjustment for Craig to have Kathleen's undergraduate staff members over for dinner. Craig was used to having a more physical and psychological distance from his work after 5 p.m. than Kathleen was. We struggled as a couple to cope with fire alarms at 3 a.m., knocks at the apartment door during dinner, and being stopped with student questions while carrying in the groceries. It became increasingly more challenging for us to handle daily job and life stressors. Where do you go to recharge as a couple when home does not feel like a relaxing place?

Looking back on our first job search as a dual-career couple, we know that we made some mistakes in our search and relocation processes, especially putting more pressure on ourselves than necessary. For example, we could have delayed our wedding to occur sometime the following year instead of three months after moving to a new city and starting two new jobs. Instead, we developed new strategies and coping skills to meet the new demands of our lives. Even now, with our two years together at Washington University behind us, we still feel as thought we cannot offer solid advice to another couple as we are still evaluating and reflecting on our decisions as a couple and as individuals. The threads of many issues we faced during the search process, relocation, and orientation continue to resurface as we find ourselves facing new tasks in our jobs or facing challenges that follow normal institutional changes and cycles. Negotiating all of these changes and challenges would have been more difficult had we not been surrounded by others who had a solid understanding and empathy for what we were facing as a couple and as two new professionals. For that we are forever grateful.

4

CROSSING THE BRIDGE
FROM GRADUATE SCHOOL
TO JOB ONE

Susan R. Jones and J. Michael Segawa

*A bridge must be well anchored on both sides, with
as much respect for where it begins as for where it ends.*
—Robert Kegan, 1994, p. 62

Introduction

The transition from graduate school to professional work is replete
with challenge, questioning, excitement, and anxiety. Although the transition itself is easily anticipated, the nature of the journey takes each
new professional into uncharted territory. We borrow Kegan's (1994)
bridge metaphor to analyze the case studies of Kevin Piskadlo,
Christana Johnson, and Kathleen Gardner and Craig Woodsmall. Each
case study illuminates the complexity of the process involved in crossing the bridge from graduate school to job one. Peter Magolda and Jill
E. Carnaghi, in the book preface, describe the process as a reflective
expedition. Our approach is also one of a reflective expedition as we
engage with the authors' stories. In our analyses, we focus on the bridge
of transitions from graduate school to the first professional position,
respecting where the bridge begins and where it ends.

Drawing upon our positions on the bridge, our professional roles
and responsibilities frame our responses. Therefore, Susan's reflective
analytical response is anchored in theory and Mike's in implications for
practice. However, we often meet in the middle of the bridge as we
integrate theory and practice, providing a more holistic interpretation of
the new professionals' compelling stories about their reflective expeditions across the bridge of transition from graduate school to job one.

A Reflective-Analytical Response from a Graduate
Preparation Faculty Member: Susan's Perspective

Many students retrospectively describe their graduate school days as steeped in the study of theoretical perspectives on student development and higher education administration. They discover that the hard work of applying theory to practice begins in earnest with their first professional position after completion of a Master's degree. I too — as a once-student affairs practitioner turned graduate preparation faculty member — find myself immersed in the world of theory and the rigorous endeavor of translating theory to practice. Thus, true to form as a faculty member, I begin my reflective case study analyses with an examination of the theoretical perspectives that influence my understanding of the cases studies.

Few graduate students escape their graduate studies in student affairs without an introduction to the luminary work of Robert Kegan. In fact, as these essays poignantly portray, some graduate students understandably find that during their job search processes they are in over their heads. In his book, In *Over Our Heads: The Mental Demands of Modern Life*, Kegan (1994) applies the bridge metaphor to convey the nature of developmental transitions, the meaning students make of such transitions, and the educational conditions necessary to support such meaning making. Kegan's metaphor provides a theoretical lens through which to read and understand the preceding essays. Further, Kegan (1994) suggested, to successfully cross the bridge, support mechanisms must be in place to serve as anchors for change. Kegan referred to these supports as "an evolutionary bridge, a context for crossing over. It fosters developmental transformation, or the process by which the whole ('how I am') becomes gradually a part ('how I was') of a new whole ('how I am now')" (p. 43).

Closely connected to the process of crossing over the bridge, and negotiating the relationships between "how I was" and "how I want to be," is the role of self-authorship (Baxter Magolda, 1999; Kegan, 1994) in the transition and change process. "Self-authorship is simultaneously a cognitive (how one makes meaning of knowledge), interpersonal (how one views oneself in relationship to others), and intrapersonal (how one perceives one's sense of identity) matter" (Baxter Magolda, 1999, p. 10). Writing explicitly about work life demands, Kegan (1994) articulated, "When we look into this collection of expectations for success at work we discover that each actually demands something more than a particular behavior or skill. Each is a claim on our minds" (p.

185). As students negotiate the transition from graduate school to the role of new professional, new claims are made on the process of meaning making, which are more complex than those previously experienced. One's capacity to organize and make sense of the diversity of experiences represents an "internal identity, a self-authorship that can coordinate, integrate, act upon, or invent values, beliefs, convictions, generalizations, ideals, abstractions, interpersonal loyalties, and intrapersonal states. It is no longer authored by them, it authors them and thereby achieves a personal authority" (Kegan, 1994, p. 185).

Drawing on Kegan's work and then extending it based upon her own research, Baxter Magolda (1999) asserted:

Self-authorship, then, is a complicated phenomenon. It is simultaneously an ability to construct knowledge in a contextual world, an ability to construct an internal identity separate from external influences, and an ability to engage in relationships without losing one's internal identity. (p. 12)

The role of self-authorship and the challenges of authoring one's own life become most poignant in the context of making important career and life decisions and in navigating the transition inherent in crossing the bridge.

While Kegan and Baxter Magolda illuminate the developmental process of growth and change, Schlossberg, Waters, and Goodman's (1995) model focuses on the nature of transitions and the potential resources from which individuals may draw to cope with transitions. Anchored in theories of adult development, this framework enriches understanding of the nature of transitions new professionals may experience and provides suggestions for negotiating such transitions. Schlossberg et al. defined a transition as "any event, or non-event, that results in changed relationships, routines, assumptions, and roles" (p. 27). Further, they identified four factors that influence an individual's coping abilities during a transition: situation, self, support, and strategies. Briefly defined, these factors constitute a support system and the presence or absence of each influence how the individual copes with change and transition. Situation refers to environmental and perceptual factors that vary by individual, such as what triggers the transition, control over the transition, duration, accompanying role change and stress. Self defines personal and demographic characteristics as well as psychological resources (e.g., self-efficacy, commitment, values, optimism) upon which the individual may draw. Support refers to the types and range of support available to the individual in the transition. Strategies include the behaviors used by individuals to respond to stressful situations (Schlossberg et al., 1995, pp. 53-77).

Connecting the work of Kegan and Baxter Magolda with that of Schlossberg et al., we might presume that the transition from graduate school to the first professional position is one that is expected and for which preparation occurs. Interpersonal maturity and the capacity for self-authorship will influence how new professionals understand and negotiate the transition, as well as the coping resources upon which they have to draw to successfully navigate the transition.

The Bridge

The authors of the three preceding case studies stand on one side of the metaphorical and developmental bridge, as they reflect on the process of crossing over. While each story is unique, because the individuals authoring each narrative bring their own stories and life experiences to the bridge crossing, overarching themes emerge regarding the nature of the journey and the structures of support that facilitate the process of crossing over. Embedded in these three case studies are important lessons regarding the development of a professional identity, effective job search strategies, and navigating life on the other side of the bridge—the beginnings of a career in student affairs.

Self-Authorship

Essential in all three case studies was the importance of knowing one's self. In fact, the job search process tested the strength of one's internal voice or authority as multiple external influences operated in the sometimes-competitive career decision-making and job search arena. Choosing the right paper for a resume, appearing too ethnic, fielding difficult interview questions, negotiating the web of professional and personal lives, or confronting a fear of the unknown made claims on a soon-to-be new professional's sense of self and tested the capacity for self-authorship.

Conducting a successful job search focuses an individual on what is truly important in one's life. Personal values then become the foundation for professional commitments. These in turn, inform the parameters of one's career decision-making and the scope of a job search. For example, Christana knew she did not want to work at a religious institution if doing so meant compromising her philosophy regarding gay and lesbian issues. She wrote, "If I worked at an institution strongly affiliated with the Catholic Church, I did not want to be prevented from being an ally for lesbian, gay, or bisexual ·students..." In so stating, Christana affirmed an important personal value that then informed her job search process. Similarly, Kevin realized that a religious institution like Notre Dame was a good fit because of the institution's ethic of care and philosophy of education.

Kathleen and Craig had an additional layer of complexity as they negotiated a dual-career search and blended their personal values. As they embarked on job searches as a couple, it was important that each defined their own individual identities, as well as their identities as a couple. They explained:

> It took much inward reflection and values clarification individually to determine negotiable and non-negotiable issues... we replaced the freedom to follow individual needs and values with some constraints to finding a place that will support the shared needs and values of us both.

The ability to integrate these two identities depends upon interpersonal maturity, which is an outcome of self-authorship (Baxter Magolda, 2000).

Another poignant example of the capacity for self-authorship appears in Christana's narrative, when she grapples with her racial identity in the context of her job search. Christana's racial identity intersected with job search decisions such as "how ethnic" she would look when interviewing to concerns that she would be "pigeonholed into only being able to work with students of color." Seeking advice from a mentor, Christana found in the mentor's response an enduring value that serves as an anchor for all when crossing the bridge: "That reminder, to be myself, was one of the most important pieces of advice I received during my job search."

Determining how much of one's identity, racial or otherwise, a person is willing to compromise in an environment where it feels like the employer holds all the power, is a complex decision that requires the ability to author one's own life rather than be authored by the perceptions, biases, and expectations of others. The job search and career decision-making process make claims on a person's sense of self and constructions of identity. In fact, in each of these stories written by Kevin, Christana, and Kathleen and Craig, we see how the transition from "how I am" to "how I am now" is navigated as the job search process makes claims on their thinking about who they are and who they are to become. However, the nature of the transition varies for each.

Coping with Transitions

All three case studies pulse with the emotions associated with transitions: to graduate school, to a new job, new city, new colleagues, or a new institutional culture. Kevin refers to this as moving from "comfortable familiarity" to "the unknown." Although certainly not without anxiety and stress, Kevin, Christana, Kathleen and Craig utilized resources available to them and coped well with their transitions. Perhaps due to the benefits of retrospective thinking, or the availability of support networks and psychological as well as physical resources, all successfully navigated the sometimes-stressful journeys of transition.

All anticipated the transition, at least intellectually, of the move from graduate school to professional work and were therefore prepared. However, Christana, Kevin, Kathleen and Craig all acknowledged dynamics of the transition for which they were not prepared. Kathleen and Craig experienced multiple sources of stress because they were seeking new jobs at the same time they were planning their wedding (a decision that in hindsight they realized they might have made differently!). Each story contained elements of feeling out of control during the job search process (i.e., the difficult environment of conference placement interviewing, waiting for institutions to make decisions); fortunately, careful preparation aided Christana, Kathleen and Craig, and Kevin to handle job search stresses.

The presence of support was perhaps the greatest resource for all case study authors in their transitions. Christana's reliance on very supportive and knowledgeable mentors helped her keep the job search in proper perspective and navigate the logistics of the search process. Kathleen and Craig, experiencing great stress and anxiety in negotiating the decisions associated with a dual career search, identified the support of "colleagues, supervisors, and faculty members" as comforting as well as helping to "normalize our experience," because many of these individuals had crossed a similar bridge. Kevin turned to his mentors and family when self-doubt about his decision to attend graduate school haunted him. He also acknowledged that his graduate faculty challenged him, thereby helping him develop skills that would serve him well as he sorted through the dilemmas and ambiguities associated with professional identity and work.

Implicit in the stories of Christana, Kathleen, Craig, and Kevin is the reminder that the transition from graduate school to job one is buttressed greatly by the presence of support systems and networks and that the job search process and transition to professional work is the time to maximize these systems' potential.

Each case study author also revealed a variety of strategies used to cope with transitions. Kathleen and Craig actively learned about their new city by exploring social and community groups with which they might become involved. They also identified effective communication as a strategy and skill essential to their dual-career job search. Seeking information and taking action to alleviate the stress associated with the transition were other strategies utilized. Good preparation was a strategy Christana successfully employed as she geared up for on-campus interviews. She also sought out the advice and guidance of mentors and colleagues to "draw on the lessons they learned from their job searches."

Finally, the resource of self, demographic characteristics as well as psychological resources was evident in many of the case study reflections. Christana conveyed her experience as a person of color, both in terms of her own racial identity as well as others' perceptions of her and the impact this had on her job search process. In so doing, she communicated her pride as a professional of color and what that means to her. Her pride, sense of self, and self-efficacy were sources of strength throughout the job search process. Clarity about one's values, as reflected in the story of Kathleen and Craig, served as a psychological resource as did commitment to the work each wanted to do. Kevin's engagement with the idea of crossroads led him to a more intentional process of thinking about his professional goals and career decision-making. Graduate school experiences further equipped each of these new professionals with a sense of self and self-efficacy that served them well in the job search process and job one.

A Reflective-Analytical Response from a Senior Student Affairs Administrator: Mike's Perspective

The perspective Susan brings, as a graduate preparation faculty member, to the narratives of Kevin, Christana, and Kathleen and Craig serves as the foundation for my discussion of the three case studies as a senior student affairs administrator on the other side of the bridge. Reflecting the interplay between theory and practice, my analysis is grounded in the theory set forth by Susan but tempered by administrative challenges! The case studies reveal the many strengths, struggles, and values that guide graduate students and new professionals. The degree to which new and experienced professionals travel together across the bridge from graduate school to job one in the student affairs profession has important implications for three primary stakeholders—aspiring new professionals, employers of new professionals, and the profession.

Considerations for Aspiring New Professionals

Embedded in the three case studies are four considerations, that if addressed, enhance the likelihood of a positive job one experience: the importance of knowing oneself, while maintaining an openness to change; resisting seductions of the interview process; understanding institutional culture; and developing networks.

Self-Knowledge and Openness to Change

An awareness of needs, values, and desires is perhaps the most important consideration for new professionals in their transition from graduate school to job one. Christana reinforced this concept when describing the need to present "my true self to employers." That, however, is balanced with an openness to change, to see things differently, and to be flexible. In fact, all four case study authors convey the importance of being open to change. Kathleen and Craig found the need to change their views on the role geographical location played in their search process. The needs of students of color and how that factored into her decision-making process evolved in surprising ways for Christana. Kevin's understanding of how change occurs in established organizations evolved during his Notre Dame journey. New learning came with some struggle as emerging professionals were challenged not only to understand new perspectives but also to determine, at the same time, their own individual needs and values. In Kegan's language, the job search process made great claims on individuals' sense of self—the transition from "how I was to how I want to be".

Seductions of the Interview Process

For the aspiring new professional, the job interview process can be seductive. Candidates and employers are on their best behaviors throughout these processes. Candidates might be seduced by jobs that seem too good to be true and by unsolicited flattery that might not have come their way as a graduate student. For example, in one of her interviews, a vice president told Christana that she was his top candidate. These dynamics place an undue physical and mental strain on candidates that might cause them to act hastily, accepting or declining a position for the wrong reasons. In assessing job opportunities, we recom-

mend that aspiring new professionals do not allow employers to undu-
ly rush, either intentionally or unintentionally, important decisions.
Allocating reflection time is a critical part of any job search process. In
the example given above, Christana resisted seduction by the compli-
ment she received from the vice president, carefully considered all
aspects of the interview and proceeded with an open mind to her next
interview. Her deliberative style resulted in her first job offer, and then
after further consideration, her first job.

Resisting seduction, however, is a more difficult task than it might
appear, even when ample reflection time is allocated. Not only is it
tempting to accept a position to ease the strain of the job search process,
but as with other challenges inherent in the job search, resisting seduction depends in large measure on the job candidate's ability to author his
or her own life as well as to manage the transition to job one. Without
the ability to resist, candidates may be more likely to accept a position
that might be impressive to others or that boosts self-esteem through the
lure of flattery. Checking in with supportive faculty, peers, and family
members, as our case study authors did, can help candidates assess if
job offers are considered for internally defined reasons rather than
external pressures.

Institutional Culture

Part of determining whether a job opportunity is the right fit
requires diligently exploring the culture of a potential work environment. Even when the norms, expectations, and habits of a work place
are explicitly presented to candidates, it is important that they form their
own judgment about the culture. Conducting cultural audits is more
than gathering information about, for example, salary, institutional reputation, department size, and organizational structure. Although these
elements are important, it is critical to examine, for example, institutional core values or beliefs and the institution's assumptions about students. Institutional artifacts (e.g., strategic plans, budgets, accreditation
reports, mission statements, surveys) are helpful for conducting cultural audits and are readily available on campuses.

All of the case study authors made efforts to better understand the
cultures of the institutions with which they interviewed. Christana, during a campus interview, used the student newspaper as an artifact to better understand the culture of the institution, asked students and staff to
discuss their favorite campus traditions, and informally chatted with
students in the hallways. Craig and Kathleen pointed to the existence of

a policy on domestic partners that extended to campus housing staff as an important indication of campus culture. Kevin and Christana noted the influence of a mission statement on their career deliberations.

The case study authors learned that sometimes paying attention to culture reveals the imperfections of a potential job setting. When imperfections are revealed, it is necessary to determine whether these shortcomings are important enough to warrant not accepting a job offer. These are difficult decisions that require the ability to create and live one's own values and beliefs and to determine whether these self-authored values and beliefs are congruent with the institution.

Networks

Student affairs work is rarely a solitary endeavor. It is important for aspiring new professionals to seek out collegial advice, perspectives and support. Peers, faculty, and colleagues are invaluable resources who offer a diversity of perspectives on the transitions associated with job one. The case study authors discussed the importance of mentors and teachers from graduate school who then formed the beginning of a supportive network. Kevin fondly recalled the influence of mentors from his undergraduate institution. Christana pointed to the critical support and advice she received from mentors about job search factors. Craig and Kathleen shared how their network of colleagues, supervisors and faculty provided them with the greatest comfort and support in their process. It is important for candidates to begin building their own network of colleagues that will serve them well for many years to come.

Establishing a network takes time, but with careful consideration of specific strategies for creating a web of support, networks take shape. Staying in touch with graduate school classmates is a good place to begin. Taking some risks and initiative to become involved in regional and national professional associations and conferences is a strategy for not only staying in touch with classmates but also strengthening a network that may seem tenuous at best when one leaves graduate school.

Other than a brief reference by Kathleen, the case study authors did not speak directly to networking. The absence of this reference highlights the paucity of networking that occurs among new professionals. Further, developing a network sometimes feels like an arduous task for those new to the profession, especially for new professionals who do not know many others similar to them in important ways, such as in Christana's case, other professionals of color. Yet, each case study author showed an appreciation for the assistance of faculty mentors in the job search process. These faculty mentors, whom Susan noted in her section, were important supports in the transition process and can become valuable resources as students begin to develop professional networks beyond their faculty.

The case study authors provide testimony to the challenges inherent in these noble ideas, as well as to the interrelationships among these considerations and to self-authorship and transition. For example, one's capacity for self-authorship will greatly influence how one manages the challenges associated with the job search process. The stressful nature of the job search has the ability to make claims on an individual's sense of self and will affect the decisions made. Further, the resources each person has to draw upon will also influence the nature of the transition and how each individual negotiates the transition.

The case study authors realize that no Camelot work setting exists. Still, they create optimism about the possibilities of new opportunities. The importance of knowing oneself while being open to change, resisting the seductions of the job search process, understanding institutional culture, and developing and sustaining networks all make positive contributions to the journeys of new professionals.

Considerations for Employers of New Professionals

Employers of new professionals anchor the other side of the job one bridge. Experienced colleagues recognize that they are more than simply supervisors. Employers assume the roles of role models, coaches, mentors, guides, sounding boards, and sources of challenge and support. Through these multiple roles, employers travel to the new professionals' side of the bridge and provide them with good company as they make their journey into the student affairs profession. Employers who recognize and respond to these expanded roles strengthen the profession.

The case study authors offer invaluable reminders of what it means to be new to this profession and how employers can help or hinder them in their first steps into new, uncharted territory. Specifically, Christana, Kevin, Kathleen and Craig remind experienced professionals of the importance of job one, being fair with candidates, facilitating access to networks and resources, and spending quality time with new professionals.

The Importance of Job One

Perhaps the most noteworthy message common to all three case studies is the importance new professionals place on their first job in student affairs. As experienced employers and supervisors become further removed from the experiences of new professionals, it is easy to forget the job search process and the pressures associated with the transition from graduate school to the world of full-time employment. The job one process can be all consuming for new professionals who often depend upon more experienced colleagues to provide much-needed support and guidance. As Susan discussed in her section on transitions, Kathleen and Craig valued advice from supervisors who helped normalize their search experience. Christana described the importance of being able to draw upon the lessons she learned from mentors or the help of mentors who could sometimes make an initial job contact.

One of the most important ways for employers to help new professionals cross over the bridge from graduate school to job one is to take a genuine interest. Unfortunately, this seemingly common-sense advice is too often not followed. Not only do more experienced professionals tend to forget the issues faced by new professionals on their first job, but they also tend to fill their calendars with other responsibilities that may take them away from helping new professionals transition into their new positions. It is important for administrators working with new professionals to realize that they are modeling administrative practices, values, and professional values in their treatment and socialization of new professionals.

Fairness

It is in the best interest of all stakeholders (e.g., graduate students, employers, new professionals, and graduate preparation faculty) and the profession to be fair with candidates, providing them with balanced and complete information about job opportunities and allowing them ample time to contemplate options. Every institution has strengths and liabilities that should be explicitly discussed with candidates during the interview process. Well-informed candidates are likely to make better decisions than those with incomplete or skewed perspectives. Employers hell-bent on wrapping up their job searches sooner rather than later by pressuring candidates for quick decisions not only increase the chances of a candidate making a poor choice but also symbolically convey that the needs of the employer supersede the needs of the staff.

Christana declined an on-campus interview because of an interviewer's honest response to a question she posed about why the institution was interested in hiring her (to diversify the staff). While in the short run this may seem like a loss for the employer, in the long run

Christana' ability to make a well-considered decision based on her values is in everyone's best interest including the employer's. In Kathleen and Craig's situation, the sensitive handling of their interview processes and job offers by their eventual employer enabled them to feel confident and reassured about the choices they were making in spite of some initial reservations. Fairness, while representing a value and norm of ethical behavior, also relates to self-authorship and managing transitions. When candidates can count on being treated fairly through the job search and transition to job one processes, the likelihood of self-authorship is promoted and a successful transition facilitated.

Access to Networks and Resources

Many experienced student affairs professionals take their support networks and resources for granted. Helping younger colleagues make connections is critical to their career development and success. Kathleen described the impact of having colleagues use their networks to support her search. Christana found the experiences of her mentors helpful. Beyond what our case study authors experienced, other examples include inviting staff members to campus events and introducing them to colleagues; inviting new employees to meetings they normally might not attend; encouraging involvement in regional and/or national professional organizations and providing contact information for those groups; nominating staff members for recognition and awards; and identifying local community organizations in need of volunteers. Too often, important opportunities for facilitating connections are overlooked. For instance, Christana was not provided an opportunity at any of her three interviews to meet with staff of color, despite the fact that such interactions could have helped her begin to establish important connections.

Quality Time with New Professionals

The time senior administrators spend with new professionals is often allocated to supervision issues. Solving day-to-day problems can consume what little time supervisors and supervisees spend together. Taking time to interact with new professionals where the focus is solely on the new professional or non-crisis issues is time well spent for both parties. Conversations centering on new professionals' student affairs philosophies, self-authorship, identity and transitions are examples of worthy discussion topics. The content of these conversations has direct application to potential staff development topics. As each case study author suggests, both implicitly as well as explicitly, supervisor anticipation of issues they confront as new professionals would have aided them in their transitions.

Conversations of this nature benefit the more experienced professional as well through exposure to new ideas, deepening their understanding of a different generation of colleagues, and staying current with the literature of the field. Allocating time for these kinds of conversations has the potential to revitalize both the new professionals and their mentors.

Employers must not underestimate the intensity of the transition that new professionals are making from graduate school to job one. Each new professional's ability to cope with the transition will be influenced, as the Schlossberg et al. model suggests, by the situation, self, support, and strategies. In turn, employers have an opportunity to influence these factors by being fair throughout the interview process, spending quality time with new professionals, anticipating issues that they will experience, and facilitating access to people and resources to support the transition.

Considerations for the Profession

The job one process is an important introduction of new colleagues to the student affairs profession. This process says much about the values of the profession.

Anchoring Both Sides of the Bridge

As described by Susan, one side of the bridge are candidates and their graduate school experience and the other side are employers who are ready to receive these newest colleagues into their work environments. It is imperative that all stakeholders in this venture anchor both sides of the bridge to improve the nature of the transition across the bridge. This includes improving the effectiveness of both graduate programs and employing organizations. Initiating conversations among individuals helping to prepare aspiring new professionals for a career in student affairs (e.g., faculty, assistantship and internship supervisors) and employers of these new professionals would enhance the quality of everyone's work life, including the lives of undergraduate students.

Unfortunately, genuine and ongoing dialogue among the four stakeholder groups (graduate students, faculty, new professionals, and supervisors) rarely occurs. Such a conversation among all the stakeholders might lead to this initial question: How could a new professional's transition be enhanced? Kevin in particular articulated the need for improvement in helping "students learn how to navigate the entry level." Kathleen's and Craig's experience, while having a successful conclusion, reminds us of how difficult a dual career search is and the need to collectively look for better ways to meet the needs of colleagues engaged in a dual career search. Certainly Christana's experience points to the added complications our colleagues of color face in the job one process. All the stakeholders in this endeavor need to be engaged in these conversations to find viable solutions to these issues.

Ethics

Student affairs professional associations have published numerous statements of ethics. For the most part, however, they do not directly address the job search process for new professionals. Ethical statements should be amended to include explicit guidelines for candidates, faculty, and employers. As the case study authors demonstrated, candidates struggle with composing a fair and impressive resume, contemplating job offers, and negotiating compensation packages. It is interesting to note that none of the case studies spoke to any set of ethics related to the job search process. Each case study author wrestled with a number of ethical dilemmas. For example, Kathleen in deciding how long she could keep a potential employer waiting after a job offer; Christana is weighing how her ethnicity influenced the interview process; and Kevin's struggles with how his ideal notions conflicted with the realities of his situation. However, none of the authors cast their dilemmas in terms of professional ethics, which suggests an absence of an awareness of applicable codes and standards.

Job Search Processes for New Professionals

The transition from graduate student to new professional has not changed in decades. For example, the conference placement center approach to securing a job (affectionately known as a meat market) remains a popular route to securing employment. Yet, it has inherent limitations. As Christana, who had an interview at the bottom of an escalator illustrated, the physical setting of placement services is impersonal, lacks privacy, and may have an overwhelming feel. Candidates experience a physically and emotionally draining few days that are not conducive to the truest representation of self. Employers look at so many candidates in a short amount of time that they often have trouble even remembering them.

Advances in technology (e.g., on-line job postings, electronic resumes, teleconferencing, etc.) may be the impetus for altering this process to better support the needs of new professionals. For example, candidates are becoming increasingly able to conduct electronic searches for positions that best meet their interests and needs (e.g. based upon geographical location, functional responsibilities, salary range, required experience). Teleconferencing may become a more inexpensive way for candidates to conduct initial interviews with employers rather than traveling to national conferences. Christana's search process reflected some of the early efforts to better utilize technology in the placement service process and she mentioned web pages as a future tool for improving her ability to showcase her skills and accomplishments. Given candidates' increasing sophistication with technology, it is also likely that those institutions that effectively use technology in their recruitment processes (e.g. web versus printed material, virtual tours of campus, availability/encouragement of email contacts) will have an advantage.

Job search processes should be redesigned to combine the strengths of the old world and those of the new. For example, technology tools could be used to enhance the first step screening process; teleconferencing replaces telephone interviews; CDs replace paper resumes. Conference placement then could be utilized more effectively for interviewing that enables greater exchange of information and relationship building between candidate and employer.

We all have an investment in how the transition from graduate school to first job goes and thus have a responsibility for the condition of the bridge that is being crossed by our newest colleagues. Aspiring new professionals, employers, and faculty all stand to gain from a deeper understanding of how this process is supposed to work and how it is working in actuality. Case study authors have provided us with a valuable snapshot of what occurs during this time. While most of the experiences they report are well worth celebrating and encouraging, there are elements that bear further scrutiny and revision. The transition from graduate school to job one will be enhanced by increased communication between faculty and practitioners, the articulation of a set of ethics and standards for the job one process, and reconsideration of how job searches are conducted in an age of technology.

CONCLUSION: GRADUATE PREPARATION FACULTY AND STUDENT AFFAIRS ADMINISTRATORS ON THE BRIDGE TOGETHER

As we conclude our reflective expedition examining the bridge of transition from both theoretical and practical perspectives, we revisit the structure of the bridge itself. Returning to the metaphor of the bridge introduced earlier in our chapter, Robert Kegan (1994), building upon the work of William Perry, suggested:

> Perry understood that if developmental education is a matter of collaboratively building a consciousness bridge, then the bridge builder must have an equal respect for both ends, creating a firm foundation on both sides of the chasm students will traverse. Firmly anchoring the bridge on one end by welcoming rather than disdaining the way they understand, as Kierkegard put it, Perry then invited his students to join him in constructing what they would only gradually come to see was a bridge they could choose to walk out on. (p. 278-279)

Implicit in the case studies is the suggestion that student affairs work could be strengthened when graduate students, faculty, new professionals and employers collectively evaluate the structural integrity of the bridge. In a world that becomes increasingly, we need to improve the quantity and quality of our conversations about the work we share.

We hope that graduate preparation programs, in collaboration with the student affairs professionals with whom graduate students interact, create a firm foundation for traversing the bridge. Part of this process, however, is helping soon-to-be new professionals to understand, in more complex ways who the self is that is poised to walk out on to the bridge and to provide students with new ways of thinking about the journey and their resources. The theoretical perspectives offered by concepts of self-authorship and the four factors influencing transitions ground and help explain the perspectives offered by the case study authors.

The most effective way to anchor the bridge on both sides is for graduate preparation programs and student affairs professionals to join together in substantive and meaningful ways to develop curriculum and professional development experiences that complement one another and integrate with the core values and contemporary issues of the profession. The distance between graduate preparation programs and professional work, or from theory to practice, should be a short one. Graduate preparation faculty and student affairs administrators should model this more integrative and mutually reinforcing approach in their work.

Through our reflective-analytic responses, we hope we modeled the spirit of collaboratively building and anchoring the bridge of transition from graduate school to job one. This approach took shape as we collaborated on each case study as well as in the way we co-wrote our chapter: beginning from our own professional standpoints but meeting in the middle. Each individual story, however, illuminating the results of reflection on the process of stepping out on to the bridge and looking back from the other side, formed the core of our analysis and led us to integrate theory with practice in ways to make sense of the nature of the journey. Along the way, we realized these individual narratives tell the story of our profession and suggest important implications for how graduate preparation faculty and student affairs administrators must meet more often on the bridge to enhance the professional development and anchor the transition of our future leaders from graduate school to job one.

***

The authors thank Elisa Abes for reading and offering constructive feedback about this chapter.

Section Two Introduction

In Chapters Five through Seven, new professionals have crossed the bridge, leaving their community of scholars and colleagues from graduate school behind and entering their first professional positions within Student Affairs. Molly Reas focuses on her transition into a position where she actually felt like she had less responsibility and autonomy than when she was a graduate student. Stephanie Kurtzman reflects on her challenges, self-doubts, and successes of establishing professional credibility and self-confidence. And, Diana Jaramillo discusses her attempts to find her professional niche within an orientation office while struggling to establish a good working relationship with her supervisor. Two themes, common in all three narratives, are the importance of building solid supervisor-supervisee relationships and finding a place in already-established and defined work settings while attempting to establish a professional identity and credibility with colleagues.

Michael Ignelzi and Patricia Whitely use the conceptual frameworks of a *synergistic supervision model* (Winston & Creamer, 1997) and *constructivist developmental theory*, particularly Kegan's (1982,1994) theory to interpret these three narratives. Michael and Patricia highlight the importance of consistency regarding a new professional's professional and personal development and one's ability to be reflective on his or her experiences and interactions.

5

THE EARLY DAYS IN THE *REAL WORLD*: ESTABLISHING A PROFESSIONAL IDENTITY

Molly Reas

> The two primary elements that form the core of my leadership philosophy are value and empowerment. ... The first component of my leadership philosophy is that each person in a group or organization is valuable. As a leader, one of my jobs is to let people know, both through my words and actions, that they are valued members of the organization. ... The second component of my leadership philosophy is that my role as a leader is to empower others.

This passage is from one of my last assignments in graduate school, a paper reflecting on my journey as a leader and describing my personal leadership philosophy. In my final student services administration class, we explored topics such as shared leadership and spirituality in leadership and discussed our own experiences working in different types of organizations. We also discussed various organizational models and management practices employed in higher education and the corporate world. Earning my Master's degree in student affairs and working in a variety of offices shaped my views on leadership in unexpected ways.

My philosophy not only described the type of student affairs leader I wanted to be, but the type of environment I desired in my search for job one — a place where I, as well as others, would be valued members of the organization and empowered to grow as professionals. If my future organization met these two conditions, I felt there was a good chance I would be satisfied professionally.

I was intent on finding a good fit between my values and those of my future office and university. I was specifically searching for a job in admissions, and since a major component of admissions work is representing a university, it was extremely important that I believed in the mission and values of my new institution. Initially, the student-centered language used in Radford University's (RU) institutional goals and publications attracted me to the university. When I interviewed for an Assistant Director position in the Office of Admissions at RU, I was pleased to find that the interview process involved everyone in the office, including support staff. I interpreted this to be an outward sign of shared leadership and that senior office staff valued everyone's opinion. When I learned that every professional staff member in the office had travel, application review, and programming responsibilities, my impression of a collaborative work environment was enhanced. I thought that an office in which each person had significant responsibilities would most likely be an empowering environment.

My interview experience at RU was in sharp contrast to an interview at another university, where I was told that the successful applicant would primarily be giving information sessions and meeting with prospective students and families (basically, admissions grunt work), while more challenging tasks such as application review would be assigned to more experienced staff members. Similar to the feeling I had experienced as a prospective student when I walked across the campus of my undergraduate alma mater, Indiana University and things just felt right, things felt right at RU. People were genuine and the office staff interacted with students much more than at other schools I had visited. Upon comparing and contrasting my job prospects after a round of interviews, I felt that RU would provide me with the most opportunities to be a valued, empowered staff member. Although RU was located in a rural area away from my family, boyfriend, and the vast majority of my friends, I was ready to leave the Midwest and try something new. When RU offered me a position as an Assistant Director of Admissions, I decided to start my full-time student affairs career in Virginia.

I would now be part of an office staff comprised of eleven professional staff members and eight support staff members. Most of the professional staff were in their 20s or early 30s, and this was another of the position's major attractions. Since I was moving to an area where I knew no one, I hoped I would be able to make a few friends through work. While a few professional staff members had significant admissions or student affairs experience, five of the eleven were new hires (myself included), and the few remaining staff members had limited admissions / student affairs experience. The admissions director spent much of his time and energy on big picture items such as university enrollment goals and external relations, while the associate director was responsible for the day-to-day functioning of the office. Thus, during my first year in the Office of Admissions, I had two general supervisors instead of one direct supervisor.

About a month after accepting the position, I reported for work at RU. From my experiences as a graduate assistant and graduate intern, I expected to be thrown into the office mix immediately and to receive a list of projects and responsibilities. It seemed logical that my responsibilities and workload would be greater than what I had experienced in graduate school, but surprisingly, this was not the case. While special projects had been assigned to the vast majority of my colleagues, there were no projects waiting in the wings for me. It seemed as though very little thought or preparation had gone into my arrival and orientation. I felt my supervisors were not quite sure what to do with me. During my first several weeks on the job I kept myself busy reading publications, asking students and fellow staff members about their experiences at RU, and sitting at the front desk welcoming visitors — basically doing anything that would help me to learn about my new university and contribute to the office. I knew it was extremely important that I learn a great deal of information about the university in a short amount of time, but I soon grew tired of devising ways to stay busy and longed for a project to call my own.

Feelings of Being Underutilized

With the start of travel season in the fall, I finally had enough assigned tasks to fill my work day. I kept busy scheduling high school visits, making travel arrangements, and talking to prospective students and their parents at college fairs, but I still hoped for a special assignment. It took me awhile to realize that my feelings of dissatisfaction stemmed from being underutilized. While the tasks I completed were important, they did not utilize any of my special skills or the knowledge I had acquired from my college degrees. I had skills and talents to contribute to the office that were left untapped, and I did not understand why I was not called upon to do more. If my supervisors thought I was incompetent, then why had they hired me? If they thought I was competent, then why weren't my skills being utilized?

Coming from a student affairs graduate preparation program in which I had frequently analyzed different work environments from a variety of organizational perspectives, I could not help but analyze my current work environment using different organizational models and theories. I found similarities between my work environment and quite a few of the organizational metaphors outlined in Gareth Morgan's (1998) book, *Images of Organization*. In my frustration at being underutilized, I would frequently return to Morgan's view of organizations as machines. Since my work responsibilities included planning and executing travel assignments, representing the university at college fairs and high school visits, meeting with prospective students and families who were visiting campus, and reviewing applications, I did not do anything that could not have easily been done by my colleagues. I felt as though I was little more than a cog in the machine — someone who could easily be replaced. If I were to leave the office one day and never come back, I believed that things would carry on just the same. In short, I felt neither valued nor empowered. I had moved away from family and friends to grow professionally and this was not happening.

Although I was expected to make good decisions when meeting with prospective students and families, high school guidance counselors, and the public in general, the main focus of my job was to do rather than to think, another characteristic of Morgan's machine metaphor. In terms of the office culture, my initial impression of a collaborative office environment had been correct. However, while the doing in the office was shared, thinking tasks such as what work should be done and who should do it only involved senior office staff. My opinion was rarely asked and I had no input into project assignments. I only implemented the tasks that had been assigned to me. I had spent six years in higher education honing my critical thinking skills, and now all that was required of me was common sense. Except for scheduling my recruitment visits at high schools and making my hotel accommodations, I felt very little ownership of my work.

This job one experience was in stark contrast to the world of graduate school in which faculty members and supervisors encouraged and expected me to think and be accountable at all times. I now realized how important ownership and autonomy were to me in a work setting. Although I knew my situation was not unique, more idealistic management theories and organizational structures filled my mind; the mismatch between the classroom and the working world was a major frustration.

I began to realize that I had made many false assumptions regarding how my Master's degree in College Student Personnel would be received in the *real world*. At RU, my degree appeared to be nothing more than a credential that entitled me to a slightly higher starting salary than my colleagues who had been hired with undergraduate degrees. Although I realized that my Master's degree was not a substitute for full-time work experience in the field, I anticipated that it would demonstrate a certain knowledge base and level of competency as a student affairs professional. It was probably naïve of me to believe this, but I had expected to start with at least one or two assigned projects. As a graduate assistant, I had spent one year working in Greek Affairs and another teaching career development seminars for undergraduates. I had also completed graduate internships in Alumni and Admissions. These experiences played a huge role in shaping my professional identity and in preparing me to contribute to my new work environment. It was frustrating to think that the many hours of work I had contributed to the university as a graduate student each week for nearly two years were not considered by others to be real work experience.

I had gained so much personally from my graduate school experience, yet I now questioned whether it had been a good decision to pursue graduate school immediately after earning my bachelor's degree in psychology and sociology. I did not use much of the knowledge and skills I had gained as an undergraduate during my first year on the job, and having earned my Master's degree only served to make my feelings of underutilization that much worse. I had more responsibility as a graduate assistant than as a full-time professional, and at times, this realization was hard to accept. I thought that earning my Master's degree would allow me to be a more effective and polished professional, better able to contribute to my office and the field in general, but this was a view that many of those around me did not seem to share.

I am the first to admit that I was an inexperienced full-time professional when compared to senior staff members with 15 and 20 years of admissions experience. However, senior office staff did not acknowledge that I did have more student affairs experience than my new colleagues who had started working in the office immediately after earning undergraduate degrees. During my first year of work, I was the only person in my office with a degree in student affairs. If colleagues in my new office had been more familiar with the rigor and content of my student affairs preparation program, would my skills and potential to contribute to the office have been recognized sooner? Although I will never know the answer, I think this is an interesting question.

One unforeseen consequence of completing my Master's degree in student affairs before starting work in the Office of Admissions was that it raised my expectations of my work environment, supervisors, co-workers, and myself. To me, it seemed that I had a slightly different set of expectations from others with different academic backgrounds. Whereas some of my colleagues could look at an unfavorable situation and conclude, "I don't really like this, but that's just the way things are," I knew that things did not have be one certain way — that there were many different ways of operating within organizations. Rather than sitting back in relative contentment, I felt the need to take action even when others did not. All things considered, had I not learned to look at things from so many different perspectives in graduate school, I would not have been as frustrated with being underutilized at the beginning of job one.

Establishing a Professional Identity

In addition to feeling underutilized, another major job one frustration was establishing a professional identity. I knew I looked quite a bit younger than my actual age of 24, but I did not expect my physical appearance to have a significant impact on how others viewed my capabilities. I was caught by surprise the first few times I introduced myself to a colleague or the parent of a prospective student with my name and title and a few minutes later the individual would ask me "What's your major?" or "What year are you in school?" I would then be compelled to remind this person "I am a full-time professional." Unfortunately, I found that many people correlate a youthful appearance with not being knowledgeable or competent and thus do not treat young professionals with the respect they deserve.

One time during a high school visit I was meeting with a handful of students in a room across from the guidance office when a teacher opened the door to the room and said in a gruff voice, "You guys know you aren't supposed to be in this room with the door shut. What are you doing in here?" Before he could reprimand us further, I explained that I was a college representative and had permission from the guidance office to conduct my information session in the room. His tone immediately changed as he said, "Oh, I thought you were a student" and left the room, shutting the door behind him. Another time, I had dropped by the office on a Sunday afternoon to prepare for a recruiting trip when a high-ranking university official stopped me in the building lobby and demanded to know what I was doing. When I replied that I worked in the Office of Admissions, this individual looked at me skeptically and asked if I had keys to the office.

While many people found my mistaken identity stories amusing (especially when shared with people at least a few years older than myself), for me they were no laughing matter. These cases of mistaken identity angered me. While a student, I had become frustrated with people taking me too seriously at times; now that I was in the working world, suddenly people were not taking me seriously enough. I was simply not prepared for others to make decisions about my professional competencies based upon my appearance. Of all the things that surprised me during my first year on the job, this was the biggest shock.

Even people who respected my work and were generally supportive of my efforts would sometimes make comments about my youthful appearance at the expense of my professional credibility. Once, two of my twenty-something colleagues and I were giving tours of campus to a group of high school guidance counselors who were visiting RU on a retreat. Each of us had spent an hour with a small group of counselors, providing them with information about the university and answering dozens of questions before the individual groups reconvened for a large group session. To bring a little humor to the session, the opening speaker announced after the tours, "I know we weren't able to have students give you campus tours today, but your guides do look like students." My two colleagues and I were then left feeling that much of what we had done that afternoon to convey our professional competencies had been wiped out with one sentence. If we had tried to get a laugh out of the counselors by referring to the speaker's age and graying hair with "Hasn't he retired yet?" I doubt that neither the speaker nor the audience would have found this to be funny. If it isn't funny to joke about a professional being older than he or she is, then why it is funny to joke about a professional being younger than he or she is? In my view, both statements attempt to undermine a person's credibility and competencies.

I find it interesting that age-related comments such as the one above in which my colleagues and I were referred to as students often come from individuals who are very sensitive about derogatory and discriminatory comments in general and would never think about making a sexist or racist remark. This has led me to believe that some professionals do not realize how their comments are heard by new professionals, and the negative impact that a few words can make. With so many people operating under the assumption that a youthful appearance equals inexperience and/or incompetence, it is important that colleagues do not further this belief.

Surprisingly, one thing that both helped and hurt my quest to establish a professional identity was the travel component of my job. The amount of time I spent away from campus made it virtually impossible to serve on campus committees, teach an introduction to higher education class for new students, or advise a student organization — all responsibilities that would have helped convey my professional competencies to others on campus. Many faculty members and other student affairs staff rarely saw me, making it more difficult for them to know the real me. Thus, my frequent absences made it even harder to combat the youthful appearance stereotype.

Luckily for me, however, the world of admissions and student affairs is a very small place. While my travel responsibilities hindered my efforts to establish a professional identity on campus, traveling helped me to develop credibility within my own office. Admissions work is different from many other student affairs areas in that supervisors are often unable to see their staff members' efforts firsthand. They are not usually present when staff make presentations at high schools or answer questions at college fairs. At times, the only way an admissions supervisor can evaluate a staff member's performance is through feedback from admissions personnel at other colleges and universities, guidance counselors, and prospective students and families.

After working in the office for a few months, I slowly became aware of how frequently information was exchanged between my office and other college and university admissions offices. Although I do not know much of the content that was exchanged during my first year on the job, I learned there were times when my supervisors received positive comments regarding my performance through admissions counselors representing other schools and high school guidance counselors. These comments may have helped more than anything in demonstrating to my supervisors my professional competencies, strong work ethic, and ability to work independently. Perhaps doing the right thing when no one is watching is sometimes more valuable than doing the right thing when a whole room is watching your every move.

Coping Strategies

While I heard many of my fellow admissions counselors complain about the amount of travel involved in the profession, traveling also helped me to cope during my underutilization period. During the fall semester, I was frequently away from the office talking with prospective students, parents, and high school guidance counselors. While I was involved in very little decision-making when in the office, I was my own boss when attending college fairs and visiting high schools. On the road, I was once again able to enjoy the autonomy I had taken for granted as a graduate student. As I scheduled all of my own school visits, I had a great deal of control over my schedule and was able to make my own decisions. Traveling helped me to keep my cool in the office when my frustrations ran high, because if I could just make it through a few more days or weeks, I would be back on the road again, busy and happy.

By the middle of the spring semester, my frustrations reached an all-time high. I had tried a few different strategies during the year to convey that I was capable of handling additional responsibilities. The first strategy involved casually asking senior staff members at regular intervals if there was anything I could do to help. Soon after joining the office I had asked one of my supervisors how project assignments were made, and I was told that senior staff liked to wait and determine people's strengths before assigning projects. Thus, I knew it was important that I find as many opportunities as possible to demonstrate my capabilities. This strategy brought me a few small assignments such as designing a flyer to advertise a campus-wide event and creating a scavenger hunt for a special tour group, but it did little to alleviate my frustration.

The second strategy involved directly playing up one of my strengths by volunteering my services as a copy editor for admissions publications and letters. My abilities as an editor and proofreader had allowed me to contribute to others (and other organizations) in the past, and I hoped this skill would enable me to make a more substantial contribution to my new work environment. Happily, this strategy worked, and I began updating information for college guidebooks and proofreading office publications such as admissions newsletters and brochures during the spring semester.

The third strategy centered on being patient and consistent — ultimately letting my conscientious nature speak for itself. Although this strategy did not improve my situation in the short-term, it served me well in the long-term by helping me to earn additional job responsibilities in my second year of full-time work.

Speaking Up

It felt like I had tried just about everything except for sharing with my supervisors how I truly felt. Before moving Virginia, I had made the decision to stay with my new job for a year before making any major decisions. Although I had watched friends and graduate school colleagues change jobs after five or six months, I chose to follow my brother's advice that I should try to make the best of a new situation for a year before deciding to stay or make a change. I have always been the type of person who prefers to get the lay of the land before voicing strong opinions, and this situation was no different. I believed that if I assessed factors such as organizational culture and supervisory style first, then I would be more effective when I did assert myself and voice my opinions.

Other important factors influencing my decision not to voice my feelings sooner were the cyclical nature of admissions work and, once again, the amount of travel performed by professional staff. Since I was only on campus for approximately half of the fall semester and also traveled for a few weeks during spring semester, it took me longer to assess the office culture and how things really worked than if I had been on campus every day. Even when I was in the office, many of my colleagues were not, so my interactions with some individuals were few and far between during my first several months. Due to the amount of time spent traveling during fall semester and reviewing applications during spring semester, most of the planning and evaluation in the Office of Admissions occurred during the summer. At this time, project assignments were typically made for the entire year so that unless there were personnel changes, there were limited opportunities for new responsibilities mid-cycle.

Once the academic year began winding down, the time came for me to speak my mind. Although there were so many aspects of my job that I liked — my colleagues, the variety of tasks, and the ability to work both independently and collaboratively — the bottom line was that I did not feel valued or empowered. I had searched for an office environment in which I would be able to work to my potential and grow professionally, and neither of these things were happening.

Change had been sweeping through the office at the end of the spring semester, with three staff members leaving — one to pursue a Master's degree, one to move with a spouse, and a third to pursue a new career. This meant that several plum projects were now up for grabs, and I hoped at least one of them would land on my desk. When I was asked to join my supervisors to talk about project assignments one spring day, I found myself in an ideal situation to talk about my experiences during the past year and share my hopes for the next. I had prepared for this conversation for months and gone over my words time and time again, yet it was still difficult to tell my supervisors how I truly felt. I respected them and I did not want to put them on the defensive. I was looking for a dialogue, not a confrontation.

When I was finally asked for my thoughts on project assignments for the upcoming admissions cycle, I told my supervisors that I had felt underutilized all year, and I did not understand why I had not been given more responsibility. If my performance at work had been lacking, I really wanted to know how I could improve. I had a strong desire to contribute, and it was important to me that I had more opportunities to do this in the near future. Although I believed this was already understood, I wanted to make it clear that I had not moved to Virginia for the benefit of my personal life. I had come to work, and I was ready and willing to do more.

My supervisors listened to what I had to say, and they took my words seriously. My patience and persistence had paid off. I had proven myself to be a capable employee, and my supervisors agreed that I would be given more opportunities to contribute in the coming year. While senior office staff had assigned projects for the previous year with limited information on how the office's five new hires would perform, they agreed that office responsibilities had been divided in such a way that some people had been given more than they could handle, while others had been underutilized. I not only left this meeting with a commitment from my supervisors that my level of involvement in special projects would increase, but with the knowledge that I could assert myself in an appropriate manner and have an honest conversation with my supervisors. I have used this latter knowledge several times since.

Arriving as a Professional

Although this was a difficult conversation for me to have on a few different levels, it ended up being one of the best things I have ever done professionally. Not only did it boost my confidence, it helped pave the way for a more collegial relationship with my supervisors and a second year in the office that looked and felt very different from the first. By the time fall travel season rolled around again, my role had changed from someone who was underutilized to someone who had been given multiple opportunities for professional growth and development. These opportunities included working with admissions staff from seven other colleges and universities to plan a program for high school guidance counselors and to travel abroad to recruit international students.

I do not think that my supervisors knew just how frustrated I was with my lack of responsibility in the office until our spring conversation. Although travel responsibilities made evaluation activities more difficult to conduct, I do believe it would have been helpful to have had regular meetings with at least one of my supervisors to talk about issues such as my transition to the office and my work performance. While I talked with my supervisors on a regular basis and was frequently asked how I was doing, an informal "How are you?" is not the same as sitting down with a supervisor to talk about your professional goals and your progress toward them. While the office did utilize an annual review process, meeting with new staff more regularly would have made troubleshooting much easier and allow for certain issues to be addressed in a more effective, timely fashion. While a year may seem like a relatively short time to a more seasoned professional, a year can be very long to a new professional who is being underutilized.

Voicing my opinions also helped to emphasize that the orientation and transition of new staff members is a critical issue that needs to be addressed in a proactive manner. A few of my colleagues voiced similar concerns about the underutilization of new staff members during the office's annual review process, and together, we made an impact. Once again, I think supervisors often forget what it is like to be a new professional. With frequent turnover and a hectic office environment, I recognize that it is often easier for an experienced staff member to complete a task than train a less experienced staff member. However, I also know that if more untapped potential can be utilized, work can be more evenly distributed, lightening everyone's workload. If individuals do not have the opportunity to utilize their unique skills and talents in an organization they will not feel valued or empowered, resulting in a greater likelihood they will leave when another opportunity comes their way. Now that I am a more experienced staff member, I can appreciate the difficulty in training new staff when there are few experienced staff members. One of the challenges in the next phase of my professional development is to make training and developing new staff a priority, despite deadlines and a hectic schedule. I am now in a position to be a resource for new professionals, and I hope I can somehow live up to the expectations I had for others when I began job one.

When I look back at my graduate school experience and the pieces that have been the most valuable to me in the world of work, a few things immediately come to mind. One is that in learning how to advocate for students, I learned to advocate for myself. I had developed confidence in myself as a student as far back as kindergarten, but it was not until graduate school that I developed confidence in myself as a professional. I now know I have the knowledge and skills necessary to make a significant contribution to my work environment.

Another thing I learned in graduate school is that I do have the ability to effect positive change, and this is something I tried to do while in the Office of Admissions. I might not have transformed students' lives directly in my job, but I could help transform the organization I was a part of to better fit the needs of students, the university, my colleagues, and myself. While I have held onto much of my idealism, I now have a better understanding of how things work in the real world. I have a more realistic view of the things I can change, and the things that I cannot change. This understanding has made me more grounded as a professional and enables me to work more effectively. Another of my goals is to continue to effect positive change.

I am glad I gave my first job a chance before striking out for something new. While I know that sometimes it is best to leave a negative situation, choosing to stay at my first student affairs job for three years was more rewarding than frustrating or disappointing. In contrast to my underutilization period, I felt valued and empowered the majority of the time during my last two years in the office. As my responsibilities increased, I was able to think more, do more, and provide more input into office decisions. Everyone operates differently, but waiting to voice my opinions until I had the opportunity to assess my new surroundings and develop a rapport with my supervisors was a good decision for me. I do not regret the timing of my conversation and would make the same decision if I were to do it all again.

In revisiting my graduate paper *Reflections on my Leadership Journey: My Leadership Philosophy* while writing this chapter, I was both surprised and pleased to find how little my leadership philosophy had changed since graduate school, especially considering the strides I made in my journey as a leader. Although I wish my expectations had been more realistic entering job one, perhaps in some ways, I actually knew more than I gave myself credit for in terms of what is truly important to me and what I need to be satisfied in my professional life. Of all the things I gained from graduate school that affected my job one experience, taking the *journey within* and defining who I am and what is most important to me as a professional have been the most valuable of all.

6

GETTING FROM DAY ONE
TO YEAR FOUR: PERSPECTIVES ON MY
FIRST THREE YEARS AS A STUDENT
AFFAIRS PROFESSIONAL

Stephanie N. Kurtzman

Boxes surround me! This is not so different from three years of storing t-shirts, canvas gloves, binders, books, and items students have accidentally left behind   all in my humble office. This time, though, I am packed to move upstairs to an office more than double the size of my current space. The process of packing, sorting through files, and watching my office dismantled before my eyes, gives me pause for much needed reflection three years after arriving at Washington University in St. Louis (Wash U) as a very, very green new professional.

Before I departed The University of Vermont (UVM), where I completed my Master's degree, I recall asking a friend who had a few years of professional experience under her belt: "What do I *do* on Day One?" How do I begin? Where do I begin? How will I *ever* become comfortable in this new professional role? With two years of graduate school behind me – which included an assistantship in Residential Life, four distinct practica, a summer internship, as well as four years of co-curricular involvement as an undergraduate – I had no idea how to begin!

"You just walk into your office and start going through files," my friend replied. "You make your space your own. You move furniture around, you decorate, and you start making sense of your new job." Okay – I can do that. And so I did. On a rainy, humid June day in 1998 in a new city far west of my graduate school home and far east of my residence for 23 years in California, I walked into my new home away from home in Student Activities. I said my "hellos," sat down at my desk, and started rummaging through files.

I found nothing less than a goldmine as I proceeded nervously to acclimate myself to my new job as Coordinator for Women's Programs and Community Service. Opening the file drawer under my desk, I discovered a file with my name on it and large capital letters: "LOOK HERE FIRST!" In this manila folder I found my predecessor's semester reports, a list of key contacts and people I should meet, a tentative timeline for the semester, and suggested summer projects. The stars were in my favor, and I tentatively concluded that I would survive.

***

This transition was not just about starting my first job. It was about moving to a new city, living with relatives while I searched for an apartment, earning my first real paycheck, figuring out how to date after graduate school, continuing the exploration of Judaism that focused my job search around metropolitan areas, and struggling to fit into professional clothes and to be the professional that everyone expected me to be. I was lucky to find an outstanding first job, but the transition was anything but easy.

One of my new experiences upon moving to St. Louis was actually renting an apartment and living off campus – a first after six years in the residence halls. Along with this came the opportunity to build a life completely separate from my life on campus. Particularly during the early days when I felt as though work was coming at me from all directions, it was critical that I had a place to go, a dog to pet, and friends to be with who helped me balance other important aspects of my life. Each person I met introduced me to new and interesting people, and I encountered many individuals who truly reached out to help me adjust. I would hope to be as generous to other newcomers as they were to me.

***

Because I coordinate community service at Washington University, students assume that I was heavily involved in community service as an undergraduate. The truth is, my involvement throughout college and graduate school was incredibly skewed toward residential life, for no other reason than because it was my first and most happy home as a college student leader. When I began the job search process during my second year in Vermont, I struggled deeply about what I wanted to do in my professional life.

I knew residential life like the back of my hand and to this day value the work of resident advisors and hall directors immensely. I did not know if I wanted to continue down that career path, but I sure felt tracked into residential life as I began the job search process. I didn't want to work in student activities either, being much more concerned about what I considered the meaty issues of student development as opposed to the planning and monitoring of parties. Although I completed an internship in the Center for Career Development at UVM, and in the Dean's office at Middlebury College, these experiences seemed so far removed and unfamiliar to my world of residential life that I wondered if I would fit there either.

I did know that social issues concerned me deeply. I had been heavily influenced by my undergraduate years at Occidental College in Los Angeles, where I enrolled in such courses as "Cross-Cultural Issues in American Society," where I sat under curfew during the Los Angeles riots following the Rodney King verdict, where whites were the minority among students of color, and where cross-cultural dialogue and interaction was a major institutional priority. I knew I wanted to change the world, and I knew I was driven by both intellectual study and practical application of efforts to understand and improve upon our communities. I completed an internship with the service-learning program at UVM and knew that this concept fascinated me. I loved my Women's Center internship experience at UVM because it allowed me to act on my feminist values. I also knew residential life is where the jobs are, and women's centers are where the jobs are not.

During my job search process in the spring of 1998, I was like a runaway train. I applied to dozens of jobs in any city that seemed large enough to support a vibrant Jewish community, and every single job opportunity was in residential life. At the American College Personnel Association's (ACPA) annual convention, I interviewed back-to-back for these jobs. I was always most interested in residential life positions that included 10-15 hours per week in a related office on campus, such as the career center or community service – anything that would draw me away from a pure residential life position. I told my friends that in an ideal world, I would work in a women's center and that my second choice was to work with a community service program.

Somewhere between job supplement postings 1 and 30 in the ACPA placement center, which happened to be in St. Louis that year, I spotted a job only angels could have created: Coordinator for Women's Programs and Community Service. It was too good to be true! And, it was at Washington University in St. Louis, a high caliber, mid-sized institution – just what I was hoping for. This job was for me. But who would hire me? I had one semester of practicum experience in the Women's Center, and one of the same with service-learning. That was it!

Luckily, I was smart enough to submit my resume and let them decide if I was a viable candidate. The rest of the story is a wonderful blur. I interviewed during the last available interview slot during the convention and felt I had done as well as possible. A few days later, a Washington University representative called to schedule a phone interview. I organized my thoughts, conversed with friends and colleagues working in student activities, in community service, and in the non-profit world, and crossed my fingers. The phone interview went well enough to warrant an invitation to campus. During my campus interview, I met with scores of interesting people during a marathon day of interviews, and I flew back to Vermont to conclude my graduate career.

And I was offered the job!

And I accepted.

Since then, I have never doubted that good preparation and a courageous leap of faith are the only ways to find your dreams. If I did not dream big enough to apply for this job, I would not be where I am today — in the middle of an office full of boxes.

***

I learned quickly that landing a job is only the first step and transitioning to the world of work is difficult. I often recalled an experience from my senior year at Occidental. I was one of ten undergraduate hall directors – a tremendous experience that solidified my desire to pursue a career in student affairs. During our fall retreat, our supervisor asked us to read an article written by Peggy McIntosh entitled *Feeling Like a Fraud*. Our discussion about the article impressed me more than the content of the article. People did not understand why we had to read it. Several people rejected the notion that women have a different experience than men in the workforce. Many questioned the use of theory to prepare us for our work. Most worried about the nuts-and-bolts details of our job and resented devoting time to a conceptual discussion. It was nothing short of ugly. I have not revisited this article since and do not even know its whereabouts. Although our supervisor's purpose for using the article was lost on us then, it is as clear to me today as it was the first day I started at Wash U. I felt like a fraud!

And what a fraud I was. Only 25 and no prior full-time experience.

Only a few years older than most seniors, and younger than the vast majority of my colleagues. No basis for coordinating community service on campus. No basis for coordinating women's programs on campus (except for being an avid reader of *Ms.* Magazine). No idea how to manage my work life. No clue how to make job-related decisions. In short, no confidence and no perceived reason to have confidence.

I felt like a fraud. I felt I was playing dress-up or make-believe. I was a child in adult clothing, a student pretending to be a professional, and a passionate novice expected to act as an expert. Someone would surely expose me as a fraud – it was only a matter of time.

My only recourse was to do my best, be honest, and keep pushing ahead one day at a time. "The expert in anything was once a beginner," one of my colleagues had said during graduate school. I sure felt like a beginner, but I was determined to face new challenges as they came and stay on what became a wild ride.

My first year at Wash U was a cross between an out-of-control treadmill that I could not get off and an ocean of waves crashing over me from all directions. Like most anything in life, this sense of frenetic pace and confusion did abate and having survived it, I now know that I can survive almost anything. I had to learn to trust in my life foundation – to trust I was hired for a reason, to build on a range of life experiences that led me to St. Louis, to listen to my own voice and develop my own style, and to find courage to keep moving forward (and even enjoy the adventure!). It was very easy to doubt my preparation, my skills, and myself. I decided I would have to live and work with confidence to make me believe in myself.

***

During my first meeting with my supervisor, she gave me two documents. The first was a list of about 15 items she had accumulated for me to pursue, explore, or complete. I learned quickly that meetings create tasks, and I don't know if I have ever been short on tasks since that first meeting. My supervisor also gave me my various program budgets. I discovered I had three times the amount of funding for community service than for women's programs. However, more of my defined job responsibilities were with women's programs and most event money at Wash U comes from student government to the student groups I would advise.

"What am I supposed to be doing with that budget?" I asked.

"Build a community service program," she replied.

With that concise answer, I began my journey of the past three years (and counting) to build, conceptualize, explore, implement, create, articulate, promote, organize, and grow a community service program at Washington University. It has been an incredible opportunity that I know we all dream of in our own way. I have had autonomy; I have felt trusted and respected as a growing expert (imagine that!) in community service; I have been able to build partnerships and coalitions across campus and in the community; I have learned and come to understand complex urban issues and potential avenues for social change and community revitalization; I have been supported by an abundance of student staff, funding, and open doors; and I have enjoyed it all.

I know I am lucky. But I also know I had earned this opportunity. I assume I was hired because of my organizational skills, knowledge of student development theories, philosophies about student affairs and higher education, critical thinking and writing skills, and ability to transition to a new functional area. A liberal arts education! Aha! All of the concern I held three years ago about feeling tracked into residential life has dissipated. I now know that residential life, as well as a number of other rich curricular and co-curricular experiences, were foundations upon which I built my student affairs professional identity.

My successes at Wash U did not just come with time or support. They came with hard work and a lot of humility. One of my biggest ongoing challenges has been accepting and honoring my inclination to be introverted, particularly in an active and interactive office of student activities. Every winter and summer when students are away from campus, I comment to a colleague: "Isn't this time wonderful? I'm getting so much done without all the interruptions!" Just as predictably, every winter and summer I am told by my colleagues that they are about to climb the walls because it is too quiet. They miss the interaction; they miss the chaos; and they cannot sit still for eight hours at their desk.

I had to come to grips with the notion that enjoying my quiet does not mean I love the students any less. Enjoying administrative tasks does not mean I am in the wrong field. Needing to shut my door sometimes to find focus does not make me inaccessible. Rather, being an introvert means I have to find balance between the verbal, highly interactive, constant stream of people and information – and the ability to focus, to reflect, to think, and to rejuvenate. Sometimes this means balancing the activity of the academic semester with the peacefulness of times when students are on vacation. Other times, it means balancing a full day of meetings with a quiet night of snuggling with my dog and reading. At times it means blocking out time to do the work that requires my undivided attention. Often it means recognizing and supporting others who are introverts in a student culture that usually values extroverts.

Another area of professional growth involved budgets. Although I had worked with many budgets before arriving at Wash U, I still had a difficult time learning how to manage my funds. I was acutely aware that I was feeling like a fraud and I really had no idea how to discern appropriate uses of these funds. I discovered that the answer is largely dictated by institutional culture and by the values and directives of a supervisor. I had to step very cautiously at first, and still do: is it all right to take my work-study student out to lunch as a "thank you"? Can I get reimbursed for mileage while traveling to meetings at community agencies? How much can I spend per person on a closing banquet? Is it appropriate to lure students to meetings and programs with food funded by our office? Can I help fund students who want to go to conferences? And the list goes on...

Like everything else in my job, learning to manage my budgets and discern appropriate expenditures required asking good questions, double-checking, and observing patterns. It is different at every institution, but the transferable lesson is that this was an important area for me to ask questions about. These were questions that did not occur to me during the interview process.

With a large dose of humility, I learned to ask a lot of questions and to run a lot of information by my supervisor. I learned how to admit to others when I was doing something for the first time and how to ask others for help. I learned to get up and try again the next day. I learned to acknowledge my mistakes and to contextualize my failures. I figured that if at the very least I didn't repeat my mistakes, I was in decent shape. I learned that my job was never going to be done, and I learned how to put it aside and go home to rest.

***

I have been lucky to have an incredibly supportive supervisor – one who is consistent, principled, honest, and kind. My supervisor balances guidance with autonomy. She demonstrates trust in my abilities and my good sense. And she defers to me as the expert but she is also the first to advocate for me or for students when necessary. Many of my friends in a variety of professions have not experienced such quality supervisors or positive work environments. I realize now how important it is to refine excellent managerial skills. While I was quite lucky to connect with an outstanding supervisor, I know now that I should have more carefully scrutinized my potential supervisors during the interview process. In retrospect I think I focused too exclusively on job title/description and geographical location, both of which are important elements of a career, but neither of which fully define the quality of my professional life. Quality supervision influences my work life more than I ever expected.

As I have developed professionally and my supervisor has become busier, I have learned to make more decisions myself and to feel confident in them. I ask myself what my supervisor would say to me if we had a chance to meet or how she would respond in a similar situation. I ask myself what I have done in the past and what my justifications are. This was easier in graduate school courses and case studies where the stakes were not so high, but when working with the real lives of students it matters greatly.

Another key element of a smooth transition (as smooth as possible) was a quality orientation and training. Although my orientation was not as structured as I had experienced during residential life training, it was important to be introduced to basic information and key people essential to performing my job well. I also had time over the summer to transition into my new role, to read countless files, and to meet with colleagues and students before the rush of the fall.

My prior internship experiences also proved immensely helpful in my transition, because I had already learned to step into new situations, to transition into new office environments, and to adjust to the styles of new colleagues. These internships also provided the opportunity to conduct valuable informational interviews that helped me shape my professional philosophies. At both University of Missouri-Columbia (where I interned for the summer between my two years in graduate school) and Middlebury College (where I interned in the dean's office for a semester), I met with colleagues from across the university just to learn about their work, the evolution of their departments, the challenges they perceived in their areas, and the philosophies that guided their work. These conversations have stayed with me and guided me more than any other single experience during graduate school.

***

One of the main things I have done professionally since arriving at Wash U is build new programs, a task that is always new even if I have

built a dozen programs in the past. Each program requires its own supporters, has a different future at the University, and emerges in response
to a unique need. At the same time, I have been able to move from my
leap-of-faith perspective to an "I have faced and succeeded with similar
challenges before" approach. At the beginning of my work at Wash U,
every new task involved uncharted territory. I was never certain if I
could really pull it off, really think *that big*, or really manage so many
overwhelming details.

Now that I have created tutoring programs, chaired the first three
years of a campus-wide day of community service, funded mini-grants
to help pilot new student initiatives in the community, developed a
Community Service Resource Team for the campus, and responded to
countless calls, letters, and other requests that I have no idea what to do
with – now I know I have built some skills to handle new and ambiguous projects. For me, it requires framing my idea – usually in writing –
and developing a master list of timelines, tasks, and questions to pursue.
It means knowing sometimes even a good idea flops, and occasionally
poorly developed ideas take flight. It requires being open to feedback,
to including new ideas, and to sharing ownership of the final product. It
opens me up to a wave of criticism after the first round and asks me to
swallow my pride, shed my defenses, and do what is best for the students and the community.

***

My work at Wash U has been dependent on learning to understand
university culture and organizational dynamics. I take the role of the
life-long learner by asking a lot of questions and relishing opportunities
to observe my colleagues' communication styles and decision-making
processes. My higher education administration course during graduate
school and our many conversations about organizational cultures did
not seem particularly relevant until I began to maneuver the culture of
Wash U. I often reflect upon my decision to essentially go "straight to
graduate school" after a year off of doing unrelated work. Many of my
courses at UVM would have been more valuable to me had I already
had a few years of professional experience in higher education behind
me. The questions we discussed were all hypothetical to me when they
could have been based on real experiences and memories, and it was too
easy to fit case studies into a tidy box despite our professors' attempts
to muddy the waters.

For me, understanding institutional culture has been about understanding how decisions are made, how conflict is handled (or not), who is *really* in charge, how to inform but bypass those who do not have decision-making power, who the gatekeepers are, how we as an organization perceive ourselves, the image of ourselves we perpetuate in our public relations and admissions processes, and what the institution *really* values. There is a lot of history at Washington University, just as at any institution, that defines our sense of self and directs our vision for the future. It has been valuable to learn from those who have been at the institution the longest, to actually read historical information about the University, and to suspend assumptions about the way things work that I might have tried to apply from external experiences.

***

I don't know that a day has gone by that I haven't pondered whether I am in the right place. Am I in the right place geographically? How much does a great job offset the lack of mountains, the distance from my family, and the less progressive Midwestern culture? What could I or would I be doing if I had more intentionally explored and pursued career options as an undergraduate? What about those math skills that were so refined when I graduated from high school that I thought (ha!) I would major in mathematics? Could I be making more of a difference in the world through another venue? Am I more aligned with social change or with student affairs? Am I a hypocrite for sitting in a true ivory tower while I claim to be an advocate for social justice and equity? Are my students smarter than me? Who would I have been if I had attended Washington University? Did I make optimal use of my college years? Did I attend the right college? Did I really deserve the honors I received in college, or did I manage to fake it there, too? Couldn't I be using my administrative skills to earn a lot more money in the corporate world? How much of what I do is instinct and common sense, and how much do I really use theories I learned as a graduate student? Should I have gotten a graduate degree in social work? If I were to get an advanced degree, what degree would I pursue? How could I possibly be a mother while balancing a job like this? Could I ever find a better job? What if I get stale here? How can I find time to read professional literature when I have students at my door and emails to respond to? When is it okay to say "no"? When is it wise to say "yes"? What do I do when "joy" doesn't pay the bills? What if passion doesn't earn enough to fly me home to California? What are all the things I could be doing if I only worked forty hours a week? What next?

Sometimes these questions roll in and out of my brain, and sometimes they tug at my heart. They have caused me to clarify why I'm here and to accept the path ahead of me is undefined. I have learned to live with the questions without demanding answers of myself. I see options now that I did not see five years ago – skills, interests, and possibilities I would not or could not see as a graduating college senior. Sometimes, just when I hit a slump and the questions are plaguing me and burnout is looming, I find renewed energy for my career in student affairs.

The work I do is such a gift. More than my ability to influence the lives of my students, I am often touched by their capacity to affect my life. The students I have had the privilege to work most closely with are gracious, patient, and thoughtful. They are willing to challenge me respectfully and they are here to learn. They are not just looking for a career; they are choosing from among multiple career options and seeking ways to make sense of their multiple talents and passions. I consider my students to be my friends. They are not the friends I choose to socialize with outside of work, but the depth of friendship they offer me is extraordinary. I consider them my friends because they trust me and I trust them, because they enlighten my thinking and they add joy to my life, and because we are working together toward a shared vision of social justice.

At the end of every month when I pay my bills, I am forced to recall while we all know money doesn't buy happiness, neither does happiness always pay the bills. Choosing a career in student affairs has meant living more frugally than many of my friends in other professions. It means I have a big retirement account waiting for me but I have to scrimp and save to take a real vacation. It means I live paycheck to paycheck until I pay off my student loans. It means outstanding performance does not always lead to salary increases or promotions. I think this is a real conundrum for student affairs professionals. As an undergraduate and graduate student, it was easy to stay naïve about the cost of living in the world, particularly when travel is required to visit family. This made it easy to be idealistic about the line of work I was going into. Now, I have to make a conscious decision about why I am here despite the costs, and I have to determine a way to balance the intangible rewards of the work with the undeniable cost of living.

I think about the world differently than I did three years ago, and I owe a lot of my growth to students and colleagues. I work in an environment where we can celebrate together and we also understand tears. We laugh a lot and we work incredibly hard. We get to think outside the box all the time. These are intangible rewards that sometimes go unnoticed or unappreciated in the hectic pace of the campus, but they would be undeniably missed in another field.

***

Just like the questions that loom about whether I am in the right place, I often ponder what I would do differently if I had graduate school to relive in better preparation for my first job. I would have worked in the field first so graduate school would have felt less academic and more real to me. Although I loved the academic and intellectual experience at UVM, it was sometimes difficult to make hypothetical discussions real and to test my professional philosophies in a somewhat forced setting.

I would have admitted earlier that I did not want to stay in residential life and sought more opportunities for exposure to other functional areas. I devoted a lot of mental energy to the question of whether I *belonged* in residential life, perhaps out of loyalty to the area that had given me my home (literally and figuratively) at Occidental.

I wish I had been more patient with myself during my first year at Washington University. My supervisor always told us, and still tells us, that we are usually harder on ourselves than she is. I have high standards for myself and, like everyone else, I want to do the best job I can. I recognize now the importance of acknowledging that the first year is still a year of exploration, exposure, and development. Mistakes happen, and they will continue to happen. I did not have to *produce* to do well, and I did not have to defend my existence at the university.

***

So here I sit – still surrounded by boxes. I am turning a corner in my professional life as I move to a new and bigger office. It provides me the much-needed opportunity to reflect on how far I have come in three years. I find notes from meetings where I asked questions that seem silly, self-evident, or irrelevant now. I uncover evidence of past programs and initiatives that either no longer exist or are now overseen by other offices. I flip through piles of semester reports, performance appraisals, and lists of goals and objectives. I can see ghosts of the many students who have sat on my couch – or stood in the doorway out of deference to my time   sharing a piece of their lives with me. I can look ambiguity in the eye and know for right now, I *am* in the right place.

7

THE PERFECT JOB

Diana Jaramillo

It was love at first sight: Program Coordinator for New Student Programs. As I read the ad in the *Chronicle of Higher Education*, I nearly fell out of my seat. The job description seemed to have been crafted just for me. I would be responsible for maintaining some existing programs, growing some new ones, and delivering a very comprehensive series of orientation sessions. The student body contained a significant number of Latina and Latino students, a population with whom I was highly interested in working. To top it all off, I would even get to teach a course each semester, congruent with my long-term goal of becoming a faculty member.

The Program Coordinator for New Student Programs was a newly created position in orientation at a mid-sized public university. I was thrilled, as orientation was the functional area that initially drew me to student affairs. While an undergraduate, I was involved in a variety of leadership roles: resident advisor for two years, member of the lesbian, gay, bi student organization, committee chair for the student programming body, among other activities that were all highly fulfilling and fun. However, it was not until my work in new student orientation that I saw a future for myself as a student affairs professional.

In applying for admission to Miami University Master's program in College Student Personnel, my stated objective was to obtain the degree to become an orientation professional. This goal was further reinforced by my studies and practical experiences as a graduate student. Through reflective assignments, I had several occasions to examine my values and strengths, and the orientation function was an excellent fit. The power of a strong new student orientation process and related programming appealed to me, as I could easily see its role in retention and empowering students to make a new setting theirs. Successful orientation programs hinge on strong collaboration with a variety of areas, including a very significant link with the academic side of the house. For a comprehensive, institution-wide orientation program, the population served is as diverse as the entire student body. I knew what this work was about and I was clear that it was what I wanted.

Starting Out
My on-campus interview for my first full-time position was great. I asked all the right questions about collaboration within the student affairs division, opportunities for professional development, resource allocation, supervisory style, and leadership within the institution. I learned creativity, ownership, and collaboration were valued in the department. While many of my projects would be independently managed, there were several opportunities to work closely with my prospective supervisor, Mary, and with other colleagues on campus. Mary (not her real name) was well liked and respected at the institution and influential in a national professional association.

I liked what I heard during the interview, and more importantly, I felt I had developed a genuine connection with Mary. I ascertained she was a dedicated, competent professional who wanted a colleague to expand the department she had built almost single-handedly. Her role at the national level provided additional assurance that I would be working with one of the most capable professionals in the field. Thinking strategically, I believed that developing a good relationship with Mary could work to my advantage in future career moves. Mary had wholeheartedly invested herself in the department and expressed her excitement at having another professional with whom to problem-solve and take the office to a new level. We agreed I would be that person.

As a native Californian – and more specifically, a Los Angelino – my move to a large Texas city was geographically closer to home than my more recent graduate student residence in a rural, small town in southwestern Ohio. My time in Ohio was wonderful. I had gained greater confidence and a deeper understanding of myself through academic work in my graduate program and the practical experiences that complemented it; however, I knew it was time to move on and I wanted to explore a different part of the country. I conducted a national job search, because I knew orientation jobs were not plentiful and I had to be open to a variety of settings.

While I had misgivings about living in a conservative Texas city, given my liberal political leanings and my commitment to a life consistent with my values as a vegan, I was ready and willing to make some quality of life sacrifices for a job I would love. I knew it might be a problem to find vegan-friendly dining options in a town that has a B-B-Q joint on nearly every corner. I figured it would be an adjustment to settle in a city that did not have the vast cultural offerings I knew from my life in Los Angeles. Despite my concerns, I was confident I would make a great start to my career in this position. I reminded myself that one of my strengths is adaptability. While this was not the liberal enclave where I dreamed of moving, I knew it was an opportunity to learn even more about myself. I anticipated some challenges in acclimating to this different environment, yet I was confident. I knew I was ready to show my mettle as a student affairs educator and that this was the right opportunity.

I started my position with lots of energy and enthusiasm. I quickly needed to learn the ins and outs of the office and institution as my supervisor was expecting a baby in less than three months. I knew that very soon I would be on my own, other than the support of our administrative assistant and the student staff. On my first day, I picked up the phone and answered questions for new students and their family members, learning along the way, and I was commended for diving in. Once Mary's maternity leave began, I would need to assume some of her responsibilities and keep the office running smoothly. The timing of my start date in early August was ideal. I was able to observe two remaining orientation sessions for that cycle, attend the camp for new students that I would eventually manage, and experience the beginning of the academic year in my first three weeks.

The whirlwind of activity during my first few weeks on the job was a great immersion into the department, and it gave me the chance to interact with several of the student affairs colleagues with whom I would work closely throughout the year. The college success seminar I taught was full of new students whom I was thrilled to get to know, support, and challenge. I inherited a mentor program with a set of workshops to implement and freedom to nurture in new directions. I was off to a good start at work, and I was also busy settling into my new apartment and learning all about the new city I was making my home. My first three months passed quickly and I hardly had a chance to catch my breath.

Days prior to my supervisor's maternity leave, I was confident I had the know-how to handle things well. In fact, I was determined to show I could do it all with little or no help. I really thought this was a great opportunity to prove myself as a capable professional. I prepared extensively for the meetings I attended on my supervisor's behalf and made sure reports I needed to deliver were thorough and professional. Once, the Vice President's office contacted me to provide information to a professional at another institution who was conducting a benchmarking study. I must have spent half a day crafting the perfect response to this request, and I signed my name with pride. Not only did I feel pressure to produce excellent work, I enjoyed the challenge and did my best to meet it.

Even when things were not so great, I tried to frame my circumstances in the most positive light. The first orientation program I led completely alone was difficult. It felt like a nightmare, as I was highly stressed throughout the day. The program occurred while classes were in session and the majority of our student orientation leaders were unavailable when I needed them most. I had a group of 120 orientation participants and only one orientation leader present during the scheduled campus tour. Somehow, with creativity, flexibility and quick thinking, we were able to pull it off. When my supervisor called for a report on how things went, I admitted it had been a rough session and made sure she knew I handled it beautifully.

Mary, being an excellent planner, had her child during the closest thing to downtime in our office. Consequently, I did not require her assistance while she was away. I became comfortable being very autonomous, and in all honesty the independence suited my personality well. I must have completed the Myers-Briggs Type Indicator at least five times before finishing my graduate degree. I knew myself to be an independent thinker. The problem, which I did not see at the time, was I was developing my professional identity in a setting that was temporary.

During the first three months, with Mary's support, I was focused on learning the office, the institution, and the students. It was not until she was on maternity leave that I focused on who I was as a professional, a pivotal point in my career development. My identity as an independent, capable leader was being solidified as my professional identity while my supervisor was away. While independent and capable are not problematic characteristics, Mary's return was difficult for me. I had gotten used to having the office to myself and now I had to relinquish control literally and figuratively. In her absence, I became used to making decisions about the programs I managed. With Mary back in the office, I felt an unspoken directive to run things by her. While this was a relief in some ways, I also felt constrained. The pressure to be perfect was lessened, but I felt a new pressure to be connected with her on a personal level while being a good subordinate.

How could I be capable and independent, and a good subordinate and connected with her all at the same time? In my mind, being capable and independent meant doing things with little or no help. Yet suddenly I had a supervisor and she liked being closely connected with her staff. I also wanted that, but I could not understand how to put the pieces together.

I wanted to be who I was in her absence, and I wanted to be whom I thought she wanted me to be. How did I know what she wanted in the first place? It was all my conjecture. Mary and I did not have a conversation about who we were or about our mutual expectations regarding how we would interact with each other. We regularly discussed my projects, their history, what resources I should seek out and so on. We had some very basic get-to-know-you talks. Those conversations were important, but they were not enough to create a structure for how we would support each other and work together. We did not talk about what was important to us, what made us tick, how we worked through our problems, what kind of support we wanted, or countless other important topics. We had not defined our collegial relationship. At a time when intentional awareness of and explicit communication about our process was critical, we both overlooked it. We were missing a framework, a structure for our relationship.

Trouble in Paradise

It was the start of the spring semester, a busy time in preparing for the frenetic pace of the summer, when I first noticed things were amiss. Along with initially not having set a framework for our relationship, the everyday conversations Mary and I had felt awkward. Our work-related talks were very task-focused; however, our non-work conversations revolved around her infant. While I was happy for her joy at being a new mother, not having experience or much interest in babies made it difficult for me to connect with her on that level. Eventually, I found myself becoming tense whenever she mentioned the baby's name. This was uncomfortable for me because I wanted to be connected with her and supportive and I knew she wanted this, too. I did not want to offend her by asking her not to talk about her child and motherhood. I wanted to say, "I know there's more to you than being a mom," but even phrased more elegantly, sending that message was a risk I did not want to take.

Eventually, I determined that we really did not have much in common. Mary was a wife and mother and so were most of her friends and our administrative assistant. I did not watch television and could not contribute to the discussions about last night's *ER* episode. I did not play Bunko, a popular dice game that, as it was explained to me, was an opportunity for gossip among friends. I did not own a home, so I could not share stories of dealing with the homeowner's association. If being connected on a personal level was about having things in common, we were not. I felt something was wrong and I believed Mary felt it, although we did not talk about it.

Our relationship took a really negative turn for me as we prepared to co-teach the orientation leader training course. I expected we would work very collaboratively to design the course. Largely due to limited time before the start of the course and the fact Mary had conceptualized and taught the course many times prior, we worked from the previous year's syllabus. I understood the need to do this, but I was still frustrated to have so little influence in the training of the student staff I would supervise. I knew my best option was to set aside my frustration and set my sights on making a strong impact as a co-instructor.

As the course unfolded, I became increasingly uncomfortable with the process. Mary would begin each class with announcements and orientation-related business items; depending on the topic, she would lecture or pass that duty to me. We had negotiated the topics we wanted to cover and developed our lectures independently. This plan worked very well for me. What bothered me was that student staff directed questions and discussion toward her. Now I see there are many reasons why this behavior was quite natural; however, at the time I was hurt and resentful. Mary was the one who had interviewed and hired these students, and some of them were continuing as orientation leaders for the second or third time. Also, Mary lectured more than I did. In the face of these logical explanations, I felt like a glorified teaching assistant instead of a co-instructor. I had little power in the classroom and was concerned when the time came for me to be the students' direct supervisor, I would not be taken seriously. By the time Mary and I had a conversation about my concerns and frustration, it seemed all we could do was plan to do things differently the next time.

In addition to my relationship with Mary being less than ideal, I struggled with my life outside of work. Before I moved to Texas, I knew only the people I had met when interviewing on campus. I had initially met several other colleagues in student affairs but was disappointed the division was not as collegial as I had anticipated. Because I have always been an independent person, I did not worry about making friends until this time when I most needed one. The aerobics class I took connected me with another student affairs professional who was also less than thrilled with her work experience. Nothing brings people together like a shared complaint, right? Beyond my contact with her, I had failed to find a personal network of support and a sense of community in my new home.

Making Friends

It had been so much easier in graduate school. Similar to my situation in Texas, I knew no one before I moved to Ohio other than the faculty and staff I had met when interviewing. The big difference in adjusting to graduate school was I had an instant family as soon as I arrived. Not only did I quickly meet several of my classmates-to-be, but we also bonded during the rigorous residence life training with a "we're all in this together" mentality. There were so many of us that I easily found a niche of comfort and support. Contrasting this with my experience in Texas, with no such structure in place and joining a very small office, I can now understand how it was a more difficult transition. My significant other, friends, and family were thousands of miles from me and I had the long distance bills to prove it. I used my time on the phone with my loved ones as an opportunity to escape my situation, albeit briefly.

Expectations and Disappointment

Maintaining optimism, I hoped a shift in circumstances would make for a better work experience. A shift to the summer's focus on delivering numerous orientation programs would be different. I went into the summer with high expectations. The student staff was excited, and I looked forward to supervising and supporting them in their role and was thrilled for a change of pace. While I had facilitated orientation programs for spring and summer semester starters, the fall orientation programs constituted the big leagues. Those sessions involved more participants, more staff, and more excitement, energy and fun. I was terrified. Yet, after the first few tries and being fully engaged with problem solving and tweaking the schedule, it was a veritable walk in the park. It was not until I was in the throes of the summer orientation season, I realized I was unfulfilled.

Most days, we had an orientation session of one kind or another, and my primary role was to ensure the sessions ran smoothly. This required little effort, as good planning and good initial problem solving paid off. I quickly and unconsciously diminished what I was doing, and my work became creating detailed schedules and directing traffic. My perspective was that my talents were underutilized, as I knew a well-trained student could easily fill the role. So much of my job was consumed by the orientation sessions that I had little time left for other responsibilities. Of course, those other responsibilities, like creating publications and planning the camp and mentor program, were what I viewed as more stimulating and more important. Those were the responsibilities worth my time, the ones I really deserved. I was frustrated and it showed. To make matters worse, I was deeply disappointed in myself for allowing others to become aware of my dissatisfaction and even more embarrassed that I was frustrated in the first place. Was I not competent? A true professional would find a way to improve the situation.

The summer was grinding to a halt, and I was relieved to see it end. Yet, just when I thought things were looking up, they got infinitely worse. Mary and I had a confrontation at the orientation camp immediately before the start of classes. It was not a flattering exchange for either of us and, as with most arguments, it was not really about the apparent topic. Ultimately, which students would be honored as Mr. and Ms. Camp was the pretense for an argument about our relationship and my growing dissatisfaction with feeling underutilized and unfulfilled.

We did not really have a conversation addressing those true concerns until the following week during my one-year evaluation meeting. Asked to put together a summary of my experience and accomplishments in my first year as program coordinator, I decided to make clear how I made sense of things. I spent several days crafting a narrative that detailed what I did and how I felt about it, taking care to use candor and tact. Soon after it was submitted, I learned what I had written did not meet Mary's expectations. She wanted to see a list of items, a more objective representation of what I did without my interpretation. I revised my one-year summary using the guidelines Mary presented and we met.

The meeting was tense and emotional. Mary questioned my dedication. She told me that I was difficult to read. She brought up several situations from the past where things I said and did were misconstrued. Mary suggested I did not respect her. I learned our relationship was so problematic for her that she literally lost sleep over it. I was not expecting to hear this and I felt attacked. I rebutted, explaining past situations and actions to the best of my ability. I was deeply hurt that I did not have the chance to respond to these ill assumptions at the time they were made. I communicated that I cared very much about my job, indicating it was primarily where I directed my energy. In an uncharacteristic show of emotion, I cried. And it seemed it was really at that point Mary understood me at a different level. We concluded our conversation in a much better place, both assured we understood the other.

Moving On

We both declared we would start fresh with better communication. While I felt things were moving in a positive direction, shortly after this turning point, I chose to seek other job opportunities. I wanted to be back in Los Angeles and decided I would start a job search as soon as possible. I told Mary I would leave at the beginning of May, planning to leave before the next summer orientation season began. The frustration I experienced peaked during that last summer and I did not think I could endure it once more. Additionally, I thought that would be the ideal timing for hiring and training a new program coordinator. Mary was appreciative to have several months to find a person and she supported my decision.

When the committee was formed to select my successor, I was disappointed I was not asked to participate. At the time, I did not know it was unusual for someone to participate in helping select his or her own replacement. Who knew the position better? As interview time came and the candidates' schedules were circulated, I was again surprised to learn the candidates had no time scheduled to meet with me. I told Mary that if I was interviewing for a position where the person vacating the role was still present, I would find it strange not to get a chance to ask that person questions. I told her I would likely be suspicious that there was something purposefully being hidden from me. Mary decided to make it an option for candidates to meet with me and I was pleased she heard me.

Of the three candidates who came to campus, I met with two. Holly (not her real name), who ultimately accepted the offer, had several questions. When she asked me about Mary's supervision, I took a deep breath. I chose my words carefully and gave what I believed was the most fair answer possible. I complimented Mary's skill in supervising student staff and spoke generously about her strong points. I also disclosed that I was the first student affairs professional she had supervised. I talked about how we did not work particularly well together, and I took a great deal of responsibility for not making my own needs and expectations clear. Following Holly's exit from my office, I congratulated myself for handling a potentially charged topic with tact.

Later that day, Mary came into my office livid. I learned that one reason I was not originally asked to help with selecting the new program coordinator was because Mary was concerned I would sabotage the process. She had asked Holly what we discussed, and Holly relayed my comment about Mary's inexperience in supervising a student affairs professional. I did not know if Mary had only heard that small piece of what I said or whether she was addressing only the piece with which she had taken issue. I told Mary about the rest of my response to Holly's questions, and Mary appeared relieved and somewhat embarrassed. I was sad. I got the impression that Mary believed I was bitter and out to undermine her program. I genuinely wanted someone great to fill my position. I believed in the programs and services we had developed and I honestly thought it was an amazing job. I told Mary this and also how I felt to be cast in the role of betrayer.

Mary and I made our peace again and my remaining weeks were calm. My departure from the university was very quiet. In fact, Mary was not in the office on my last day. I was relieved to part company with her. I felt as if a weight had been lifted from my shoulders when I said goodbye to the office staff, because I no longer had to feel the strain of a relationship gone bad.

As I packed for my move to Los Angeles, I alternated between feeling happy about going home and feeling like I was running away from a challenge. Was I simply escaping? I hoped that a return to familiar surroundings would allow a return to myself. The self I knew leaving graduate school only two years earlier seemed like a distant memory; I had felt disconnected for several months. What happened to the strong person I was? It was almost like I was a shell of my former self. I was not at my best and I was anxious to return home to heal and rediscover my voice.

What Really Happened

Time and distance have been of tremendous benefit to me. I am now able to look back and see what I did, how I was instrumental in creating my experience, and how I was responsible. Rather than believing it was poor supervision or a bad set of circumstances, I now know I had power in my first job that I simply did not use. The power I had was in trusting myself, in speaking up about what was not working for me, and in choosing to be at peace in spite of my circumstances.

How was it that I had lost touch with my true self and inner strength? With fresh eyes, I see that I had simply stopped trusting myself. When my job was not how I wanted it, I got scared; and lacking a quick fix, I lost faith. I worried I could not handle being a professional, and I started to believe I was in over my head. My fear was real, but rather than express it, I kept it inside. The voice of insecurity echoed louder still until it obscured the strength that had been there all along. I believed admitting my fear was tantamount to admitting failure. If I told Mary how I was feeling, she would know I did not have all the answers. Worse, I would be admitting to myself that I did not have what it took to be a capable, independent professional.

The irony astounds me. The missing connection with Mary had little to do with our not having much in common. More than a year later, I know Mary and I did not connect because I did not show her all of me. I shared with her fragments of who I was, those slivers I thought were most admirable, and my insecurities were missing. While she caught a glimpse of my humanity when I cried in her office, that small glimpse was all I would allow. What kept me from sharing myself fully with Mary was my insecurity, what it would say about me if I expressed my fear. Yet, sharing my insecurity would have made possible a real connection with Mary and in that lived the possibility of having the support I needed to allay my doubts and fears.

Upon reflection, I see how I contributed to the disappointment of my first job, and I take responsibility. However, I do not feel ashamed or embarrassed. Having been through this experience and a few other lessons since then, I am much more generous with myself. I can now be at peace in circumstances that are less than ideal because I can identify and appreciate my feelings, whatever they are. I am no longer concerned with projecting just the right image. I now focus on trusting myself and being true to my feelings. The freedom I experience in expressing myself honestly, without worry about my petty judgment or the potentially negative assessment of another is tremendous. It is easy for life to be peaceful when that constant worry is gone.

The lesson I have learned from my experience with Mary is job satisfaction begins with honesty. I knew this to some extent before I took that first job. I was honest about the kind of work I wanted to do, and I found that kind of work. Clearly, it is more than the duties and responsibilities of a job that matter. There is a whole package to consider. Being honest about all pieces of the package along the way is critical.

There are compromises one makes in choosing a job, and being open about which work and which do not is key.

It truly was the perfect job, just the right start to my career. I know, in a way I might not have known without this job that I have a tremendous amount of power to create an extraordinary experience for myself and those around me. Trusting myself, being honest with others and myself, and taking responsibility are essential ingredients in realizing that power. I know these ingredients will make the greatest difference in my continual development as a professional and as a human.

8

SUPPORTIVE SUPERVISION FOR NEW PROFESSIONALS

Michael G. Ignelzi and Patricia A. Whitely

Introduction

"The supervision that developing professionals receive is important for learning and mastering the craft of their profession, and ultimately in providing quality service to their constituents" (Ignelzi, 1994, p.1). As such, the importance of new professionals' job satisfaction and experience with their new supervisors and work environments cannot be overestimated. Staff success and satisfaction are two of the most important resources of student affairs, and supervisors and senior student affairs officers must try to create work environments that will lead to staff members' success and satisfaction. The three previous case studies by Molly Reas, Stephanie Kurtzman and Diana Jaramillo offer rich personal accounts of how issues related to supervision and the supervisory relationship influence the nature and quality of the transition from graduate school to full-time professional employment.

As these three narratives demonstrate, adjusting to a new job and work environment during the first year as a full-time professional is challenging. Although graduate schools provide new professionals with a body of knowledge and a variety of experiences, academic programs cannot completely prepare them for the expectations of their first professional student affairs job and the adjustment issues associated with being full-time staff members. In some real sense, student affairs preparation faculty *pass the baton* upon graduation to the new professionals' supervisors and with it significant responsibility for continuing to facilitate professional development.

Although supervisors clearly bear significant responsibility for the success or failure of new professionals, we acknowledge that these staff members also must be responsible for their own adjustment to new jobs.

However, we contend it is critical to utilize a constructive developmental view (as we do in this chapter) that considers how new professionals understand or make sense of their experience, which directly influences exactly what they are able to take responsibility for effectively.

While there are significant similarities in Molly's, Stephanie's, and Diana's narratives, they also illustrate somewhat different experiences and outcomes related to the first-year professional transition. We believe that this is largely a result of two interrelated factors: [1] the differences in the work and supervisory environment provided each new professional, and [2] their particular ways of reflecting upon, understanding, and making sense of those environments.

In this chapter, we utilize two areas of the professional literature to analyze these three new professionals' stories: student affairs supervision literature and constructive developmental theory. Within the student affairs supervision literature, there is a paucity of published work on the topic of supervision, particularly in comparison to the rich body of literature existing in other human relations fields (e.g., counseling, social work, teaching). However, there is a *synergistic supervision* model (Winston & Creamer, 1997) that provides a comprehensive treatment of supervision of student affairs professionals; it contains several components useful in analyzing these three case studies.

Constructive developmental theory contends that individuals actively construct their own sense of reality. An event does not have a particular singular meaning that simply gets transferred to the individual. Instead, meaning is created between the event and the individual's reaction to it. Constructive developmental theory further asserts that the individual's internal cognitive structure utilized to organize the sense of reality evolves in regular and systematic ways. As such, the general course and direction of development is predictable over time and experience.

The student affairs profession has effectively made use of a number of these theories (e.g., Piaget, 1967; Perry, 1970; Kohlberg, 1984; Kegan, 1982, 1994; Baxter Magolda, 1992, 2001; and King & Kitchner, 1994) to better understand how students make sense of their experience and themselves as well as what that understanding suggests for creating environments supportive of students' learning and development. We have seldom used these theories to aid our knowledge of how student affairs professionals make sense of their experience and themselves as new professionals.

Using this developmental lens enhances our knowledge of how new professionals understand their work (including the supervision they receive) and what may support their on-going development as satisfied, competent student affairs professionals. We use Robert Kegan's theory of meaning-making development (1982, 1994), in conjunction with research that has been conducted by one of us (Ignelzi, 1994) on the professional development and supervision of student affairs professionals to interpret Molly's, Stephanie's and Diana's stories.

The organization of this chapter is as follows. First, we review aspects of the synergistic supervision model (Winston & Creamer, 1997), of meaning-making development (Kegan, 1982, 1994), and of related developmental research on student affairs professionals (Ignelzi, 1994). We then use this material to analyze and illuminate our understanding of the new student affairs professionals' experiences, particularly as related to supervision and the supervisor-supervisee relationship, as detailed in the previous three chapters. We also reflect upon and recommend strategies that may contribute to creating more supportive environments for new professionals such as Molly, Stephanie and Diana as they meet the challenges of effectively managing their first full-time jobs.

Synergistic Supervision

Winston and Creamer (1997) define *synergistic supervision* as an approach that includes a "dual focus on accomplishment of the organization's goals and support of staff in accomplishment of their personal and professional development goals" (p. 196). They view these two objectives as interrelated and assert that supervisors should emphasize both. Both goals involve staff in helping set organizational goals and strategies so that they become personally identified with them and assist staff in identifying and working toward their own personal and professional objectives in the context of the organization.

Other characteristics of synergistic supervision include: "joint effort, two-way communication, a focus on competence, growth orientation, proactivity, goal-based, systematic and ongoing processes, and holism" (Winston & Creamer, 1997, p. 197). These characteristics are briefly defined below.

Joint effort is the principle that supervision is a cooperative endeavor where both supervisor and staff "must be willing to invest time and energy in the process" (p. 198). Winston and Creamer (1997) assert that this shared commitment is what makes supervision synergistic. "Its cooperative nature allows joint effects to exceed the combination of individual efforts" (p. 196).

Two-way communication, requiring substantial trust between the supervisor and staff member, refers to the importance of learning about each other and sharing direct feedback with each other. *A focus on competence* concentrates supervision on "four areas of staff competence: knowledge and information, work-related skills, personal and professional development skills, and attitudes" (p. 199). Winston and Creamer (1997) particularly focus on the importance of attitudes, stating: "Whether a staff member approaches tasks with an attitude of enthusiasm or sarcasm often determines his or her ultimate success. Attitudes are, therefore, an important subject of supervision" (p. 200).

"Just as successful student affairs practitioners base their work with students on an understanding of developmental theory, successful supervisors need an understanding of adult development theory as they work with their staffs" (Winston & Creamer, 1997, p. 203). In support of a *growth orientation* to supervision, Winston and Creamer (1997) present a chart of psychosocial development life tasks and career/professional tasks for student affairs professionals at various age ranges (pp. 204-207). This chart is based on the work of Schein (1978), Chickering and Havighurst (1981), Levinson and Levinson (1996), Carpenter (1991), and others.

By *proactivity*, Winston and Creamer (1997) refer to the importance of identifying problem situations early so that the supervisor and staff member can collaboratively address them. Supervisory sessions are viewed as opportunities to consider alternative intervention strategies as well as to provide a forum for processing mistakes that may have already occurred.

Goal-based supervision is achieved through staff members periodically developing both short-term and long-range professional and personal goals in conjunction with their supervisors. Progress on these goals (and revision of them, when necessary) is then regularly monitored and reviewed during supervisory meetings. In this way, "both supervisors and their staffs...have a clear understanding about the expectations each has of the other" (Winston & Creamer, 1997, p. 209).

Winston and Creamer (1997) assert that *systematic and ongoing processes* of supervision should be "a routine part of professional life" (p. 210). These processes should include both individual and group supervisory meetings, which they distinguish from staff meetings where staff come together "for coordinating activities and work assignments" (p. 211).

Lastly, a *holistic* approach is advocated as "fundamental" to syner-

gistic supervision. Winston and Creamer state:
>It is impossible to separate people and their attitudes and beliefs from their professional positions. Who one is determines to a large extent the kind of job one is able to do. Synergistic supervision concentrates on helping staff become more effective in their jobs and personal lives, and supports them in their quest for career advancement. (p. 211)

Synergistic supervision is viewed as appropriate for all student affairs professionals. They do, however, contend:
>Supervision must be tailored to the individual and the context. As Hershey and Blanchard (1977) argue in their theory of effective leadership, the level of direction required is dependent on the supervisee's skills and knowledge of the tasks to be performed, experience in dealing with a given situation, level of personal maturity, and developmental stage. (p. 212)

Meaning-Making Development

Robert Kegan's (1982, 1994) theory of meaning-making provides a valuable developmental companion piece to Winston and Creamer's (1997) model of synergistic supervision. Kegan's developmental model is a conceptualization of how human beings make meaning of themselves, of others, and of their experiences throughout the life span. As distinct from psychosocial developmental models that identify what the life tasks are within a particular age group, constructive developmental models, like Kegan's, focus on how individuals internally understand or make sense of those tasks and their experiences. Stages or positions within constructive developmental models are less age-related than those within psychosocial models. Constructive models assert that individuals within the same age range and/or level of experience can be at different stages of development and, as such, make meaning of their experience in qualitatively different ways. Having some awareness as to how supervisees are currently making meaning of their work, their supervision, and themselves has important implications for supervisor-supervisee relationships as well as what might constitute effective supervision.

Orders of Consciousness

Kegan proposes a series of six (orders 0-5) holistic (i.e., each with its own internal logic) and qualitatively different forms of meaning-making that individuals may evolve through during their lifetime. He calls these major places along the path of self-evolution, "orders of consciousness" (Kegan, 1994). As a person's development proceeds between and through these orders, meaning-making undergoes changes that affect the person's view of the self, relations to others, and understanding of experience.

Kegan contends and research on his theory supports (Kegan, 1994) that the majority of the adult population (from late adolescence through adulthood) makes meaning at or between order 3 and order 4. The story of adult meaning-making development seems to be largely described by the slow evolution of the self from order 3 to order 4. Hence, it is useful to consider these orders and the transition from one to the other in the context of new professional experiences and supervision.

Order 3 meaning-makers co-construct their sense of meaning with other persons and sources (e.g., books read, ideas exposed to) in their environment. They are not psychologically differentiated from these co-constructions. That is, the individual's sense of self is based upon a *fusion* of others' expectations, theories and ideas and those expectations become integrated into how one thinks about the self. The individual's sense of meaning-making partially resides in other people/sources and partially within the self, so there is no coherent sense of meaning-making or self apart from other people/sources. An order 3 meaning-maker is masterful at coordinating others' points of view and can create a shared reality with others, but is limited in her or his ability to reflect on that shared reality and how it is influencing or determining her or his view (Kegan, Noam, & Rogers, 1982). When an order 3 meaning-maker shares what she or he thinks, believes or feels, another (person or source) is always implicated.

Order 4 meaning-makers construct their sense of meaning and the self such that self-authorship is the key feature. The order 4 individual transcends the co-constructed self of order 3 by developing the ability to differentiate a self-standard apart from, but in relation to, other people and sources. That is, the self can internalize multiple points of view, reflect on them and construct them into one's own theory about self and experience. Thus, the individual's meaning-making is influenced by, but not determined by, external sources. The self becomes identified through these self-authored conceptualizations, giving the self an enduring identity that largely remains stable across contexts and interpersonal relationships.

Order 3-4 transition between stages is about the process of making what was subject into object (Kegan, 1982), or transforming the old construction of self to a new one. Development from order 3 toward order 4 meaning-making consists of gradually becoming able to take a perspective on or make object the co-constructed, shared realities that one is subject to at order 3. This growing ability allows the individual to begin to reflect upon and coordinate multiple points of view, constructing them into one's own theory about oneself and one's experience. The central conflict in the order 3 to 4 transition is between defining the self in terms of others' expectations (as at order 3) and "an emerging orientation toward considering 'what it is I want' independent of others' expectations" (Kegan, Noam, & Rogers, 1982, p. 114). Both sides of this conflict or ambivalence are manifest in the individual's meaning-making during the transition as neither the co-constructed mutuality psychologic of order 3 nor the self-authored system psychologic of order 4 is firmly in place.

Meaning-Making in the Supervisory Context

Ignelzi (1994) found that the ways that student affairs professionals understand their experiences and themselves as professionals have underlying constructive developmental bases consistent with Kegan's theory of meaning-making outlined above. He interviewed 30 student affairs professionals about their understanding of three main professional development issues: their work with students, the supervision they receive, and their use of theory in their practice. The professionals interviewed were at three different experience levels in their early careers. Ten had recently finished their first year in a student personnel graduate preparation program; ten had just completed their first year as full-time student affairs professionals; and ten had between three to five years of professional experience in the field. Ignelzi's research yielded a model of professional development that essentially describes and illustrates how meaning-making is manifested in the understanding early professionals have about their work, their supervision, and their use of theory. For the purposes of this chapter, we will focus on the supervision portion of the model.

Ignelzi (1994) found that a professional's understanding of many of the aspects of the supervision she or he receives as well as the supervisor-supervisee relationship can be described by three distinct perspectives (Ignelzi, 1994):

Autonomy, structure, and support:	Relationship with supervisor:
Perspective 1	**Perspective 1**
Supervisee depends on supervisor for direction, advice, answers, and personal and/or emotional support; may want some autonomy but with supervisor readily available for assistance/backup.	Supervisee wants supervisor who takes a personal interest in the professional and the professional's learning; has difficulty relating to and feeling supported by supervisor who is perceived to have different personality style than the professional's and/or with whom a personal relationship is not established..
Perspective 2	
Supervisee wants to be given increasing autonomy to use creativity and do things differently; needs her competence to be trusted and does not want to feel supervisor is watching over her; depends on supervisor to be available to provide guidance, organizational and political expertise, and decision options; and personal and emotional support.	**Perspective 2**
	Having a personal relationship with supervisor helps motivate the new professional in her work; wants to feel comfortable (be able to trust) honestly venting to and confiding in supervisor about job-related and personal problems and opinions, but may not due to concerns about negatively affecting supervisor's view of the professional or concerns about how supervisor may use information (may not trust supervisor); wants supervisor who encourages and supports her to take care of herself..
Perspective 3	
Supervisee wants broad autonomy in defining and carrying out job responsibilities; values supervisor as a resource and consultant and decides how best to utilize supervisor in service of achieving organizational and personal goals.	
	Perspective 3
	Supervisor is seen more as a colleague and equal than as a superior.

Supporting view/position	Disagreements and conflicts:
Perspective 1 Supervisee wants supervisor to support the professional's position and feelings about important issues and to unconditionally back her up with others which affirms the professional's confidence in her position and her self-esteem.	**Perspective 1** Supervisee reports few conflicts or disagreements with supervisor with whom issues and situations are often viewed similarly; disagreements that do exist are seldom raised and feedback is rarely given for fear of hurting supervisor's feelings, relationship with supervisor, and/or supervisor's view of professional; most likely to raise disagreement with or give feedback to supervisor if professional has backing of others (e.g., colleagues, friends) or if supervisor asks for feedback; when disagreement is raised, professional's position and feelings about voicing her opinion are greatly influenced by supervisor's position and response.
Perspective 2 Supervisee wants supervisor who will support and advocate professional's position publicly, sharing any criticisms or differences privately with professional to protect her credibility; feels supported by supervisor who is willing to back up the professional's position in difficult situations and who advocates positions that advance her professionally.	**Perspective 2** Disagreements with supervisor become more identifiable and there is a greater willingness to raise these or to follow the professional's own belief particularly if professional thinks she has the support of others; willing to compromise with supervisor or adjust approach to reach acceptable agreement.
Perspective 3 Supervisee expects supervisor to hear, understand, and consider the professional's viewpoint in a disagreement or in making important decisions, but, afterwards, can accept supervisor taking a position the professional may not agree with; important to professional that supervisor make decisions based on principle, conviction, or well-articulated rationale.	**Perspective 3** Disagreements or conflicts with supervisor are addressed directly and assertively; being honest is seen as strengthening the product and the working relationship.

Supervisor feedback

Perspective 1

Frequent and explicit feedback is needed to gauge or validate self-performance; supervisor praise is highly motivating; appreciates supervisor who is non-judgmental and non-critical of professional's performance.

Perspective 2

Supervisor feedback is used in affirming growing sense of self evaluation and direction; wants on-going feedback to be aware of supervisor's view and to avoid any surprises.

Perspective 3

Supervisor feedback is compared with own self evaluation; may engage supervisor in discussing or processing differing views, but the professional ultimately decides validity of feedback and how to make use of it.

The model of student affairs professional development as related to supervision presented in the table is reflective of the combined interview responses of 30 student affairs professionals using qualitative case analyses. It does not *perfectly* describe the way any particular individual thought about and understood her or his supervision. In other words, few, if any, research participants represented their understanding of the issues in exactly the way described in one of the three perspectives. There were individual nuances and differences. The model outlines the general characteristics of the three different ways (i.e., perspectives) professionals described their thinking about the supervisory context. Ignelzi (1994) did find that an individual participant's *predominant* way of thinking about these issues could be identified using the model.

Significant logical and empirical associations were found (Ignelzi, 1994) between the perspectives identified above and Kegan's meaning-making orders. Perspective 1 is closely associated with order 3, perspective 2 with order 3-4 (transitional), and perspective 3 with order 4. As such, the perspectives provide context-specific characteristics related to how meaning-making is evidenced in the supervisory setting.

Putting our attention directly on where meaning-making meets the experiences of new first-year student affairs professionals, Ignelzi (1994) found that the predominant way of thinking of the majority of first-year professionals in his study was order 3-4 and perspective 2. Most of these professionals were struggling with somewhat mixed and ambivalent ideas about what they wanted from supervision as they moved away from (but still between) co-constructed meaning-making toward self-authorship. Knowing this has potentially important implications for supervising new professionals, as does knowing that some new professionals' predominant ways of thinking are more consistent with order 3 and perspective 1 or order 4 and perspective 3. This model strongly suggests a supervisor cannot simply assume, based on age or number of years of professional experience, what a particular supervisee needs to be supported in his or her work and development. Supporting new professionals' development first requires comprehending and valuing how they understand their experiences. Kegan (1982) suggests that to be of effective help to another, we need to first be able to communicate that we understand how it is for them.

Meaning-making theory and research also suggest that supervisors must have reasonable expectations of staff members based on the current positions of staff in their own developmental processes. For a supervisor to uncritically and/or unconsciously assume that new first-year staff are or should be thinking or behaving consistent with order 4 or perspective 3 meaning-making, would be placing most of those staff in a situation Kegan (1994) aptly describes as being *"in over our heads."* Kegan refers to this as the experience all human beings have when environmental expectations require understandings beyond the current way of making-meaning. It typically leads to feelings of anxiety, frustration, doubt and helplessness. These feelings are not conducive to doing effective work or facilitating professional growth. It is important to remember that professional difficulties experienced by staff are usually not the result of character flaws or learning deficits (Kegan, 1994). Instead, they often have developmental bases. As Kegan (1994) points out, many demands of the hidden curriculum at work and in our personal lives are actually demands on our mind. They are demands on how we think and know which cannot be changed simply or quickly. How we think and how we organize our experience evolves somewhat slowly over time and experience.

What We Might Learn About Effective Supervision From the New Professionals' Stories

We now turn directly to the revealing personal accounts of Molly, Stephanie, and Diana as they describe their experiences of transitioning from graduate students to full-time professionals during their first year of work. These extremely rich stories contain insightful analyses by the three new professionals. The depth and quality of reflection each author brings to her own experience is impressive. We are reminded by these stories of the critical nature of personal reflection in our continued learning and developmental growth as professionals and persons.

While we use the constructive developmental lens to enhance our understanding of Molly's, Stephanie's, and Diana's stories, we do not use it to individually assess or score their developmental level. The appropriate and ethical practice of individual developmental assessment includes some shared agreement between the parties and follow-up with the individuals to check the interpretive integrity. We have not met with or interviewed Molly, Stephanie, and Diana. Our understanding of them is based solely on the stories they have so graciously shared in the preceding three chapters. As such, for the purposes of analysis, we assume that all three are somewhere in the transition from order 3 to order 4 and perspective 1 to perspective 3. Again, this is consistent with the research on meaning-making reported (Kegan, 1994; Ignelzi, 1994).

Frequency of Supervision

It is a widely-held truism that a key component to success at most any endeavor is showing up. Based upon research reported by Winston and Creamer (1997) and Saunders, Cooper, Winston, and Chernow (2000) as well as the accounts shared by Molly and Diana, many supervisors of student affairs professionals are not showing up or are not showing up often enough.

While Winston and Creamer (1997) advocate weekly supervisory sessions for new staff, that does not appear to be the norm. Combining the results of two-large scale studies on the frequency of supervision, Winston and Creamer (1997) and Saunders, Cooper, Winston, and Chernow (2000) found that staff members surveyed, across all levels, reported having individual meetings with their supervisors less than once a month. More alarmingly, 47% reported five or less supervisory sessions in the past year. We wholeheartedly agree with their conclusions:

> One could argue that supervision could not possibly produce the outcomes of continuous learning and holistic development if it occurs so infrequently. The student affairs profession has as one of its explicit values to enhance the development of staff as well as students. Limited time spent with individual staff supervision is inconsistent with that purported value (Saunders, Cooper, Winston, & Chernow, 2000, p. 188).

Molly reports that she had two supervisors, neither of whom had regular meetings with her; thus initially she was not provided much direction or mentoring. Additionally, it did not appear that her supervisors formally oriented her. This contributed to her frustration level and feelings of being underutilized.

Diana had to make work adjustments during the first months due to her supervisor's maternity leave. During the three months of her supervisor's maternity leave, Diana handled significant responsibilities with little, if any, direct supervision. She viewed this as an opportunity to prove herself, despite it being a highly-stressful time. Although she eventually enjoyed her autonomy, she also missed out on receiving feedback on her first few programs and projects. When her supervisor returned, Diana was ambivalent; it became a significant adjustment for Diana to re-establish a relationship with her supervisor.

In contrast, Stephanie's supervisor spent ample time with her early on, helping her to navigate the challenges of her new job. Stephanie's supervisor also provided a substantial orientation and training program.

Stephanie states that her supervisor "balances guidance with autonomy, she demonstrates trust in my abilities and my good sense, she defers to me as the 'expert' but she is also the first to advocate for me or for our students when necessary."

From a constructive developmental view, while each of these new professionals values a certain amount of autonomy, that does not mean that they wish to be (or that it is of benefit to them to be) left largely unattended by their supervisor. New professionals in the midst of the order 3-4 meaning-making transition (moving toward self-authorship) need some structure and support as described in perspective 2 of Ignelzi's (1994) model. Stephanie's supervisor understood this, and Stephanie directly benefited from that approach.

Content of Supervisory Sessions

Winston and Creamer (1997) assert that supervisory sessions should have a substantial focus on issues related to professional and personal goals/development as well as addressing supervisor-supervisee expectations. Survey research conducted by Winston and Creamer (1997) indicates that: "Across all levels of staff, there seems to be relatively frequent attention to short-term work assignments (things to be done in the next few days or weeks), new knowledge or information, and little else" (p. 109). As such, supervision is not used for facilitating staff development, but strictly as a vehicle to get work done (Saunders, Cooper, Winston, & Chernow, 2000).

Based on Molly's account, it appears her supervisors did not subscribe to the synergistic supervision model. Molly states: "While I talked with my supervisors on a regular basis and was frequently asked how I was doing, an informal 'How are you?' is not the same as sitting down with a supervisor to talk about your professional goals and your progress toward them." Molly went from feeling valued and empowered during the interview process to quickly feeling underutilized and that her opinions were neither solicited nor valued.

It may be tempting to fault Molly for waiting ten months to raise her concerns directly with her supervisors, but Ignelzi (1994) found that it was often difficult for individuals below perspective 3 to initiate discussion of such concerns. Perspective 2 thinkers, for example, generally want to honestly confide in their supervisor about job-related problems, but may not due to concerns about negatively affecting the supervisor's view of them. This is somewhat threatening for individuals who are in the 3-4 order transition, because they at least partly co-construct their view of themselves based on what they think others (whom they value) think of them. Thus, a perceived negative evaluation by one's supervisor will likely lead to a negative evaluation of the self.

Supervisors of new professionals need to establish strong relationships with their supervisees in the initial stages of their transition to a new job. Staff members must feel comfortable enough with the supervisor/supervisee relationship to risk and share personal and professional interests (Bryan & Schwartz, 1998, p. 92). Perhaps, if one of Molly's supervisors had made an effort to establish a more formal, yet personal and friendly relationship with Molly, it would have led to better joint effort and two-way communication as described in the synergistic supervision model (Winston & Creamer, 1997). Certainly, Molly would not have experienced so much frustration, self-doubt, and boredom if she had been provided better avenues to discuss work issues with her supervisors.

Diana's story is largely one of unspoken and untested expectations. Given time, distance, and critical reflection, she recognizes and accepts responsibility for her role in the difficulty she experienced in her relationship with her supervisor. She later understands that some of her unspoken expectations of her supervisor were unreasonable, that she projected a somewhat false image of herself and her feelings and did not trust herself enough to be more honest. From a constructive developmental perspective, Diana is now able to take as *object* and critically examine her meaning-making, as it existed during that first year when she was subject to it. She has evolved beyond that way of thinking and, as such, is no longer captured by it.

Diana now understands that her projected image of independence and having everything under control hid her true feelings of insecurity and fear regarding the significant challenges she faced in her new job. She states: "I worried that I could not handle being a professional, and started to believe that I was in over my head." She felt she could not share these concerns with her supervisor because admitting her fears might adversely affect her supervisor's confidence in her, which, in turn, would worsen her confidence in herself. Diana's attempt to portray a confident, capable image to her supervisor was an attempt, however futile, to hold onto that view of herself. This, again, demonstrates the characteristic of co-constructed meaning-making that is the hallmark of order 3 and the order 3 side of the 3-4 transition.

Diana now understands that sharing her insecurity with her supervisor "would have made a real connection with Mary (her supervisor), and in that lived the possibility of having the support I needed to allay my doubts and fears." Could Diana's supervisor have done anything to better facilitate such sharing? Diana posits a possible supervision strategy when she discusses how she and her supervisor never had any conversations about expectations of the other including how they would interact, work together, and support one another. Diana states: "We did not talk about what was important to us, what made us tick, how we worked through our problems, what kind of support we wanted, or countless other important topics." The goal-based supervision component of the synergistic supervision model emphasizes the importance of supervisors initiating explicit discussions about such matters (Winston & Creamer, 1997). Perhaps, if Diana's supervisor had made discussion of such matters a central part of their supervisory sessions, Diana's somewhat unrealistic expectations as well as her real concerns would have surfaced and could have been more directly addressed.

Stephanie also lacked confidence when she started her new job. She reports having no idea how to manage her work life or how to make job-related decisions. She felt "like a fraud" and was certain someone would eventually expose her. She, however, tried to focus on a more realistic view bolstered through the support of internalizing at least one key piece of advice in addition to the support of her supervisor. The piece of advice came from one of her graduate school colleagues who had told her, "the expert in anything was once a beginner." Stephanie adopted this view as well as the strategy "to do my best, be honest, and keep pushing ahead one day at a time." Order 3-4 meaning-makers can and often do partly co-construct their meaning with significant ideas, beliefs or concepts to which they have been exposed. Stephanie's internalization of this advice as well as some of her own more self-authored reflections helped her work through the tough, initial transition to her job.

Although Stephanie had to traverse through a challenging process, both intellectually and personally, it was clear from her account that her supervisor spent much time helping Stephanie navigate the significant challenges of her new job. Her supervisor helped explain the institutional culture, provided the autonomy for Stephanie to make decisions and take reasonable risks in her job, and was very supportive and understanding of her new role (all highly valued as supportive by individuals at perspective 2). Stephanie concluded that her supervisor trusted and respected her. Stephanie's supervisor provided her with appropriate direction necessary to attain success including support, funding, and encouragement to network and take risks. Stephanie was not afraid to ask questions, experiment and, most importantly, think reflectively about her experiences. Stephanie's approach, encouraged by the active support and mentoring of her supervisor, helped her adjust in a healthy way and make great strides in her first job. Stephanie came to realize through her experience that: "Quality supervision influences my work life more than I ever expected."

Group Supervision

Winston and Creamer (1997) assert that: "Group supervision sessions may be useful if there are several staff members being supervised who have comparable job responsibilities" (p. 210). Within student affairs, this method of complementing individual supervision has been utilized most in the supervision of paraprofessionals and, in particular, resident advisors. While none of the new professional stories report use of group supervision, the utilization of such supervision and/or group support structures may have been helpful to Molly, Stephanie, and Diana.

Molly was one of five new professional staff hires in the Office of Admissions. She relocated to an area where she knew no one and hoped that she could make some friends at work. Stephanie was also living in a new city far from family and home taking on the responsibilities as a coordinator of two programs—women's programs and community service. Diana, who selected her job based on her perceived resonance with her supervisor, defines herself as politically liberal and a vegan yet moved to a conservative city in Texas. She was one of three staff members (including her supervisor) in the Orientation office. All three of these new professionals faced considerable adjustments in transitioning to new jobs and new work and personal environments.

Molly may have benefited from an effort by her supervisors to bring new admissions staff together for supervisory sessions (i.e., to supplement, not replace individual supervision). Each of these staff likely shared some job/personal adjustment issues that could have been discussed and addressed during group sessions. Group settings are also useful for conducting on-going orientation and training. If supervisors used these sessions to set and monitor professional goals, Molly's underutilization and interest in more challenging project work may have surfaced sooner. Collaborative possibilities between staff on projects or other work-related issues might be discovered as staff discuss their interests and goals. Periodically, inviting more experienced staff to these sessions could facilitate both professional modeling and mentoring opportunities.

Since both Stephanie and Diana worked in smaller offices with no other new professionals, they may have benefited from a more student affairs division-wide effort to bring together new professionals for professional/personal networking as well as more project-focused collaborations. Although Stephanie identifies herself as an introvert and used her position to effectively network with other professionals across campus, such a group support structure may have accelerated her efforts and adjustment. Diana had difficulty creating a "personal network of support" at work, which she contrasts with the built-in graduate school community. Diana's need to make significant connections at work and in her community became more pronounced as her anticipated close connection with her supervisor did not materialize. Diana would have clearly valued a structure that facilitated her job/life transition through helping her more easily connect with new colleagues and potential friends. Such intentionally structured groups have the potential to ease the significant transition from graduate programs to full-time work through attempting to create supportive professional communities for new professionals.

Another potential benefit of such groups is to provide a forum for new professionals to continue to reflect on and discuss what they learned in their graduate programs and how that knowledge can be used in their professional practice. Many student affairs professionals come to greatly appreciate the value of their learning when they are confronted with the real-life situations and dilemmas of full-time work. Becoming a more reflective practitioner is facilitated through active discussion with others. Perhaps a senior student affairs administrator and/or faculty member could facilitate periodic discussions with new professionals about the application of theory to their ongoing work.

The three personal accounts written by Molly, Stephanie, and Diana also illustrate the value of personal reflection in understanding the meaning of one's experiences and oneself. Attentive, on-going reflection is an effective means of enhancing complexity of thought, self-understanding, and personal and professional development. To the extent that we in student affairs can effect the creation and maintenance of groups that would facilitate such on-going personal reflection, we would be making a significant contribution to the development of new professionals.

Concluding Thoughts

The new professional stories as told by Molly, Stephanie and Diana illustrate the importance of effective supervision to the continued professional and personal growth and development of new student affairs staff. We have demonstrated, using characteristics of the synergistic supervision model (Winston & Creamer, 1997) and components of meaning-making development (Kegan 1982, 1994; Ignelzi, 1994), that structured models and theories may inform both our understanding of a supervisee's experience and suggest appropriate approaches to her or his supervision.

The synergistic supervision model asserts that supervision should have a dual focus on professional and personal development. Constructive developmental theory supports this viewpoint, as professional and personal development are seen as being influenced by the same underlying meaning-making structure. The relationship demonstrated between Kegan's orders and Ignelzi's perspectives further supports this view. As such, it may be largely assumed that supporting a supervisee's personal development is supporting professional development and vice-versa.

We contend that the work and life transitions associated with the first few years of full-time employment in student affairs provide almost all of the developmental *challenge* necessary for professional and personal growth. What may be lacking, in many cases, is adequate developmental *support* to provide the necessary balance so crucial to creating healthy learning environments. It is a major responsibility of student affairs supervisors to effectively contribute to providing such support for their supervisees.

What are the characteristics of support new professionals need? Ignelzi (1994) concluded that one way to find out is to ask them. The 30 participants in his study were quite articulate about what they viewed as supportive supervision consistent with their developmental level, as described earlier in the three perspectives. Providing effective developmental support is largely about meeting individuals consistent with how they currently make meaning. Providing support consistent with an individual's meaning-making powerfully communicates that he/she is understood and accepted. Such support provides solid grounding from which the individual can naturally move toward more complex ways of understanding work and self.

Kegan (1994) contends that management has a preference for hiring individuals who are psychologically self-authored. Applied to the topic of supervision this statement suggests that supervisors would like to hire staff members who do not need much, if any, supervision. This is an unrealistic and anti-developmental position to assume when considering new student affairs professionals. Individuals cannot be expected to be fully self-authored as they begin their careers. Self-authorship is a developmental goal that we all work toward during our adult lives, and we need appropriate, sensitive support to effectively navigate the journey. Kegan (1994) states: "It is a poor school whose favorite students are the ones it doesn't have to teach" (p. 171). Similarly, we contend that it is a poor student affairs division whose favorite staff are the ones it does not have to supervise.

Providing effective supervision is a complex task requiring adequate information, skill and experience. Winston and Creamer (1997) report that only half of the student affairs professionals they polled "ever received any formal training in providing supervision" (p. 111). Effective supervision is too important to the growth of professionals in our field and the quality of their work to leave its development unattended. Graduate preparation programs, professional associations, and student affairs divisions need to more systematically integrate what we know about the practice of good supervision into coursework, professional development opportunities, and in-service training.

Supervising and training new professionals requires time, energy, and patience, but the willingness of supervisors to make that investment in new professionals such as Molly, Stephanie, and Diana can reap enormous benefits not only for the staff member, but also for the overall organization and the students they serve.

Section Three Introduction
In Chapters Nine and Ten, Deborah McCarthy and William Simpkins share parts of their job search processes and their first days in *job one*, explicitly discussing how their personal identities influenced their choices of deciding on geographical locations and institutional fit, on degree of risk taking and vulnerability, and on determining their interests and potential roles as advocates. Deborah explores her identity as a residence hall professional and reflects upon balancing a personal disability with a professional identity. William is an out gay male and discusses the importance of being a student affairs professional who serves *all* students, advocates for social justice issues and the rights of lesbian, gay, bisexual and transgendered individuals, and lives his personal and professional life with integrity.

Anna Ortiz and Rich Shintaku examine Deborah's and William's narratives as well as revisiting questions raised by Christana in Chapter One. Their analysis sheds light on how personal identity influences a new professional's quest for professional growth and development, achievement, and job satisfaction. They call upon a number of theories as bases to discuss and analyze the new professionals' journeys, taking into consideration the nuances of traditionally oppressed and marginalized social identities in career decision-making and early work experiences.

9

PLAYING IT SAFE OR BEING REAL: INTEGRATING A DISABILITY AND A PROFESSION

Deborah McCarthy

When I turned sixteen, my parents gave me a paperback book entitled, *No Apologies* (Weiner, 1986). It is a collection of narratives about living with a disability. The book was my family's way of encouraging me to explore my own experience with my disability – cerebral palsy.

Cerebral palsy is a disability caused by lack of oxygen to the brain. In my case, as a six-week premature infant in 1970, it is likely that my system was deprived of oxygen during or just after birth. The resulting brain damage is permanent. I will not experience any further deterioration of ability nor will I be able to reverse the brain damage with treatment or time. At the age of 33, I have the exact same damage to the nerve endings controlling my legs as I did the day I was born.

What I remember most about the first time I skimmed *No Apologies* is a quote from a doctor attempting to explain why an individual has a disability. The doctor wrote, "After all is said and done, your situation is a riddle. Your birth was a riddle. Your childhood and adulthood will be riddles. You will know riddles as few able-bodied people know them" (Weiner, 1986, p.7). That quote has been in the back of my mind and my heart for over fifteen years now. Each of us has riddles to explore. Sometimes, we are lucky enough to find answers. Other times, it is the people we meet while searching that become the benefit.

It is perhaps a bit unusual to begin a chapter on my first student affairs job with an explanation of cerebral palsy and a discussion of life's mysteries. And yet, as I look back on my journey through my first professional position, I recognize that my disability was a key factor in my career development.

In his book, *In Over Our Heads*, Robert Kegan (1994) asserts that the mental demands of life in the 20th and 21st centuries exceed our ordinary coping capacities. At no time in my life did I feel as *in over my head* as I did while looking for my first professional position in student affairs. I would like to say that my first job search was incredibly systematic. In fact, it was only one step above throwing a dart at a United States map and hoping for the best. Having grown up in St. Louis, gone to college in Kansas City, Missouri, and navigated the Ohio winters during graduate school, I decided against living or working in any location where snow or ice would persist for more than twenty-four hours at a time. My friends teased me about not liking cold weather.

What truly guided my decision was the knowledge that if I were going to be an independent person, I had to live in a location where my physical mobility was not going to be an issue. I had to face the reality that despite my tendency to downplay cerebral palsy, my disability made a difference. While my colleagues explored the details of large versus small schools, private versus public institutions, and the finer details of on-campus apartments, I negotiated American geography. I simply did not apply for any positions in the Northeast or the Midwest, and I limited my west coast search to California and Washington.

Many people use geography as a way to limit a first job search. For me, the decision to draw what I affectionately termed the *snow-line* across the United States was monumental. Drawing the *snow-line* was the first time I consciously made a decision to allow cerebral palsy to actively influence my direction in life. At the time I was single and I knew that living alone and building a life in a climate with ice and snow would cause me undue stress. Prior to my first job search in student affairs, I ignored, worked around, or resented any difficulties cerebral palsy brought. To actively limit my options based on a disability that I had attempted, until graduate school, to minimize as much as possible was a growth experience. It was the first sign of my willingness to acknowledge and act upon a new set of demands and challenges that would continue to grow as I began my professional career. Kegan expresses these new demands as "the demand that we be in control of our issues rather than having our issues in be in control of us" (1994, p. 133).

Interviewing and resume development presented its own unique set of challenges. To paraphrase the famous Shakespearean phrase, *to tell or not to tell* become a focal point for me. My disability is such that I do not need specific accommodations to be able to navigate a college campus. Similarly, if an interviewer meets me when I am sitting down there is no way he or she would know that I have cerebral palsy until I rise to walk. When I am walking, an unusual gait and a limp give away my disability. I struggled in my first job search, and I still struggle with how much information about my disability to divulge on paper.

Within the student affairs arena there are definite advantages to making a disability known prior to an interview. We work in a sensitive and usually accepting profession. Thus, a potential employer might see having a person with a disability on staff as an asset. I also knew the benefit of personal experience in leading discussions about disability issues and/or mentoring students with disabilities. For these reasons, I wanted my future employers to know that I had cerebral palsy.

Yet, my personal integrity was also at stake. I wanted to be hired for my competencies and my commitment to the field. I did not want to be a champion of disability issues or even an educator on the topic (I would later grow into my role as an educator). I wanted to ensure that I emphasized my strengths without making more of my disability than necessary. I chose, after advice from a colleague with a more limiting disability, to address the issue of my disability in my resume and cover letters by focusing on my interest in disability issues rather than my own cerebral palsy. At first, it was like attempting to split a strand of hair, but it was an effective strategy. I could make my own interest in disability issues known while protecting myself from unnecessary or unethical questions in an interview or from the subtle but pervasive *curiosity factor*. I could demonstrate sensitivity to and an awareness of disability issues without drawing undue attention to the difficulties of my daily life.

After a series of interviews spanning from San Francisco to Atlanta, I accepted a newly-created position as a hall director at a large southern university. I was to be one of the first full-time hall directors in a collegiate system with nearly 50,000 students, 5,500 campus residents and a new Director of Housing. The position brought excitement and worry at the same time. Leaving the relatively safe environment of graduate school for a rapidly changing housing system concerned me. After several consultations with mentors, I crossed my fingers and moved south.

Dismay is probably the most appropriate word for my first few weeks on the job. Like most professionals, I believed (as I still do) in the value of student communities, student empowerment, and student interactions. I wanted to make a difference in students' lives. I wanted to answer the question posed by the Wingspread Group (1993) on

Higher Education, "What will we do today to ensure that next year's graduates are individuals of character more sensitive to the needs of community, more competent in their ability to contribute to society, and more civil in their habits of thought, speech and action?" (p. 9). By being open to a student's current realm of thought I could help students become individuals of character. I prized the ideal of being available to each and every student.

What I found were seemingly endless expectations and realities that did not match my ideals. With a staff of ten resident assistants and a building of over 800 residents, I simply could not learn everyone's name – never mind getting to know each student on a personal level to offer him or her the challenge and support I so desperately wanted to put into practice.

Among my colleagues I found a somewhat tenuous welcome. While no one would say it directly, it was clear that the departmental transition from graduate to full-time staff had caused some negative feelings with returning staff. I found myself caught between the excitement of a new position and the frustrations of colleagues who felt slighted. My own enthusiasm waned and my doubts of my own success increased. I attempted to be silent because I wanted to support both the institution and my newfound friends and colleagues. I thought that by being silent I could negotiate a tense situation effectively. At the time, I felt that the best way to show support for my colleagues and my employer was to be silent and allow the situation to open further. I wanted to avoid making a rash judgment. What I know now, after six years of student affairs experience is that there is a fine line between being open and appearing neutral. I believe openness engenders communication, community, and competency. Neutrality, on the other hand, is, in my opinion, a professional construct which we choose because it is safer than demonstrating our own core values or internal feelings.

Our profession values team participation and group consensus. Thus, as a new professional, I chose to remain quiet rather than voice opinions that might allow others to think of me as overly critical. Ironically, it was my disability that provided a way to recognize that no matter my audience, playing it safe was not in my best interest.

The Institutional Audience
One of the more jarring elements of my first student affairs job was that I spent far more time in meetings than I did with students. Thus, my first opportunities to be truly open were with colleagues rather than res-

idence hall students. As an auxiliary department, finances were a major concern. University pressure to build a new residence hall within the next three years heightened these concerns. When my supervisor asked me to serve on the building committee for this new residence hall, I eagerly accepted the opportunity. I had no idea that my participation in the committee would enlighten so many about disability issues.

The goal of our committee was to make recommendations about the appearance and function of a new residence hall. At our first meeting, I found myself immersed in a discussion of whether there would be elevators in the building. The conversation left me stunned! It was difficult to accept that my colleagues did not possess a keen understanding of accessibility. On an individual and social level, my colleagues responded well to my disability. They appeared responsive to the daily barriers that I encounter. We had discussed realities like: "Deb needs railings to go downstairs," or "Deb needs a disabled parking permit in addition to a staff permit," or "Meetings across campus are difficult for Deb to get to." I simply could not understand how the same people who responded so well to me neglected to make the connection between the presence of an elevator in a new building and accessibility issues for future students. In my mind there would be elevators. To build a building otherwise was to exclude a growing segment of our student population. Even more to the point, to build a building without elevators was to potentially exclude me from working in that building.

I listened to my colleagues as they debated costs, benefits, and building codes related to the elevator. I kept my inner struggles to myself. I did not want to be accused of making a professional issue personal. I was often accused of having negative reactions to new ideas and was attempting to tame this side of my professional demeanor in favor of a more team-orientated approach. As the semester continued, issues of accessibility in the new hall – from elevators to lobby furniture – continued to surface. I realized that for many of my colleagues, disability issues pertained to a small and finite number of students. There was no awareness of the potential for injury, elderly visitors or even the need for easy access. Further, if they recognized me as someone with a disability, it was simply a surface recognition of a physical limp rather than an understanding of the daily struggles.

I want to be careful here because my colleagues were bright, supportive and competent people. They simply had not been exposed to the pervasiveness of disability issues. As Joseph Shapiro (1993) quotes in his book, *No Pity*, "You can become disabled from your mother's poor nutrition or from falling off your polo pony. And since disability catches up with us in old age, it is a minority that we all, if we live long enough, join. It doesn't matter if your name is Kennedy or Rockefeller or Smith or Jones, your family's been touched" (pp. 8-9).

My co-workers' naiveté and my own inner struggle between wanting to be a cooperative team player and feeling compelled to educate others by sharing my own experience caused great frustration. Finally, toward the end of the semester, I vocalized the question I had been thinking for months: "Why would we build a new building that would, by its very design, exclude any individual with even minor mobility issues?" I attempted to present the likelihood that each of us would be – if we were not already – touched by a disability, and I suggested that we had the opportunity to remove rather than add to potential barriers.

In the end, the residence hall included elevators. Current building codes require elevators. Ultimately, I still felt defeated. While my colleagues remarked that they had learned something from my questions, I felt as though I had somehow failed. The building included an elevator because state law required it — not because my colleagues identified with the need. What I learned that day was that finances and student development or even diversity awareness do not always coexist. I also realized that I could not be true to myself and continue to be quiet about disability issues. For the sake of my own integrity, I would have to risk being seen as critical to own my disability in a new way. I was a new professional who carried the responsibility of being a disability educator both for myself and for those around me.

The Professional Colleague Audience

As part of August training my second year, our department sponsored an off-campus retreat for hall directors. En route, I learned that one of the activities was a vertical climbing wall. The activity was billed as optional, but we were expected to cheer for our colleagues. I felt torn. I needed to support my colleagues; I wanted to be part of my work community; and I knew that attempting to climb the wall would make me vulnerable. Even more, climbing the wall would be physically difficult. Because of cerebral palsy, I have minimal leg strength and my muscles are unusually tight. Thus, I am not very flexible. In general, success on a climbing wall depends in part on strength and in part on the ability to contort one's body in far-reaching stretches. I knew that climbing the wall was likely to mean muscle spasms, bruised knees and sore arms from pulling myself up the wall.

I was not sure I was open to the challenge of allowing my colleagues to see my physical frustrations with such a task. Further, I almost always have an emotional reaction to physical frustration. Often enough, I look at an activity like the climbing wall, convince myself that it is possible and then find myself betrayed by a body that simply cannot meet what many consider normal physical demands. I knew that attempting the wall and failing would bring feelings of anger or tears of frustration. I wanted to educate my colleagues, but I was not particularly interested in baring my soul.

At the retreat, I watched several colleagues scamper up the wall as if it were nothing more than a small hill. I was filled with sadness. My job was a place where I wanted to excel. It did not seem fair that my disability and my professional identity would become so entangled. To this day, my reasons for attempting the climbing wall are a mystery to me. Perhaps I did it because I had something to prove to myself. Perhaps I felt the need to prove something to my colleagues. Somehow, I forced my body up to the top of the wall. My knees were bruised from kneeling on footholds I could not reach any other way and my legs were shaking from muscle spasms. But, I had conquered the task at hand.

Looking back, the climbing wall may have been one of the most significant moments in my career. Three thoughts emerged from this experience that continue to guide some of my practices in student affairs. First and foremost, the climbing wall event was the most visible experience of the *challenge and support motto* I have experienced. For once in my professional career, I personally felt the doubt, the uncertainty and the fear that a student must face when he or she faces a challenging situation. I understood the mindset of the student who takes a risk because he or she wants to have a sense of belonging. I felt the almost desperate need to succeed that is common for so many new students.

The second thing I took away from the experience came from my colleagues. As I came off the wall, I heard words such as awesome and inspiring. I felt uneasy. I did not want to be a departmental *hero* for having climbed a wall. I walked away from the group to regain my breath and composure. Despite my best efforts, the tears streamed down my face. I cried out of frustration, out of relief and perhaps, despite my success, the climbing wall was a direct reminder of my physical limitations. One of my colleagues walked up beside me and said, "That must have hurt like hell." I responded by saying that the bruises would heal and the scrapes were minor. He looked me straight in the eye and said,

"I mean it must hurt your spirit. It was amazing to watch you keep trying, but it must have hurt." Then, he stopped talking and just sat with me. The climbing wall taught me about challenge, and my colleague taught me about true support. He did not praise me or tell me the details of how my actions affected him. That would wait. He simply sat with me and allowed me to feel a caring person's presence. In short, he shared the mystery of my disability with me.

Many times, when working with students I return to that memory. My colleague shared his real feelings. He did not shy away because he did not know what to say. He was open. He chose to allow me to dictate the support I needed most. From that day forward, I made a decision to support students by simply being present. As professionals, we are quick to provide additional resources to students. This is not bad. My colleague's reaction to my climbing wall experience taught me that true support comes from recognizing and engaging in an individual's struggle or mystery.

Earlier in this chapter, I discussed my realization that I was going to have be an educator for my colleagues. The climbing wall incident brought home the need for me to be a more pervasive educator. I could not assume that my colleagues understood disability issues because they were close to me. I would have to be direct in my educational efforts. As we processed the event, I mentioned that I knew nothing about the activity prior to the retreat. When this statement met with semi-confused stares, I explained that, had I known about the activity prior to the retreat, I would have packed different shoes, included a set of kneepads to protect my knees, or determined how I could be supportive without putting myself in physical risk or emotional uncertainty. I explained that it took me as long to prepare my mind for such a physical activity as it did to prepare my body.

Towards the end of the conversation, several colleagues mentioned how inspiring it had been to watch me climb the wall. I pressed them for further explanations. I learned something I had not expected. What inspired them was not so much the outcome as my determination. Colleagues shared that, had they been me, they would have given up long before I did. When asked why I kept going, I explained that once I accepted the challenge by mounting the wall in the first place, it became vitally important to give the task everything I had. Yes, there were many points on the wall— almost all of them in fact—when I thought about quitting. But as long as I was making progress, it was important to continue. I shared that my initial goal had been to figure out how to get my foot up to the first foothold, a good three feet off the ground. From there, my goal became to make it to the next foothold, and the next, and the one after that. Making it to the top was simply a natural outcome of having achieved each individual step along the way.

The realization that hit me from this conversation was that my disability was, if not a gift, at least a doorway to deeper professional relationships with my colleagues. If I made myself more open to integrating my disability with my professional life, I could have a more powerful effect on the education and awareness levels of my colleagues. Having a disability offers me a unique perspective regarding the concept of persistence. My nickname is Turtle. The name comes from a daily philosophy of one step at a time. The climbing wall incident was a way for me to demonstrate this philosophy to my colleagues. The experience became an important stepping-stone for discussions about how each of us could encourage students to be persistent.

The Student Staff Audience

Interestingly, I did not struggle with sharing my disability when working with students or student staff. I had assumed that colleagues who had graduate degrees in student affairs would know more than they did about disability related issues. I did not hold students to this same expectation. From day one, I expected to not only have to explain to students, but to defend my ability to be an excellent hall director despite my physical limitations.

My first group (and all subsequent staffs) of resident assistants surprised me; they were ten women with markedly diverse backgrounds and experiences. They were curious about my disability but, unlike my colleagues, were willing to openly ask questions. We spent many staff meetings discussing everything from my surgeries and the braces I wore as a child to the difficulties I faced on campus and how my staff could help minimize these difficulties. I noticed after the first month of working with these women, that the railings in my building were consistently clear. My staff took it upon themselves to train students to leave railings available for those who needed them. I noticed that doormats were no longer used to prop doors because I had a tendency to trip on them. I also noticed that when my staff and I walked somewhere together, they often matched my pace or offered to drive rather than trek across campus.

I wondered during that first year why I had so much success sharing a disability with students and less success, or at least more frustration, sharing the same disability with my professional colleagues. Here again, I faced the difference between being neutral and being open. I began the relationship with my resident assistants with a degree of openness I had not shared with professional staff. With professional staff, I assumed that if someone wanted to know he or she would ask. In contrast, I presumed my students not only wanted, but also needed, to know about my disability and I needed to begin the discussion for them. Hindsight is always a source of wisdom. Had I recognized that presenting my experience and myself with cerebral palsy to my colleagues would have engendered the same caring reaction it did from my students, I would have opted for this openness from the beginning.

The Residence Hall Audience

A similar lesson occurred when dealing with residents rather than staff. With nearly 50,000 students on campus and only 5000 on-campus housing spaces, filling the residence halls was rarely a problem. We always had a waiting list. When the University issued a directive for more freshmen housing, my department implemented a lottery system for returning residence hall students. The lottery system dictated which upper-class students remained on campus. The lottery appeared to me to be fair and objective. So, I was caught off guard when two residents of my hall who used wheelchairs came to me to discuss the lottery. They were both angry, as if someone had deliberately hurt them.

I attempted to diffuse the anger by explaining the rationale behind the lottery system. As a hall director, it was my job to help students work through frustrations while promoting the division's policies. I thought I was doing these students a service by remaining silent with regard to their disabilities. I explained that the system was not personal and that we were treating them like any other students. I stressed that impartiality and equality were our goals. I discovered, by listening to each of them, that this equal treatment was the crux of the problem. If the department did not grant a lottery space for the average residence hall student, he or she would make do off campus. For students using wheelchairs, losing the convenience of on-campus living could mean ending their education. For these women, the lottery was not simply about a place to live. It was about maintaining the resources each felt she needed to be independent.

As a woman with a disability, I understood their fear and the need to know that the university system would consider their special circumstances. I presented the case to senior residence hall administrators. For legal reasons, the department was not willing to make an official comment stating that students with disabilities would be given priority. Once again, I found myself face-to-face with what I believed to be the right service and assurance to provide to a student and the political and legal fears of an institution. I was not able to guarantee either student a space in the hall. And despite my best efforts, I could not bring them any official assurance that the department would consider their circumstances.

In many ways, I believed I had failed these students. Yet, in the weeks that followed, I learned that the best service I could offer these two was to openly share my own frustrations and fears about being a person with a disability. We shared anxieties about campus accessibility, thoughts about the lack of awareness on campus, and humor at our own ways of addressing the unforeseen difficulties of having a disability. For these women I became an individual rather than just an administrator. I learned from these students, as I learned from my staff, from my colleagues and from the job search process in general. My greatest asset as a professional with a disability is to share the reality and the mysteries of living with a disability.

Looking Forward

This chapter is not about answers. If you have a disability and need to know specific strategies for job searching, I can only offer the cliché *be yourself.* And, if you are an employer looking to hire someone with a disability, I can only offer, *be open.* Too often in my first position, I lost opportunities to connect with others by minimizing my disability. This chapter is a reflection of the values I discovered while attempting to be a committed but quiet professional. Simply put, it was impossible for me to fully engage with student staff or colleagues and play it safe. In the end, the value of acting with integrity — of being true to myself — superseded any desire I had to appear neutral.

Each of the stories I told here taught me to appreciate and to incorporate the mysteries of my personal experiences into my professional journey. My hope is that by reading this piece and by contemplating your own journey, you will begin to see that "what we can do today to ensure next year's graduates are individuals of character" is to be individuals of character ourselves. For me, being a professional of character means integrating my experience as a woman with cerebral palsy into my professional work with students. The professional challenge for each of us is to speak from the personal rather than the safe and to cultivate a willingness to engage in mystery.

10

PART OF THE CROWD: ONE MAN'S JOURNEY THROUGH IDENTITY

William D. Simpkins

Introduction

I am gay. I am also white, Southern Baptist-raised, Appalachian born and bred, from an impoverished area, and am one of thousands of people living with depression. I cannot remember a time when money was not something I worried about. I cannot remember a time when I felt totally part of the crowd. I am a white man battling his racism, his sexism, and yes, his internalized homophobia and heterosexism.

All of these identities are the weights of who I am, bound to my physical being each day, pulling me back, attempting to keep me from developing into the person I know I can be. Since the first day I understood what I wanted to do with the rest of my life, each of these identities has been called into question, challenged, weighed, re-shaped, and acknowledged.

It should be said from the beginning that I enjoy my work very much, and I look forward to traveling an hour uptown each morning to get back to work. It is such an intense feeling when I know that I have just helped a student learn something about herself. As Program Coordinator in the College Activities Office at Barnard College, a private, liberal arts college for women in New York City, I am responsible for advising many of the campus student organizations including the programming board, the Latina student group, and the yearbook. I am also charged with coordinating and advising Latina Heritage Month and Asian Pacific American Awareness Month as well as Barnard's New Student Orientation Program. Barnard College has a long history of preparing women to be leaders in business, the arts, and creating a new society. At times, this sense of tradition plays a crucial role in shaping and re-shaping programs to prepare our students to enter the world of

149

the twenty-first century. Other times, however, tradition holds us back and becomes a barrier to new experiences and programs. One colleague told me she found it difficult to create change on a campus where the administration strives to maintain the status quo.

Our students are driven, intelligent, and are very self-aware of their wants and needs. They often call us to task on the kind of advising we offer and the kinds of programs we offer. It often seems that many of our students come from privileged backgrounds in the New York City tri-state area. Many students were privately educated through high school. However, this stereotyping of our students sells the campus short; there are many students who attend Barnard and who work to cover the high costs of tuition and living expenses. More than I ever was at a public university, I am in contact with parents of our students who are involved in their daughters' lives. I work with young women who want to enter the business world, or who simply want to focus on their family life, or who want to travel to Brazil and work with indigenous people. The common thread that links all of these students' interests is their Barnard experience, which offers them role models for every occasion. Graduates like Margaret Mead '23, Zora Neale Hurston '27, Martha Stewart '63, Cynthia Nixon '88, and Edwidge Danticat '90 are admired and frequently celebrated on our campus as women who have made a difference in the world around them.

Undergraduate Experience

If I were to write a history of my professional experience – or even look at my resume – it would seem very clear where my professional interests lie. As an undergraduate student at Virginia Polytechnic Institute and State University (Virginia Tech), I was both a resident advisor (RA) and the president of the Lesbian, Gay, Bisexual and Transgender (LGBT) Alliance. I came out during my first semester in college on a midnight stroll to the duck pond, when my friend confided an attraction she had had to another woman while we were in high school together. I casually told her that was neat and yeah, I thought I was bisexual. The whole process took about three weeks, culminating on January 7, 1997 with telling my parents, who reacted much like any other parent does with initial tears at the hard life they knew I would lead, disbelief that what I was telling them was true and was not a phase, but always with the knowledge that they would love me and support me no matter what. All in all, I never had a negative reaction to my coming out; it was like a burden had been taken from my shoulders and I was finally free to explore who I wanted to become. Everyone around me was so supportive; even the roommate with whom I could not stand to be in the same room offered words of encouragement and intelligent questions. I began to incorporate my new sense of identity into my coursework and classroom discussions.

My coming out process also overlapped with the resident advisor selection process, more specifically, the semester-long course I was taking to prepare to become an RA. At first, I did not acknowledge my newfound identity to my instructors or my peers. One night, toward the middle of the course, I pulled the undergraduate Head Resident who was co-facilitating the course aside and explained my situation and asked if I should come out. She laughed and said yes, I should. My experiences would be invaluable to the rest of the class, but I should do it at my own pace. She would be there for me if I ever had any concerns. So I did. I think the moment when most of my classmates' suspicions were confirmed came when we played the game Cultural Bingo, where the goal is to find answers to culturally-related questions. There were no other out LGBT students in the class, so I was everyone's point-person and led that part of the large-group discussion for questions about pink triangles and Harvey Milk, both gay symbols of the twentieth century.

Three months later I found myself not only working as an RA, but also running for a position in the LGBT student group, becoming the Program Coordinator and Vice President. I had entered the group in January and immediately bonded with the existing leadership, which consisted of a young woman who was President, doing it all by herself. I attended the weekly group meetings as well as the weekly support meetings offered by this student organization. Those of us in the support group – about 8-10 first-year students – began to talk about ways that we could revitalize the organization. Most of us ran for positions in April when elections were held. It was such an exciting time – to finally be a part of a group of people who shared more with me than just being at the same school and to feel accepted by them! I think I have always had a drive for leadership, even in high school, and this was the perfect opportunity. This position also thrust me into more of an activist role than I was accustomed to previously. Because I had never personally dealt with negativity toward my gay identity and because I had so many supportive people around me, this came easily to me.

The two positions I held intersected at every turn. I was a role model for my fellow resident advisors. I was an educator about LGBT issues for my supervisors and peers and occasionally for the profes-

sional staff in the residence education office. During my first RA training, I had to remind a staff professional with over five years of residence
life experience that there should be someone representing LGBT
resources on campus at a diversity resources information session. My
life, my campus persona, had become the face and voice of LGBT student concerns on this rural southern campus. I was asked to be on
numerous search committees for high-level campus administrators,
including the Vice President for Multicultural Affairs as well as his
assistant. I was also asked to serve on a Sexual Harassment Policy Task
Force and the Student Advisory Panel to the Dean of Students. I presented LGBT and sexual harassment information in various situations,
including a student affairs graduate class, resident advisor training, and
a seminar in secondary vocational education.

On the day the world first heard that Matthew Sheppard had been
brutally beaten, it was me who the local television stations sought to
interview. Of course, this was the very same station that my entire family and network of family friends watched each evening. When I called
my mother later that afternoon, after yelling at me for a few minutes,
she told me to get on the phone and call my grandparents so that they
did not have to hear the news from the television. My grandparents, one
set of whom were fundamentalist Christians, all reacted well to my
news, indicating that they still thought well of me and would continue
to do so.

I was not the only LGBT voice on campus, but I was one of a very
few. I had not yet learned the skills of leadership that would help me to
pull together groups of my peers, but I had learned the skills of networking and speaking out. Professors, classmates, and supervisors all
accepted me for who I was and encouraged me to continue my leadership role on campus. People whom I remember fondly are those who
really supported me as a gay man working toward a better campus climate: the Dean of Students, the Executive Assistant to the President of
the University, the Executive Director of Equal Opportunity and
Affirmative Action, several staff members in the Residence Education
office, and several faculty members on campus.

As a leader of a student organization, I did not, however, feel supported by the staff of the Student Union and the Student Activities units.
They viewed me more as a foe than as someone with whom they could
work. I was challenging old systems of student involvement that centered on student government and Greek life. Cultural groups and advocacy groups were something new · though they had existed since the

1960s when the Black Student Union began to meet. It was only during my last year at Virginia Tech that the LGBT community was granted a seat on the Commission on Student Affairs, the main policy-making body related to student life. I often remember this feeling of not being supported in my student center as I have gone through graduate school and now work in a student center. I see it as my mission to make student activities more welcoming and challenging around issues of sexual identity. Barnard College is the perfect place for me in so many ways. We are all committed in this activities office to issues of social justice and equity. I hope that the students I work with have a better and more supportive experience than I did.

Transition to Graduate School

My undergraduate career was extremely fulfilling and taught me much about being a campus advocate and even more about myself and how I react to various situations. It was only natural for me to want to continue this avenue of growth as a student advocate. As I weighed my academic major, English, against my other major, which was being a student leader, I knew I wanted to follow in the footsteps of my mentors and go into student affairs. When I considered which graduate program to attend in the fall of 1999, I wanted to be in a place that would be accepting of who I was; I wanted to take a break from being the campus LGBT political voice. I also knew the activities I enjoyed most as an undergraduate were those that bettered the lives and climate for other students on campus. A program in student affairs would allow me to combine my two passions: the search for knowledge and social justice for LGBT persons.

I only applied to two programs, the University of Maryland (UM) and Virginia Tech. A very wise faculty member at Virginia Tech encouraged me to leave my comfortable environment in Blacksburg, Virginia and to branch out to a new campus where I could learn new things. After just one day at the University of Maryland for Preview Weekend, I knew that this place was where I wanted to be. The emphasis on multiculturalism as well as the high rigor of the academic course load impressed me. I called Virginia Tech and declined the assistantship I had been offered there in the Dean of Students office without knowing if I would be offered a position at UM.

The graduate assistantship selection process at UM was the first indication that I would be making some difficult choices. These choices did not include revealing my sexual identity to my interviewers. I had included all of my campus activism on my resume and spoken freely of it in my program interviews. Rather, these choices were between many graduate assistantship positions that interested me and one in particular that I knew I was qualified for, but not sure if I really wanted to do. As Coordinator of LGBT Student Involvement in the student activities office, I would be responsible for advising the LGBT and allied student groups, as well as working with leadership concerns in the LGBT community. At first, I was reluctant to accept their offer of this position, resisting any direction that might lead to professional pigeonholing. Would people assume that my only concern was for LGBT students and that this was the reason I had chosen student affairs as my field of choice? I did not want to always be the gay man in the room; rather, I wanted to be the terrific student advocate who happened to be gay. As I write this, I realize how cliché that statement is and how many times I have heard the exact same statement said by many of my colleagues about their own identities.

It took me a long time to realize that first I was an educator. And one of my many responsibilities was to take the struggles I encountered as a LGBT student and to work to make these challenges easier for other LGBT students. When I began writing papers and reports in my graduate program, I tried to expand my areas of interest writing on populations and issues that I had not spent much time organizing around or working with during my years as an undergraduate like Jewish students, students of color, and women. Gradually, I began to realize I was most vibrant and interested in my subject matter when I wrote about queer issues and students and then connected these issues to the struggles of other populations. By my final year, most of my papers, including my seminar paper and first publication (Simpkins, 2001), were on topics related to LGBT leadership, involvement, and development of LGBT students.

While I was not the only gay male student in my cohort, I believe that throughout graduate school, my peers began to see me as someone who only spoke to gay issues. We sometimes joked that one friend was the *good gay*, and I was the *bad gay* because of the reactions from our cohort that we each received. During a seven-hour debriefing of the activity *Starpower*, one classmate mentioned that he was frequently frustrated with me because he felt that I only talked about gay issues and that he questioned if I "really wanted to be there." More shockingly, yet another student shared the feeling that he "sometimes just wanted to kick my ass" because I was so gay all of the time. At the time, I internalized both of these comments to mean that in my everyday life I was nothing but a gay man. That both of the men who had made these comments were straight men of color hurt me even more. As one oppressed person to another, they could not understand what I was going through and they could not see the connection between our two identities. I extended this inference to the types of social activities I engaged in, the types of media that I watched or read, and to the things I talked about in everyday conversation. What I didn't think in that moment was that I was filling a void in our classroom discussions – that gay issues were not discussed as much as other issues, and some students resented the fact that I brought them up so often.

One afternoon before my job search began, I vividly recall approaching my faculty mentor and confessing I was not sure I was in the right place, going in the right direction with my life. Many in my cohort intimidated me; their knowledge and expertise astounded and challenged me. Age was another factor that contributed to my uncertainty. At 20 years old, I was young when I graduated from college; and in graduate school, I was by far the youngest person in the classroom. After my mentor assured me my work was good, she challenged me to continue my work with LGBT issues. She told me there just was not the volume of literature in student affairs about LGBT issues and my contributions could be great, I could become an expert. I carry this conversation with me each day and remember it every time I become discouraged in the work I am doing, each time I do not feel particularly appreciated, each time I question my purpose. I found the support from this faculty member, as well as other seasoned professionals, to be key in keeping my sanity through the rough times. When you consider that graduate programs should and do challenge new professionals to grow outside of their comfort circles and discover new identities as professionals, it is absolutely imperative we know and are continually reassured on an extremely personal level of our worth and ability to be successful student advocates.

The Job Search Begins

I spent the third weekend in January 2001 stuffing envelopes with resumes and cover letters, sending them to many positions listed with the American College Personnel Association and the National Association for Student Personnel Administrators conventions that spring. I spent hours scouring professional publications and websites for possible positions. I knew I wanted to work in student activities, I knew I wanted to be in a major metropolitan area on the east coast, and I knew I wanted to challenge myself to grow more as a professional through my work. I believe that this drive to challenge myself comes naturally to me, I have always been a person who looks for the next level of involvement.

I researched several position openings for directorships of LGBT resource centers in wonderful places across the nation. The pay was more than I could expect from most entry-level positions and several of these institutions were highly regarded. There was something inside of me that kept pulling me away from those positions. I began to wonder what it was about LGBT issues that made it so different from any other department within a student affairs division. For one, the qualifications needed to head up this unit at most of the schools were a Bachelor's degree with a Master's degree preferred and some experience with LGBT campus issues. On many of these campuses, most other unit directors had many years of experience and most had doctorates. What this suggested to me was that no matter how good I was at my job, no matter how many publications I put forth, because of my position I would not be taken as seriously on any campus that did not already value their LGBT office and its staff as highly trained professionals in the same light as other employees on the same level. Perhaps I was over-reacting, but I knew that if I was at the table with other directors who had terminal degrees, I would feel overwhelmed and not as worthy as those around me. I also knew that I was not ready in my profession-al development to challenge any institution to make the changes neces-sary to really establish an LGBT resource center on that campus. I was looking more for the opportunity to grow as a person and a profession-al through learning from others, than to see myself as someone who needed to train my colleagues about LGBT issues.

Throughout the interview process, I was open about my identity and the types of work I had done in my graduate program, asking ques-tions about domestic partner benefits and the types of support for LGBT students and staff offered on particular campuses. I applied for mostly student activities positions and a few residence life opportunities in the various cities in which I chose to look for positions. I began to notice that, although I had gone through the same graduate program and my graduate assistantship was as challenging as many of my peers, I did not receive as many interview offers as did they. I don't know that I origi-nally attributed this fact to the work that I had done, but to some flaw of my own. When I look back, some of the people who read my resume may have come to the conclusion that my graduate assistantship did not provide me the experience that more traditional assistantships would have in a student activities office. An LGBT advising position is far from traditional in most student activities offices.

Before my first and only campus interview at the College Activities Office of Barnard College in early April of 2001, I was asked to rewrite my cover letter to more fully explain that my graduate assistantship was in a student activities office and that my duties and skills were similar to those of any other activities advisor. These were skills such as organization advising, budget preparation and maintenance, marketing programs, and assessing and programming for the campus community. I re-wrote the letter, had my interview, and accepted the position without interviewing on another campus. I know now that the search committee at Barnard was primarily looking for someone who believed in social justice and could articulate that value to the college community. This is what, I hope, set my application apart from the rest and gained me entry into the process. After being asked to be more articulate regarding my actual job skills, I was hired.

During this interview, one of the more challenging questions asked by several of the students and staff pertained to what role I saw myself playing as a male on a women's campus. Obviously, I had given this question some forethought, knowing that Barnard was a women's college. How I view my role here is still changing as I become aware of the tendency to fall into or be put into a patriarchal role by some students. Often I realize after a meeting that the conversation sounded eerily like what I imagine a father-daughter discussion might be like. Resisting a parental role is a conscious decision on my part to advocate against hierarchy and patriarchy on a campus where these two ways of thinking are tradition.

REFLECTIONS

I find myself, almost a year later, reflecting on the first six months at my first professional position in student affairs. Those first six months were more instructive, more challenging, more growth-oriented, and more exciting than any time in my life. Sure, the pay is more than I could expect at other places but still not that great. New York City is an expensive place to live and work. My daily one-way commute is over an hour. And, my social circle is very slowly growing. But, I really enjoy my professional life. I look forward to getting on the subway and going to work each morning.

My position is perfect for what I continually need to be challenged. The 11-member staff (including three professional student affairs staff members) with whom I work is committed to students. I never doubt their commitment and belief in undergraduates. I work with a very young and progressive-thinking staff, have many responsibilities in several different areas of student activities, work with intelligent and challenging undergraduate women, and have the opportunity to create new programs and fulfill my own personal academic interests through research and professional development. I am encouraged to present at national conferences, to spend time writing, and to begin research projects on campus around diversity and campus climate issues. My office operates under a social justice mission statement, a mission that electrifies and tests me daily. This mission statement encourages staff to ask questions of any program that we coordinate or advise. These questions include "What voices aren't we hearing through this program?" "What voices are we hearing too much in this program and why?" "What does this program do to encourage positive social change on our campus?" This mission constantly challenges me to be aware of my own baggage when advising students.

As I continue to make the transition into Barnard College, my language is also changing. The word "queer" was never in my vocabulary except as a derogatory remark made by others in reference to LGBT people. I had already disowned the term "homosexual" to describe others and myself as something that sounded too clinical and placed too much emphasis on sex rather than on love and intimacy. I knew that there were others who used the term queer to describe themselves and other LGBT people, but I could not understand the draw. At Barnard College, particularly in the College Activities Office, this term is embraced as a new way to speak about Lesbian, Gay, Bisexual, and Transgender students in a way that does not pigeonhole them into a ready-made box of what each of these labels represents. I have even met straight students who refer to themselves as queer, because they do not feel as if they fit what a straight or heterosexual person should be. When I returned from my campus interview, and then subsequently as I grew into the position later, I began using the term queer more and more. Language only has a negative power over me if I allow it to, and in the circumstance of words like faggot and queer I have not felt their negative power since the first day that I came out to those around me. My general reaction to being called a faggot is   "Yeah? And?" My position within and my interactions with Barnard College have taught me about who I am and what labels I do and do not accept for myself.

As I was easing into this new position, one fact that assured me I could be successful at this institution as a gay man was knowing my direct supervisor, and her direct supervisor, are both queer and are both out on campus. On the surface, the sheer presence of these two remarkable professionals assuaged my need for security and for queer colleagues. However, as time progresses, I begin to see the simple presence of queer professionals and colleagues on a campus does not indicate a safe campus climate for gays and lesbians. There have been several instances where my faith in the college has faltered, such as when the basketball coach called another team's player a faggot, and on National Coming Out Day, when our facilities department washed away hours worth of students' campus chalking because of words that were perceived as obscenities – dyke, bitch and fag among them. There was little to no response from the college and surrounding Columbia University administration and even the queer community. On a day-to-day basis, I feel supported by my director and our dean, but I still feel the same sense of little genuine support from the upper administration.

***

It is hard for any person, me included, to try to put into words such a personal journey without first encountering and dealing with the multiple layers of identity that make up who we are. Evans and Levin (1990) explained that, while people experience multiple aspects of their identity simultaneously, the environment appears to be the critical influence in determining which aspects of identity are most important to them at any given time. During my transition from graduate school to Barnard College, there have been times when who I am as a male working at a women's college has played great importance. At other times at Barnard, it was me, a person from a lower-middle class family, working with students who for the most part come from privileged backgrounds that made me stop and ponder. I am challenged daily to break my Christian-centric view of the world being on a campus with large, vibrant Jewish and Muslim populations and communities. Still other times I wonder at how often someone points out my slight Southern drawl and ask, "Where are you from?" Certainly after the events of September 11, 2001, my beliefs about racism, religion, and what some acquaintances call my liberal, bleeding-heart views pushed me to act and speak out against the mass stereotyping of persons of Arabic descent and Muslims.

Being a gay male is what most often makes me stop and think about the role I play on campus and in students' lives. It is the times when people look at me with a knowing look as if there is a Cher or Madonna compact disc playing in my office, or when they see the pictures of my friends and family around me, or the way they have packaged me into a box of what a gay man is supposed to be – a gender-bending, flamboyant, effervescent, club-loving, not-too-deep guy. I could not even recount the number of times people have said I reminded them of the character *Jack* from the popular television show *Will & Grace*. Jack – the stereotypical, flamboyant gay man – is not how I think of myself. Certainly I think of myself as funny and occasionally even a little zany, but I also see the deep intellectual side of who I am. I wonder if others around me see this side, or if I let them see this side.

***

Two events have forced me to stop and reflect how far I have come in my development and how far I still have to go. One made me look back and weigh my experiences against those of another person, contrasting and comparing how each of us has handled our identity to this point in our lives. The other event pushed me to think about my future and my identity when looking for new challenges in working with students.

When I returned to work after a long winter holiday in 2002, I sat down to construct the mid-year evaluation for the graduate student I supervised and mentored. I also was faced with asking her questions about her pending job search. Developmentally, I realized that only a year ago I was facing similar challenges. She, too, has much to consider when finding her first professional position. As an observant Jewish woman, she will likely have to address many issues of working in our field and maintaining her Jewish identity. Already questions like "How should I deal with observing the Sabbath and being expected to work weekends?" are creeping into our one-on-one meetings. This question reminds me of similar ones I asked a year ago, "How do I ask about domestic partner benefits during my job interview?"

On another occasion I sat down to sort through a pile of 70 or so resumes – all applicants for an associate director position in the student activities office. What kinds of characteristics would I look for in a successful candidate? What kind of person would I trust to fill the void left in our three-professional office? After only six months of working in my first, full-time, professional job, was I ready to take on the responsibility of a search committee? There were many different people applying, men and women, people with Anglo surnames and people with Latin surnames, people from large colleges and people from small religious colleges. As I catch myself making assumptions about what I see on paper, I wonder what assumptions were made about me when people read my two-page résumé and cover letter. It makes me wonder now who you think I am after reading this short narrative.

11

PROFESSIONAL AND PERSONAL
IDENTITIES AT THE CROSSROADS

Anna M. Ortiz and Richard H. Shintaku

Introduction

Attracting and retaining diverse workforces that mirror ever-changing national demographics and creating culturally competent campus communities remain critical challenges in higher education. Despite strides in access and inclusion of historically under-represented student populations, there have been fewer successes in the representation and development of student affairs professionals who claim identity to various historically under-represented groups. Indeed, while the national college student population is 31% non-White (*Chronicle of Higher Education*, 2001), the latest demographic report of student affairs administrators indicate only 19% are non-White (ACPA, 2002). While the need to recruit individuals from backgrounds who mirror the national student population is great, the need to retain these individuals in the field is even greater.

In this chapter, we analyze three new professionals' stories to shed light on the effects of personal identity in their quest for professional growth and development, achievement, and job satisfaction. For purposes of this analysis and discussion, accounts from previous chapters include voices from new professionals who claim the following personal identities: a woman with a physical disability (Deborah), a gay man (William) and a woman of color (Christana). Using diverse theoretical sources, we discuss the relationship between personal and professional identities and the need for congruence between the two. We reveal tensions that arise when a new professional's personal identity confronts institutional identity and culture. In total, the analysis illuminates issues the profession must address to retain these new professionals and provides guidance for those who work with graduate students and new professionals.

Although these narratives are not inclusive of the many voices that can and should be heard, they provide a significant backdrop for understanding some of the more unique and distinctive experiences of new student affairs professionals. While writing her chapter, Deborah McCarthy, a woman with cerebral palsy, was employed as a resident director in a large, public university in the Southwest. Deborah's narrative centers on how advocacy intersected with her identity and professional development. She describes how her personal disability influenced her job choice, location, and personal struggle with whether to make her disability an integral part of her professional life. We also hear from William Simpkins, a gay, white male, whose life and campus persona, according to him, "became a face and voice of LGBT [lesbian, gay, bisexual, transgendered] concerns on campus." And, thus far, according to William, his greatest challenge has been to integrate personal and professional identities into his young career. And last, we revisit some of the experiences of Christana Johnson, an African American female who, in pursuit of her first full-time position, faced challenges relative to her desire to be viewed as a professional rather than a person of color.

It is ironic that many student affairs graduate preparation programs require course work in career development theories and graduates of these programs, as seen in these accounts, personally struggle with many of the issues present in the career development literature. A foundational belief of these theories is that wise career decisions are made when the personal values and goals, skills and abilities, and knowledge are congruent with the characteristics of the chosen careers.

These narratives suggest that even the best-prepared and most knowledgeable individuals encounter difficulty and challenges as they balance their personal and professional identities and strive to act authentically in work environments. Although there are multiple dimensions of identity development (e.g., sexual orientation, ethnic identity, gender identity, religious identity) that affect one's entry and success in student affairs, many new professionals are at the forefront of realizing the consequences of the identity development process. These new professionals experience the influences of multiple social identities on their identity and career development processes. Students of color, LGBT students, and students with disabilities routinely manage multiple agendas that mandate the blending of personal identities with career decisions. As the narratives emphasize, the influences of these multiple social identities go beyond career-related decisions, as students become new professionals.

As graduate students seek their first full-time positions, identities that they have carefully constructed and thoughtfully considered, collide full-force with well-established institutional cultures staffed with professionals who may be very different from Deborah, William, and Christana. This chapter explores the theoretical implications of the experience of these new professionals and offers insights to supervisors and graduate preparation faculty who prepare, nurture and challenge future professionals.

The Role of Identity in the Career Development Process

Central to Erikson's theory of human development is the notion that the self develops through a series of developmental challenges that marry internal psychological drives and processes within the parameters of one's social context. In *Identity, Youth and Crisis* (1969), utility, in the form of work, relationships and play, is an integral component of healthy personality development. Erikson's stage model delineates the role that work plays in how an individual comes to understand herself and her place in society. This process involves role-playing in early childhood, moves to the construction of work fantasies in the school years, and culminates in career choices made in late adolescence. Identity and work are intertwined, primarily due to a society that often equates identity with occupation.

American society has moved subtly to rely less on identity as what one does; yet, what one does is a primary component of adult identity. Erikson posits that this external force for definition of self, based on work, is integrated with an adolescent's need to choose work that is meaningful and expressive of one's emerging identity. Just as the stage of identity versus identity confusion represents the integration of the tasks of the stages before it, career choice represents the imagination and experiences of childhood, integrated with the person one is becoming. For the young adult, the cloak of identity encompasses work, so much so that some "prefer not to work at all for a while rather than be forced into an otherwise promising career which would offer success without the satisfaction of functioning with unique excellence" (p. 129).

College provides the ideal environment for the discovery of the career options that best offer the individual the opportunity to develop unique excellence. Indeed, many graduate students in student affairs have discarded career choices with more tangible chances for success that may be preferred by significant others. They rebuff pressure to pursue more traditional careers with better-known markers of prestige and early financial reward to pursue a career in student affairs, because it best fits their sense of identity and the unique contributions they want to make to society.

Career development theories more aggressively capture the contributions of identity to career decision-making and focus on the match between self-concept and occupation (Holland, 1985; Super, 1969). Individuals seek occupations that fit their views of the roles they anticipate playing as adults, their personality traits, and their abilities. Assessment of personal goals, preferences and personality, and awareness of available opportunities are paramount to making good career decisions. When conflicts arise, between abilities, personality traits, and anticipated roles, career indecision or unrest are the likely results (Yost & Corbishley, 1982).

Deborah and William's narratives demonstrate the complexity involved with integrating identity and work. William integrated being gay into his professional identity, yet he still worried he would be pigeonholed in his graduate program and professional career. The possibility that people might view him as a gay man, not as a new professional with a wealth of abilities and experiences that would make him successful in his work, troubled William.

However, the strength of his primary identity, a gay man, directed the abilities he developed, the knowledge he was drawn to, and the experiences he chose. The congruity between what he chose to do, who he was, and what he valued aligned perfectly.

Working on campuses to make them better places for LGBT students excited William. He enjoyed working with LGBT students on an individual basis and even published a LGBT manuscript in the higher education literature. Yet, William's inability to secure interviews for many generalist jobs in student activities frustrated him. William's resume and supplemental application materials likely emphasized his passions to work with LBGT students. Predictably, he secured a position in a non-traditional student activities office with a focus on social justice and staffed by individuals with similar sexual orientations. The congruity between William's abilities, goals and identity and his work at Barnard is ideal. The office's unique mission, promoting social justice, also allows William to engage in personally meaningful work. We suspect that William would not be as happy in a more traditional student activities office.

Deborah realized her disability was a key factor in the location of her first job   both geographically and in terms of accessibility.

However, Deborah did not anticipate the role her disability would play in the professional she would become. Although her narrative almost exclusively focuses on the experiences of her first job, we surmise that there were not many conflicts in her undergraduate and graduate education experiences that called for advocacy on her part. In fact, one of the reasons that working in student affairs was a good fit is its tendency to be accepting of diverse individuals and sensitivity to the issues many students and staff with disabilities experience.

Deborah did not want to get a job because of a disability; thus, she chose to mask this part of her identity in her application materials. Subsequently, in her new job, she sought a neutral stance in her work environment where her personal values were subjugated both voluntarily (i.e., by trying not to be the disability educator) and through environmental press (i.e., by realizing the limits of her student-centeredness in a large residence hall system). When she was called to advocacy through her work on the residence hall building committee, she came to understand that her personal values did affect her work environment and her professional values. The neutrality she worked hard to cultivate unraveled as she was called upon to educate this group. Two subsequent incidents (the wall climbing incident and the on-campus housing lottery) cemented her roles of educator and advocate. The authenticity she experienced in being open about her disability with her students transcended to other areas of her work. She learned that congruence between who she was, what she valued, and how she worked was paramount to job effectiveness and personal satisfaction.

Nuances of Traditionally Oppressed and Marginalized Social Identities in Career Decision-Making and Early Work Experiences

If a balanced and accurate assessment of skills, knowledge, and abilities is critical to the career development process, then infusing the challenges of oppressed and marginalized social identities into the process is necessary to shed light on the experiences of William and Deborah. A series of theories designed to explain the identity development of specific groups attest to the experiences and factors affecting identity and career decision-making. In this section we apply the contributions of racial, sexual, and disability identity theories to understand the narratives of these new professionals.

Sleeter (2001) offers a meta-analysis of theories used to describe the process by which disenfranchised groups come to realize and confront the expectations placed on them by an oppressive society and, then subsequently, develop positive identities free from internalized oppression. The process enables individuals to fully participate in their specific communities, eventually taking an activist perspective to promote their group and resist oppressive forces. Her meta-theory is based on theories such as Cross's Cycle of Nigrescence (1995), Cass's Model of Homosexual Identity Formation (1979), and Atkinson, Morten, and Sue's Minority Identity Model (1993).

Emancipatory identities are formed through a five-step process that does not necessarily need to be linear, but tends to be. The first step, conformity and passive acceptance, is one of naiveté, where there is little acknowledgment of oppression and little resistance to it if oppression has been internalized. In the second step, dissonance, individuals are confronted with the reality of oppression and the realization that this dysfunction has had a negative personal effect. Resisting societal norms that facilitate oppression, individuals often reject mainstream society and turn to their identity community for further exploration and eventual commitment to the emancipatory identity. Examples of the third step, immersion, include Black students becoming involved in the Black community and culture; LGBT students accepting and taking pride in their identities; or women embracing the ideology of feminism. After active exploration and immersion in these identity communities and cultures, individuals then move to where the new internalized identity permeates the holistic sense of self. This new identity influences other social identities and is balanced with a broader range of life goals and commitments. Individuals who become a voice for their group and work on the group's behalf for social change and progress have reached the fifth and final step of active commitment. To be successful, individuals need to act authentically and maintain a consolidated sense of identity that withstands criticism, challenge and disappointment in doing activist's work.

William had already begun to integrate his identity as a gay man into his overall sense of self. He had progressed through the developmental issues of identity tolerance, acceptance and pride (Cass, 1979), and developing a gay social identity and entering a lesbian/gay/bisexual community (D'Augelli, 1994). He was working on identity synthesis (Cass, 1979) in his job search. He feared being gay would be the only aspect of him that would be evaluated in the job search process. Blunt feedback from his peers revealed to William that others perceived him as a gay man who only advocated for LBGT issues. These perceptions accelerated his need to establish an identity where his multiple social identities were recognized and in harmony with his gay identity, representing the internalized, holistic identity that Sleeter describes.

Deborah's experiences with her disability in higher education before her first full-time job were relatively positive. She had an early introduction to books that provided insight into living with a disability, and she involved herself in disability education and assisted students with disabilities. Because she felt supported, the dissonance she encountered from multiple audiences in her first job caused her to move toward the later points in Sleeter's model, where activism becomes central.

Perhaps as a result of an absence of research and a more recently developed understanding of the personal and social experiences of people with disabilities, Olkin (1999) contends that there are parallels between disability identity development and that of other minority groups. Similar to other minority groups, the result of the treatment of people with disabilities has profound effects on the type and quality of interpersonal relationships, social interchange, and identity development. Unique to this group are the physical effects of living with a disability. Depending on the type of disability (e.g., visible or invisible, physical), the disability could involve a triad of pain, fatigue, and muscle weakness.

According to Olkin, people with disabilities follow a progression of development characterized by denial, exploration, and acceptance. Owning one's disability must eventually happen on two levels, factual and emotional. Ultimately, accepting a disability enables an individual to make more realistic attributions about his or her own successes and failures and, therefore, gain a greater sense of responsibility and control over one's life. In a professional setting, discrepancies between one's real and ideal identity, or the difference between how one actually is and how one is expected to be, contribute to the temporary loss or gain over one's professional identity. For Deborah, explaining her cerebral palsy to others and claiming that her disability did make a difference were key factors in her individual identity as well as in her professional identity. To have both her personal and professional identities entangled was a challenge that she had to overcome.

Identity Fusion and Infusion in the Work Environment

William, Deborah, and Christana all encountered the aforementioned identity issues as they accepted their first full-time positions within student affairs. They not only managed the demands of choosing a position aligned with their professional goals, they considered how their identities related to those positions. William had to find a place where he could be out. Deborah had to find an institution that she could physically manage. Christana had to find a position that did not make her feel that she was only a professional of color. Once these new professionals found positions that met these criteria, they then had to strategize how to succeed in their work environments. The narratives suggest a process where identity plays a central role in the construction of career choices and the job search process.

Further, it suggests that the integration of identity into the work environment proves to be most challenging for students who have social identities that are historically disenfranchised. Through these narratives, we observed identity intersecting with career and professional development in key transition points.

- Identity has an impact on how students construct the job search and the choices available to them. It is noteworthy that each of the students resisted seeking positions that would place them in service units directed only at students with disabilities, or LGBT students, or students of color. No one wanted to be known as a professional who could only assist members of his or her own group.

- Identity was used as a criterion for evaluating job opportunities and other professional choices. Uncertainty about the strength of their own professional identities as distinct from their identities as an African American, a gay man, or a person with a disability intersected with motivations they ascribed to their potential employers.

- Identity also served as a lens that affected how students perceived limits or boundaries in making meaning of the things that happened to them during the job search. Focused work experiences in graduate school often pigeonhole students into the functional areas for which they have prepared. For example, it may be difficult for someone with only residence life experience to get an entry-level position in career services. When functional areas and personal identities are closely aligned, it is difficult to determine which dynamics are at work during a job search.

- Institutional environments encouraged commitment to identity groups, which caused these new professionals to be called to advocacy. These narratives and our own experiences in student affairs highlight the dichotomy between being a student and being a professional when advocacy is concerned. Because sexual orientation, racial and disability identities are personal, these new professionals tried to keep them in the private domain, despite at least one of them being a student advocate during his undergraduate years. They internalized the myth in higher education that authorities are neutral and seldom act on their own personal interests in public forums.

• New professionals constructed multi-layered identities that were public, and active when needed, but no longer at risk of compromise. Each of the new professionals ended their narratives with a sense of resolve about the integration of their personal and professional identities. They no longer compartmentalized personal identities by keeping them out of the work arena. Their sense of confidence about the professionals they had become helped them to realize by allowing one's self to be "personal" with students and colleagues did not jeopardize their personal or professional identities.

Given this process, the remainder of this chapter addresses practical components of the job search and the early professional lives as modeled by Deborah, Christana, and William. Recommendations for graduate students, new professionals and their mentors and supervisors help us to learn how to better integrate personal and professional identities.

Pursuing the First Job

Understandably, the first job search produced high levels of anxiety and apprehension for these new professionals. Issues of location, job responsibilities, position, institutional type, campus demographics, and on-campus interview impressions weighed heavily on their minds as they sought the ideal first job in student affairs. But as witnessed from these personal accounts, identity intersected with the job search in ways different from most other new professionals.

For Deborah her initial job search was "the first time (she) consciously made a decision to allow cerebral palsy to actively influence (her) direction in life." William desired a sense of community that extended beyond an organizational or institutional footprint. He needed the vibrant gay community that liberal, urban centers tend to support. Like William, to tell or not to tell contributed to Deborah's anxiety throughout her job search. At what point, if any, in the job search should individuals divulge information relative to their unique identity? Would doing so make a difference in an institution's decision to extend a job offer? Many wonder if they were offered a position for the skills and abilities developed during graduate school or because they were seen as "diversity" candidates. For them, questions like these create internal dissonance, pitting personal identities against professional identities. Similar to students of color, who have to prove to others that they are not simply affirmative action admits, professionals with specific unique and distinctive personal identities are also challenged. This "professional pigeonholing" was a fear of both William and Christana. William struggled in his job search to ensure that he not be stereotyped into "LGBT (lesbian, gay, bisexual and transgendered) support" positions. Christana did not want to work only in multicultural affairs. But in making the decision to pursue more generalist positions, they also were concerned, they would seemingly avoid areas still in need of high-quality student affairs professionals.

The challenge is to assist new professionals in understanding the critical role that identity plays in their professional lives. It is equally critical for new professionals to understand the seemingly unavoidable role that they assume as a result of their personal identities. It is an individual decision whether "to tell or not to tell" one's identity during the job search. As noted earlier, the student affairs profession values multiculturalism and what individuals with diverse experiences can bring to higher education. New professionals need to learn to understand and accept that they will indeed make unique contributions and to embrace these skills and knowledge bases as assets in their professional repertoire. They should be cognizant of the decision to specialize, knowing that it can be perceived as pigeonholing. As such, new professionals who wish to avoid this pigeonholing are encouraged to diversify their experiences in graduate school and early in their professional careers.

Establishing Credibility and Professional Identity
Soon after the successful completion of their initial job search, new professionals find themselves faced with the arduous task of quickly establishing credibility. Questions new professionals pose include: Will my supervisor and institution want more from me given my identity? Will students have different expectations of me than my peers? Will I be

able to exhibit my true self in my new environment? These and other questions have meaning relative to the convergence of one's personal identity with his or her professional identities.

As noted in the introduction, Barr identifies six professional issues that warrant attention to assist in the transition to student affairs work (1990). Among these issues are mapping the environment and establishing expectations for performance. With Deborah, William and Christana, there was the added responsibility as members of historically under-represented and oppressed groups. In these instances, mapping the environment and establishing expectations for performance included much-needed introspection and risk taking. There is a need to be sensitive to the stress and expectations that are sometimes unknowingly placed upon new professionals. Supervisors need to establish reasonable expectations for performance as well as establish clear boundaries about what added roles new professionals are willing and/or not willing to take on given their personal identities and new professional status.

On the flip side of the coin, new professionals need to take responsibility for their professional well-being by initiating a professional development plan. As new professionals get pulled in different directions, a plan can keep them grounded and working toward a more balanced career and lifestyle. New professionals also are encouraged to seek out and establish personal and professional support networks. In many academic communities, these formal and informal networks may already exist (e.g. LGBT faculty and staff associations, faculty of color networks).

Building Networks

The integration of personal and professional identities helped these new professionals to define new professional relationships and networks, identify specific advocacy issues, as well as create new and unique challenges. Deborah found herself in an opportune position to build professional ties by educating her peers on disability issues. Deborah's relationship with students and her ability to establish herself as an effective educator also served as key components of her early success and satisfaction. Likewise, the presence of supportive and social justice oriented colleagues and supervisors helped William to build effective networks. Unlike his undergraduate experience, William was able to ease into his position, knowing that his supervisor and supervisor's supervisor were both queer and out. As is common with many professionals at small institutions, Christana also had to develop networks across campus. She came to understand that this was necessary, not just for the basic responsibilities of her job, but also to advocate for multi-cultural issues and students of color.

It is essential for mentors and supervisors to take an active role in helping new professionals identify potential networks. With the support of mentors and supervisors, new professionals should seek support beyond the campus boundaries to include community and local and regional professional groups. It is important to new professionals that these networks include people from their identity groups to serve as much-needed sounding boards and support systems. Professional distancing and contact with individuals from the similar identity groups provide the necessary objectivity and "break" from the immediate work environment that new professionals frequently find themselves needing soon after assuming a new position or role.

Challenging Institutional Structures

The integration of personal identity into the workplace required William to challenge institutional structures such as partner benefits. Deborah could not ignore institutional structures that were unfair to students with disabilities. For most new professionals, challenging institutional structures early in their careers is daunting. But for those who bring significant experiences and personal insights to the work place, these challenges can bring about positive change. In most instances, new professionals with these experiences and insights can ask difficult questions and propose possible solutions to institutional problems. For new professionals, exercising diplomacy, developing good judgment, and serving as an advocate are all equally critical. As such, new professionals are encouraged to work with their supervisors and colleagues in asking these difficult questions, while seeking needed allies in addressing organizational change. Supervisors should encourage new professionals to participate in committees, task forces and work groups that highlight the unique contributions that they bring to the organization.

Fusing Personal Values and Professional Values

Education, higher education, and student affairs work in particular, are all venues where personal and professional values converge for new professionals in distinct and powerful ways. For new professionals, separating personal and professional values in the work place is as challenging as integrating the two. Am I making a professional issue personal? Is it better to be neutral on issues that affect my personal identity? By minimizing my identity, will I be losing an opportunity to affect change? It is apparent that these and other questions profoundly impact the development of new professionals.

When confronted with a policy dilemma affecting students with disabilities (i.e., assessing priority housing assignments), Deborah was forced to make a decision on whether to be viewed, as she describes, as an individual or a neutral administrator. For Deborah, the growth occurred in her realization that the two cannot be separated. In sharing her disability, Deborah served as a role model, resource, and advocate for students with disabilities. Like Deborah, William's first priority was to be viewed as a competent student affairs professional and not just someone who only addressed gay issues. The fit and satisfaction in William's first professional position came from the personal and professional support of his supervisors and colleagues, a personally and professionally challenging student population, and from his new community (New York City).

Student affairs work often places professionals in the midst of difficult, and many times conflicting, issues. Although many may feel trapped by the conflict between their personal values and work values, in reality this position enables them to engage in a more comprehensive view of the problem and potential solutions. New perspectives gained from the inclusion of diverse values enhance the probability that solutions will benefit constituencies previously overlooked. To effectively lead from this position, the development of strong political acumen is necessary. Mentors, supervisors and colleagues are encouraged to work with the new professional in developing the skills and experience necessary to lead from the middle, while fusing together personal values and professional values.

Building Their Professional Capabilities

For new professionals, integrating personal identity with professional development creates professional capabilities beyond initial expectations and specific job functions. Establishing themselves in new positions is a priority; however, many bring a keen sensitivity to particular issues crucial to the work in student affairs. Deborah, William, and Christana's presence in their respective institutions added unique and significant value that others could not offer. Because of Deborah, students with disabilities were able to view their experiences more positively; and in reviewing housing procedures and facilities, colleagues were able to be more cognizant about the needs of students with disabilities. William developed the capability to address the inconsistencies of policies relative to queer issues as well as to introduce queer issues to discussions of diversity, pluralism, and multiculturalism. For Christana, it was the desire to work with students of color on a campus with few professional role models.

As noted, new professionals from under-represented groups often feel as if they have to over-compensate for the lack of people like themselves in student affairs organizations. Hence, they sometimes fail to attend to advanced skill development in their specific functional areas because they assume additional responsibility for multicultural issues on campus. Supervisors need to be aware of workload commitments and progress in skill development, in addition to nurturing the unique capacities these new professionals bring. Supervisors should not be threatened by the unique gifts that new professionals bring to the work environment, but rather embrace the capabilities these unique identities offer and acknowledge the talents that all student affairs professionals possess.

Conclusion

The paucity of research and literature on the experiences of "diverse others" in the career development process makes the lessons provided by Christana, William and Deborah important to our understanding of how to assist diverse new professionals to succeed. These professionals are often called upon to work *double duty* in our institutions. They have the same job responsibilities as their majority peers, yet are also expected to work with students from their identity group and educate others about their identity group.

The narratives expose the underlying desire of these new professionals to be treated more like others; however, environments necessitate that they take on additional roles and responsibilities. The management of these multiple identities, responsibilities, and expectations needs to be more carefully considered in the future. Like most, these new professionals want to do a good job, benefit from sound professional development, and learn from their colleagues and work environments. Ultimately, all student affairs professionals have the responsibility to ensure that new professionals are successful for the collective good.

Section Four Introduction

Chapter Twelve contains a story of someone completing job one and preparing for her next professional opportunity. Rozana Carducci explores her decision to leave her first student affairs professional position and return to graduate school as a doctoral student in higher education. She not only explores the challenges of returning to the role of a student, but more importantly, examines her assumptions and experiences of being in Student Affairs, her struggles to connect theory and practice for herself and for colleagues, and her commitment to becoming a member of the faculty.

In the concluding chapter, Peter Magolda and Jill Carnaghi synthesize the central themes of the new professionals' narratives and the respondents' analyses, provide implications for practice, and pose ideas to be further explored and tested by graduate preparation faculty, graduate students, and new professionals and their supervisors. In total, *Job One: Experiences of New Professionals in Student Affairs* is intended to stimulate discussions, more questions, and further examination of the many challenges and opportunities that will lead to a well educated and highly satisfied new professional workforce within Student Affairs.

12

IN SEARCH OF
GREENER PASTURES

Rozana Carducci

Introduction

I am in the fourth and final year of my first professional position in student affairs. If all goes well, it will be the last professional position I hold as a student affairs practitioner. Three months ago, I publicly announced my intention to leave the university at the end of the academic year to return to school full-time in pursuit of a doctorate in higher education. Currently, I am researching prospective graduate programs that offer an emphasis in higher education leadership and organizational behavior and have a proven track record of preparing their graduates for faculty and research positions. Rather than climbing the student affairs administrative ladder, I intend to secure a position in academic affairs as an educational leadership faculty member. My announcement surprised few, if any, of my colleagues. In fact, I suspect most are shocked that I lasted four years.

I was one of four entry-level professionals hired by the Department of Student Life at a Midwestern, flagship campus in the summer of 1998. Four years later, I am the only remaining member of this cohort. Soon it will be my turn to exit and I relish the opportunities that lie ahead. I have enjoyed serving as the Coordinator of Leadership Development Programs, but the roles and responsibilities of this job are no longer professionally fulfilling. Rather than spending my days and the majority of my nights and weekends facilitating co-curricular leadership workshops, training paraprofessionals, or running to the store to buy snacks and supplies, I want to immerse myself in a vocational and work environment that allows me to spend more time doing what I love: research, reflection, and writing about the future of higher education.

I have found it nearly impossible as a student affairs practitioner to carve out time to engage in continuous learning and the process of discovery. I entered the field of student affairs because I love to learn; but during the last four years, I have come to realize that the constant demands of student affairs work will not allow me to satisfy my thirst for reflection and intellectual growth. My decision to leave the student affairs field reflects a desire to pursue a vocation that is more closely aligned with my core professional values of intellectual curiosity, autonomy, and knowledge. Although there is no guarantee that the grass will be greener on the faculty side of the fence, I am ready and willing to find out. The decision to pursue a doctorate in higher education rather than seek another student affairs position was one of my easiest decisions. I can recall a number of defining moments and experiences that cumulatively influenced my vocational plans. Reflecting on these critical moments for the purpose of writing this chapter has been both challenging and cathartic. Challenging because a few of these stories evoke memories and emotions I would prefer to forget. Cathartic because they reaffirm my recent vocational decisions and serve as a source of inspiration for the next phase of my life.

Planting the Seed

I have a passion for learning and a love of college environments. This is not by any means an unusual statement for a student affairs professional to make. A quick poll of my graduate school peers or Student Life colleagues would most likely reveal that many, if not all, entered the field as a result of positive undergraduate experiences and a desire to learn in the vibrant and diverse cultures that characterize institutions of higher education. For some, it was the culture of pride and involvement associated with athletics and co-curricular activities. For others, it was the appeal of working for an organization with a rich history and well-established rituals and traditions.

The roots of my interest in higher education as a vocational choice extend far deeper than my undergraduate days. They are connected to the roots of my family tree. My father is a psychology professor and my grandmother was a part-time professor of art history. Education and a love for learning have been a part of my life from the very beginning. In 1995, I decided to seek a career in student affairs as a means of pursuing a specific lifestyle that I had observed and admired for many years — a lifestyle characterized by intellectual curiosity, professional autonomy, self-motivation, specialization, and most importantly, a life-long commitment to knowledge. My grandmother entered college at the age of fifty and completed a bachelor's degree and two master's degrees – one in art history and one in intellectual history – by the age of fifty-seven. Thirty-one years later, at the age of eighty-one, my grandmother continues to demonstrate a thirst for knowledge and the value of life-long learning. She is in the process of revising an unpublished manuscript and travels alone to Europe at least three times a year to expand her knowledge base of Baroque art. I can think of no better example to illustrate the value of knowledge, a value that is at the center of my educational and professional goals, than my grandmother's never-ending pursuit of intellectual development.

Although I did not live in the same house with my father for most of my childhood, I spent a great deal of time with him on his campus. What I loved most about the campus was the freedom it seemed to offer my father. If he wanted to spend the morning working at home editing the final draft of his personality psychology textbook or refining his lecture outlines, he could. If he wanted to go to the office before dawn or work late into the evening grading exams to attend one of my school functions, he could. I admired the flexibility and autonomy of his profession — the ability to make decisions for himself about how, when, and where to maximize his productivity and fulfill his responsibilities as a professor. In addition to his professional freedom, I also was fascinated by my father's exploration and mastery of one subject, personality psychology. Although I did not develop a firm understanding of the psychology discipline until I completed Psych 1 in college, I acquired his enthusiasm for learning and the process of scientific discovery early in my childhood. When I was ten years old I started my dad file, a folder of newspaper clippings, book reviews, and journal articles that focused on my father's research and teaching initiatives. Every time he had a publication, my dad sent me a copy for the file. With the addition of each new clipping, I would experience a burst of pride for my father's professional achievements and a growing determination to one day emulate his intellectual curiosity and success. Seventeen year later the contents of the dad file no longer fit in a single manila folder. I have dedicated an entire bookshelf in my home office to my father's publications. I continue to be amazed by his contributions to the field of psychology and have become even more determined to follow in my father's footsteps and realize my dream of becoming a university professor.

I am the first to admit my initial perceptions of higher education were a bit naive and based on the perspective of a young girl who was sheltered from the publish or perish culture that many university faculty, including my father, experience. Despite the fact that I did not have a complex understanding of my father's job, I was certainly capable of discerning the differences between his profession and my mother's work as a market research analyst for a large manufacturer. Both of my parents are extremely talented professionals, but the rhythms of their workdays and professional environments are quite different. My observations of these two diverse professional cultures were useful during my senior year of college in when it was time to pick a career and pursue a professional lifestyle of my own. Childhood memories of my father's academic freedom and intellectual curiosity, coupled with my own enlightening experiences as an undergraduate student shaped my vision for the future. I knew I wanted to remain connected to the diverse cultural resources unique to college campuses. I was raised to appreciate the educational opportunities provided by campus unions, university libraries, theater departments, and scholarly lectures. I thrived on the ability to control my daily schedule and was not ready to commit myself to an 8-5 workday. Most importantly, I desired a work environment that celebrated the pursuit of knowledge and intellectual development. Throughout college, I truly enjoyed learning – the thrill of discovering new information and reflecting upon the meaning and application of this knowledge to myself and society. I knew I was not finished learning and this fact played a significant role in the development of my career plans.

Unlike my father, I did not discover a passion for a specific academic discipline as an undergraduate. I enjoyed the coursework in both of my majors, political science and international studies, but I was not ready to commit the next 35 years of my life to scholarship in either of these areas. The lack of an academic specialty presented a rather significant career development roadblock given my interest in becoming a university professor. I stumbled upon the student affairs profession as a college senior searching for a professional path that would allow me to remain connected to the culture and values of higher education. A trusted mentor introduced me to the student affairs profession and encouraged me to research graduate programs in the field. I must admit that I was surprised to discover an academic discipline dedicated to the study of college students and student services administration.

As an undergraduate student I had participated in several co-curricular activities but had not given much thought to utilizing these experiences as a foundation for my vocation. It was my part-time work experience as the student manager of a cafeteria that provided me an introduction to the concepts of student development and served as an important source of motivation to enter the student affairs profession. In my role as student manager, I fell in love with the challenge of motivating my peers to reach their potential. This was no small task given the fact that most of the student workers believed they could learn little from fulfilling their job responsibilities of stocking the salad bar, working the dish room, and serving food. I was constantly searching for strategies to improve employee retention and increase the professional development value of this student employment experience. My student affairs mentor helped me identify the relationship between the guiding principles of the student affairs profession (e.g., co-curricular learning and student development) and my enthusiasm for developing student employees in the cafeteria. Once I made the connection, I was hooked. Student affairs would allow me to work at an institution of higher education, provide me with an academic specialty (college student development), and allow me to expand on the talents and passions I had discovered in college – student learning and leadership development.

I could not wait to start graduate school and begin my future as a student affairs professional. After a rather brief but intense graduate school interview process (three schools in four days), I made one of the most important (and as it turns out, one of the best) decisions of my life. I found a college student personnel graduate program that offered an environment, curriculum, and cohort that matched my personal and professional goals. I highlight these three specific elements of my graduate experience (environment, curriculum, and cohort), because they were instrumental in creating an educational culture that supported my passion for learning and raised the bar with respect to my expectations for future work environments. My graduate school peer group was collaborative, supportive, motivated, and most importantly, dedicated to promoting positive change in higher education. The academic coursework was interdisciplinary, self-reflective, and intellectually demanding. Professors and peers challenged me to integrate the theories of student culture, human development, and educational administration with the intended (and successful) outcomes of developing a professional philosophy for the practice of student affairs and a better understanding of myself. The campus and classroom environment (i.e., physical space, resources, learning community norms) provided an excellent laboratory within which to explore my professional and personal identity.

In addition to providing a general introduction to the principles of student affairs, my graduate school curriculum also offered an opportunity to specialize in two of three different higher education tracks (i.e., student development, administration, and student cultures). I selected the administration and student cultures tracks and immediately immersed myself in the coursework. Although I learned a tremendous amount about the field of student affairs from my practical experiences as a graduate assistant in residential life, leadership, and career services, it was the intellectual discoveries I made in the classroom that I found to be the most rewarding. My academic coursework and assistantship experiences allowed me to experience firsthand the relationship between student affairs theory and practice. However, it was in the context of my academic responsibilities, not my administrative roles, that I truly felt at home and had the opportunity to get a taste of my father's professional lifestyle. I experienced the joys of intellectual curiosity, autonomy, and the quest for specialization as a graduate student, and I was eager to continue down this path as a student affairs professional.

I am well aware that this chapter is supposed to focus on my first job in student affairs and I have yet to introduce any detailed information about my first position or work environment. This is not an oversight. My goals, educational experiences, family background, and personal values shaped the development of my identity long before I discovered student affairs. To fully understand my professional challenges, achievements, frustrations, and aspirations, I must acknowledge the lens through which they are viewed and interpreted, the lens of a woman who values knowledge, autonomy, and intellectual curiosity above all else. It should come as no surprise that these three values were high on my list of criteria when it came time to search for my first professional position in student affairs. They are also the same three values that have influenced my decision to leave the student affairs profession and seek greener pastures as an educational leadership faculty member.

Job One

In 1998, I arrived on campus fresh out of grad school and dedicated to bringing about a revolution in the university's leadership education programs. This Coordinator of Leadership Development position was at the top of my list when I left placement at the American College Personnel Association national convention, and my on-campus visit a few weeks later strengthened my enthusiasm for the position. I returned home from the campus visit on a Friday afternoon and received the job offer Monday morning. I asked for a few days to consider my options but I had already made up my mind. I made three calls Tuesday morning. Two were to cancel on-campus interviews scheduled for the following week and one to accept my first position as Coordinator of Leadership Development.

The job description was everything I had been looking for and more. Leadership development was the central theme of my undergraduate co-curricular activities and served as the focus of several graduate research papers and internships. During graduate school, my passion for leadership developed into a functionalist philosophy of student affairs. In contrast to student affairs generalists who wear multiple professional hats and juggle responsibilities for a diverse collection of student services in a single position (e.g., Greek fife advisor, orientation programming, and campus activities coordinator), a functionalist concentrates on one particular component of the student affairs profession. Perhaps this preference is connected to my appreciation for and desire to emulate my father's professional lifestyle. He is an expert in one discipline, personality psychology, and has dedicated his life to the exploration and understanding of this specific body of knowledge. I too wanted to become an expert in my field – to move beyond the surface of student affairs and become entrenched in the connection between theory and practice in a single discipline.

I searched for a professional position that would allow me to dedicate 100% of my professional work life to leadership. This was not an arbitrary decision. My adolescent fascination with the subject was reaffirmed through a diverse collection of graduate assistantship and internship experiences. During the course of my graduate program I worked as an assistant hall coordinator, career counselor, leadership educator, academic advisor, and instructor for an undergraduate career exploration course. Each of these positions provided valuable professional experience and challenged me to connect my graduate coursework to the daily practice of student development. My level of enthusiasm and investment in a particular functional area of student affairs was directly connected to the nature of my student interactions. While I had not entered the field of student affairs to become a parent, that is exactly how I felt like each time I conducted a judicial hearing or responded to a 2:00 a.m. crisis call. I thoroughly enjoyed the student staff supervision and leadership development aspects of my hall coordinator job, but the joy of working with eleven motivated resident assistants did not outweigh my frustrations with the lack of initiative and maturity frequently demonstrated by residents of my first-year learning community. In sharp contrast to my residential life assistantship, my internships in career development and leadership education allowed me to work almost exclusively with students who were actively pursuing opportunities for growth and development (e.g., internships, leadership training programs). Their participation in my programs was voluntary (not required by the code of conduct), and our conversations centered on strategies for achieving their personal and professional potential (not behavioral sanctions for policy violations).

My most meaningful internship experience was my work as the instructor of a one-credit career development course for undergraduate students. This position allowed me to gain first-hand experience in curriculum development, classroom facilitation, and the evaluation of student learning. I relished the opportunity to engage students in the process of reflection through course activities and assignments, and I discovered the difference one academic credit can make when it comes to motivating students to demonstrate their critical thinking and problem solving skills. My position as a course instructor helped me to recognize that significant differences exist between the type of reflection and learning I can facilitate in curricular and co-curricular environments. Although I am certain that active involvement both in and out of the classroom is essential for students to experience maximum cognitive, interpersonal, and intrapersonal development, I found myself drawn to the student relationships and methods of accountability that characterize curricular learning opportunities. The grass just looked greener on the inside of the classroom. This insight served as a constant source of frustration during my search for a full-time job given the fact that few entry-level student affairs positions offer professionals the chance to teach in the classroom.

The Coordinator of Leadership Development was a newly created position in the Department of Student Life. Previously, the Coordinator for Student Organizations and Activities sponsored a few leadership development initiatives. The demands of overseeing 350 clubs and a number of student activities programs prevented him from developing a coherent leadership education plan. The Division of Student Affairs hired me to develop and implement such a comprehensive leadership program. My supervisor, Tom, had minimal background in leadership programming and consequently did not offer much direction in identifying the essential components of a "comprehensive leadership education program." There were only three non-negotiables in the job description: assume responsibility for the Chancellor's Leadership Class (a highly selective first-year student leadership program); coordinate the annual Excellence in Leadership Awards program; and integrate the department's experiential education program (low and high ropes) into my programming. Outside of these three expectations, the sky was the limit and I could not have been happier. I had not expected to enjoy this level of autonomy in my first professional position, and I was quite thankful for the freedom to conceptualize and implement a program that allowed me to utilize my personal philosophy of leadership. I was thrilled that my first student affairs job offered a chance to continue developing my skills in the classroom. The Chancellor's Leadership Class was a two-credit leadership course, and I could not wait to start revising the syllabus and developing new activities for fall semester.

Perhaps the most important characteristic of my first full-time position was the nature of my relationship with students at the university. Unlike my residential life assistantship that demanded I dedicate a tremendous amount of time and energy to discipline, crisis response, and motivating students to participate in hall programming, my position as the Coordinator of Leadership Development allowed me to work closely with motivated students who were sincerely interested in achieving their leadership potential. They needed a mentor not a substitute parent. I found my work to be extremely fulfilling and was truly inspired by the notion that I was developing the next generation of leaders.

I spent my first three months focused on two objectives: developing an understanding of the campus leadership culture (i.e., how the university defined, promoted, and celebrated student leadership) and researching leadership development models from around the country. My first course of action was to sort through the contents of my office. My predecessor had left me quite a few boxes of correspondence and the file drawers in my desk overflowed with random program flyers from the last twenty years. By the time I had organized my files, I had developed a firm understanding of the University's previous leadership initiatives. To develop a vision for the future of leadership on campus, I spent hours on the internet examining model university leadership programs and identifying the common elements or themes. I read and re-read countless leadership theories, camping out in the library stacks two to three afternoons a week. To increase my understanding of the campus history and culture, I immediately scheduled information interviews with student affairs colleagues. In addition to learning more about my new work environment, I also searched for allies and collaborators. On a campus that serves 20,000 undergraduates and 5,000 graduate students, it was foolish to assume that I could single-handedly provide leadership education. Several departments and administrators were already doing a fine job of developing future leaders and I wanted to make certain my initiatives dovetailed with these outstanding offerings. The challenge of building a program that blended best practices in leadership education with the unique campus context and student culture engrossed me. It was a challenging task and I loved my job.

The First Sign of Trouble

Slowly but surely, my vision for leadership began to take shape. I outlined the core philosophical foundations (i.e., critical reflection, experiential education, social change, and collaboration) and developed specific initiatives that I intended to implement within the next six months. At weekly meetings with my supervisor, I eagerly shared my program ideas, theoretical assumptions about leadership, and my evolving understanding of the campus culture. I believe my initiative and passion for the subject matter genuinely impressed him, yet I sensed he struggled to understand why I was spending so much time researching models and theories. Tom was a self-described intuitive practitioner who preferred instinct to theory. He patiently listened as I summarized the latest leadership theories (e.g., social change, post-industrial, and servant-leadership) and described how I intended to build a leadership education curriculum around them, but I could tell he did not fully comprehend my commitment to connecting theory and practice. My intentional efforts to incorporate theoretical models of leadership into my work were the product of a powerful graduate internship in leadership education and the influence of a mentor who taught me to move beyond the traditional paradigm that depicts leadership as a collection of skills and dynamic personality traits.

I do not believe it is the responsibility of the leadership educator to teach students the correct paradigm of leadership, since there is no universal answer to the leadership question. Rather, I believe it is imperative that students are challenged to formulate a personal philosophy of leadership by engaging in the critical reflection of contemporary leadership theories and their assumptions about power, relationships, and influence. Without a firm understanding of multiple leadership theories and the diversity of perspectives that surround this subject, I feared that students would continue to operate from simplistic leadership frameworks. Although I continually attempted to share with Tom my motivations and vision for connecting leadership theory and student development, I found our one-on-one conversations to be a growing source of frustration and disappointment. We seemed to be speaking two different languages – one influenced by a commitment to exploring the theoretical assumptions of leadership, the other informed by a foundation in practical experience and current realities.

Although Tom and I agreed that effective leadership training programs must incorporate both skill development and values clarification initiatives in their curricula, we struggled to establish a balance and our philosophical differences made it difficult for us to collaborate on the development of a common vision for leadership education.

One of my most vivid professional memories will help to illustrate the philosophical differences Tom and I experienced and the influence these differences had on my decision to pursue a different career path in higher education. During its twenty-year history, the Chancellor's Leadership Class (CLC) program had taken many formats. In the early years CLC was merely a social club that gathered students together on a weekly basis for pizza and fellowship. There was little, if any, formal leadership education programming. Slowly the class evolved into a more structured leadership development experience that offered students academic credit for the participation in a variety of weekly workshops and projects. Although I was responsible for the administration of the program (i.e., student selection, registration, university correspondence), Tom and I shared facilitation responsibilities. Prior to my arrival, Tom made the decision to expand the program and offer two sections during the 1998 fall semester. Rather than team-teach both sections, we agreed to each take a section and use our weekly one-on-one meeting times to identify common themes and activities.

Given our philosophical differences it was nearly impossible for the two of us to reach consensus on the central themes and core experiences of the program. I wanted to strengthen the theoretical foundations and academic integrity of the class by introducing new readings and reformatting the class project to reflect a stronger connection to the principles of service-learning. Rather than assigning hypothetical case studies and presentations, I envisioned utilizing community service projects linked to selected readings and structured reflection activities as the means for enhancing the students' understanding and application of the course material (collaborative leadership, civic engagement, goal setting, etc.).

Tom favored facilitating an informal class structure, dedicating the majority of time to a discussion of current campus events and student concerns. I must acknowledge that both of our strategies had merit and contributed to the development of student leaders. Tom's approach to leadership education engaged students in lively discussions of contemporary events and provided a forum for students to express the challenges and rewards of campus leadership. My emphasis was on the exploration of global leadership themes (e.g., gender and leadership, citizenship, social change) and providing students with opportunities to critically reflect on their philosophical assumptions about leadership.

Although both groups were developing valuable leadership skills, the students were having two fundamentally different classroom experiences despite the fact that they were all members of the Chancellor's Leadership Class. As the year progressed, these curricular differences resulted in an unhealthy sense of competition between the two classes. I frequently heard students from different sections debating the academic rigor and credibility of the two CLC experiences and questioning the purpose of dividing the fifty participants into separate classes. Given these student concerns, I felt it was imperative that Tom and I once again attempt to reach consensus on the objectives and learning outcomes for the program. I did not believe that coordinating more closely on the development of class themes would necessitate either one of us compromising our unique leadership philosophy. Rather, I hoped it would help clarify our roles and responsibilities as CLC instructors and enhance our shared understanding of the critical leadership themes and assumptions that must be addressed. The conversation was not an easy one to initiate due to the fact that Tom was my supervisor, and we had such strong differences in our approach to the practice of student affairs. I swallowed my fears and broached the subject in a weekly one-on-one meeting.

In the context of our discussion about the CLC curriculum, Tom made a keen and prophetic observation, one that I will never forget. "Rozana, I think many of the challenges you are experiencing this year stem from the fact that you are too intellectual in your work." I felt like the wind had been knocked out of me. Too intellectual? What did that mean? I was too stunned to interject a question or defend myself, so I let him continue. Tom acknowledged my interest in remaining current in the scholarship of leadership but explained that this was most likely just a temporary phase that I would soon outgrow. He asserted that most student affairs administrators did not have time to read professional journals on a regular basis, and in his experience, the theories studied in graduate school were of little use in solving the day-to-day problems of the department. I ended the meeting as quickly as possible so I could exit before I started to cry. It is hard for me to express just how devastating and de-motivating I found this conversation. Tom had identified one of the most important principles of my professional identity, the principle of scholarship, and he characterized it as a professional limitation, a roadblock to becoming a successful and effective student affairs administrator!

What I found to be even more disheartening than my conversation with Tom was the fact that many of my Student Life colleagues appeared to share his perspective. The professional culture in the office did not place a high value on the scholar-practitioner model of student affairs. Aside from travel funds, the department did not offer regular professional development opportunities (e.g., seminars, workshops, brown-bag discussion groups, etc.), and staff meetings were merely a time to announce upcoming programming dates. There was little, if any, dialogue on critical issues in higher education or local implications of the latest research findings in student affairs. My colleagues were bright and talented professionals who demonstrated a great deal of enthusiasm and passion for their work; I just found it extremely difficult to identify individuals who shared my commitment to remaining current in the professional literature and actively integrating scholarship into the practice of student affairs.

As a result of our philosophical differences, the nature of my supervisory relationship with Tom changed dramatically in the remaining months of my first year. I accepted the fact that Tom and I held two distinct sets of professional values. I respected him as my supervisor, kept him up-to-date on leadership development initiatives, and sincerely appreciated his interest in my professional development but I did not, could not, view him as a source of inspiration, guidance, or professional growth. At the end of the spring semester, the leadership development program was transferred to a new unit within the department and as a result, I no longer reported to Tom. Although I did not know my new supervisor or colleagues very well, I enthusiastically embraced the transfer in hopes of finding a greener professional pasture in another corner of the department.

Although it has been nearly three years since Tom shared with me his views on the relationship between theory and practice, I have regularly reflected on this conversation and its implications. Here are just a few of my tentative conclusions. I am proud to be a student affairs practitioner who uses theory and scholarship to influence my work (e.g., decisions and programming). I do not view this characteristic as a professional liability; instead, it is an asset. The lack of commitment to professional scholarship is also one of the most influential factors in my decision to leave student affairs. In my experience as a professional staff member, Tom's perspective on the role of theory and scholarship in student affairs is a common one among practitioners in the field. It is to be expected that new professionals fresh out of graduate school are eager to apply their new-found knowledge to their daily work experiences. Something seems to happen, however, in the formative years of veteran student affairs administrators to convince them that professional theories are no longer relevant or appropriate tools for decision making. The demands of doing student affairs — the programming, the meetings, the advising, quickly overwhelm the desire and ability to continue learning about the profession through formal educational avenues (e.g., conducting research, teaching, writing, professional reading). Tom's assessment of my professional struggle to balance the doing with the learning was actually quite accurate. I was just not willing to accept the assumption that the concepts were mutually exclusive.

Year Two

My professional life did not change much my second year despite the department reorganization. The Assistant Director responsible for my new administrative team announced her resignation a few weeks after I was officially transferred and the position remained empty for two years. During this two-year period, I reported to the Director of Student Life and enjoyed a significant level of professional autonomy. The Director's hectic schedule and leadership style did not favor micromanagement, and I relished the opportunity to continue developing and expanding my vision of leadership education without having to justify my thinking and values. I met with the Director twice a month to discuss upcoming programs and new initiatives. The meetings were typically brief and informational in nature. We rarely delved into theoretical discussions of leadership or the field of student affairs. I was disappointed when I realized that my second supervisory relationship was, once again, not to be one characterized by intellectual mentoring or discourse. Our conversations were respectful, honest, and informative, but they did not challenge me to become a better professional.

In February 2000, I experienced another defining professional moment. A colleague forwarded me a job description for an assistant dean position at a prestigious university in the southeast. I had not given serious consideration to leaving my job after only two years, but the job description seemed to have my name written all over it. The Assistant Dean was to oversee the development of an innovative leadership education curriculum that intentionally integrated the university's strong commitment to service and citizenship. In addition to these leadership responsibilities, the Assistant Dean would share on-call and discipline responsibilities with other members of the Dean's staff. I decided to throw my hat into the ring despite the fact that they were looking for someone with significant professional experience. I doubted that my two years of full-time employment would be considered sufficient experience, but I had to try. Although the professional freedom that characterized my first two years in student affairs pleased me, I sincerely missed the mentoring relationships and professional development that defined my graduate school days. I had heard nothing but positive comments about my prospective employer, the Dean of Students, and the prospect of working for a supervisor who demonstrated visionary leadership excited me. The Dean of Students invited me to campus for an interview and ultimately offered me the position.

On paper it was the job of a lifetime that would surely solidify my place on the fast track to becoming a senior student affairs officer. The only problem was I wasn't absolutely sure I wanted to get on that particular fast track. The leadership programming responsibilities of this new position were phenomenal and would provide me with the opportunity to continue my focus on leadership. However, the inclusion of crisis management and discipline in my list of daily job responsibilities concerned me. I was not sure I wanted to travel down that road again – this time with the responsibility of serving as the first-responder for an entire campus. During my campus interview for the Assistant Dean position, I convinced my prospective employers I was capable of assuming the role of on-call administrator. I just couldn't convince myself. Ultimately, I turned down the offer. My decision was grounded in two important realizations: I was not interested in climbing the student affairs administration ladder or spending the next three to five years of my life as a student affairs practitioner. I was fairly certain that I wanted to be back in school working on a doctorate, actively contributing to the scholarship of higher education administration within two to three years, and this new position would not allow me to achieve that goal.

The interview process helped shed light on my vocational aspirations. To climb to the next rung on the student affairs administration ladder, I would have to trade in my functional practice in leadership and adopt a generalist student affairs perspective. Deans and vice chancellors of student affairs must develop a broad professional knowledge base that allows them to provide visionary leadership and supervision to a diverse collection of services and programs. I tried to imagine my personal and professional life ten years down the road if I opted to pursue the student affairs administration career track and I came to a clear and simple conclusion. I was not intrigued or inspired by the roles and responsibilities of senior student affairs officers. I was not willing to give up my pursuit of specialist expertise for the rewards of professional advancement. For once, the grass did not look greener on the other side of the fence.

Year Three

When I committed to return to my position as the Coordinator of Leadership Development for a third year, the Vice Chancellor and the Director of Student Life offered me additional responsibilities as the director for a new leadership residential college. I accepted and received additional compensation and the support of two graduate assistants. Although I was still lacking the type of mentorship and supervision I had hoped for as a new professional, the disappointment had long since turned into lower expectations of my supervisors and an acceptance of the current administrative reality. My learning curve had finally leveled off and my programming initiatives were headed in the right direction. The Chancellor's Leadership Class curriculum and the leadership peer education team I founded during my first year were taking shape. I settled into a new state of professional confidence and comfort and the months flew by. Before I knew it, March 2001 rolled around and it was time to head to my third American College Personnel Association convention as a full-time professional.

I always looked forward to the national convention as a time not only to catch up with my old graduate school friends but also as a time to fulfill my passion for learning. This particular convention, however, was even more powerful and educational than I expected. On a whim, I registered for placement. I did not intend to engage in an active job search, I just wanted to keep my options open and see what types of positions were available. I read through nearly 600 job descriptions posted throughout the convention and could not find a single one that interested me. Not one. True, the majority of the positions targeted entry-level professionals in residential life, but there were at least 20-30 assistant director opportunities designed for professionals with my level of experience. Again, I realized that moving up in student affairs would most likely mean moving out of my specialization in leadership development. In fact, I began to question my continued commitment to the discipline of student affairs. These doubts were raised and confirmed repeatedly during the convention as I made decisions about what educational sessions to attend. Programs highlighting best practices or model programs no longer interested me. Instead, I found myself attending sessions that explored the more theoretical and big picture issues in higher education (e.g., organizational development in higher education, the partnership between college student personnel graduate programs and student affairs divisions, spirituality and leadership).

Perhaps the most valuable session I attended during the convention was a session entitled, "Do I need a Ph.D.?" A current doctoral student and two higher education faculty members facilitated this highly informative program that explored the diverse motivations and methods for pursuing a doctorate. A great deal of time was dedicated to the review of important questions that must be addressed before making a final decision: Why do I want a doctorate? What can I bring to a doctoral learning community? What do I really know about doctoral work? What keeps me from making this commitment? I soaked up the material and at the end of the program I was able to definitively answer the question posed in the session title: YES, I did want and need a Ph.D. and pursuing one immediately became my number one professional priority.

When I returned home from the convention, I sat down and attempted to develop a plan for returning to school full-time. Although my institution has a reputable educational leadership and policy analysis doctoral program and several of my Student Life colleagues were pursuing degrees on a part-time basis, balancing a full-time job and doctoral studies did not interest me. I was ready to make a permanent transition from student affairs scholar-practitioner to full-time student and scholar. My professional aspirations beyond the doctoral degree were to obtain a university faculty or research position, not to return to the field as a student affairs administrator. After three years of full-time experience working with undergraduate students on a daily basis, I came to the conclusion that I was now interested in addressing the critical issues facing higher education (e.g., leadership, student learning, civic engagement) from a macro level that transcended the boundaries of a particular institution. I wanted to shift my attention to the study of higher education trends and the use of this scholarship to develop skilled and innovative educational administrators. Although I would no longer have daily contact with undergraduate students, my work would still have a significant influence on the creation of a positive college experience for students around the country. Given my professional goals, completely immersing myself in the academic culture while in graduate school was the best course of action.

Year Four

Making the decision to return to school came quite naturally; the actual transition was a bit more complicated. Fortunately, I am at a place in my life, both financially and emotionally, that will support this radical life change. I am single so I am free to relocate to attend school without having to factor in the implications of this move on a partner. I have not been very diligent about building up my savings since graduate school; on the flip side, I have managed to keep my credit card debt relatively low and make steady progress paying down my car and educational loans. During the last three years I have enjoyed financial freedom and become accustomed to a comfortable lifestyle that allows me to eat out or catch a movie without worrying about the ramifications on my checking account. I have taken steps during my fourth and final year as a student affairs professional to prepare myself as best I can for the drastic change in income I will experience next summer. I attended a personal financial planning workshop offered by the human resources department on campus with the goal of increasing my ability and commitment to living within a budget. I have already scaled back on my personal expenditures in the non-essentials category (i.e., entertainment, clothing, and decorations for my apartment) and have placed a few items on my holiday gift list that I know will be out of reach once I return to school. Saving has never been one of my strengths, but I feel good about the fact that I am at least cognizant of the financial implications of this career decision and am actively preparing myself for the change.

In addition to making financial preparations, it was important to use my final year of full-time employment to prepare myself mentally for the transition to the role of full-time student. With that end in mind, I enrolled in a four-week graduate summer school class, Introduction to Educational Research. I chose statistics since my Master's degree curriculum did not include any coursework in quantitative research methods. I worry about struggling to catch up with other doctoral students who may already be familiar with the principles of educational research. Given the more relaxed pace of student affairs in the summer, it was a perfect time to get re-acquainted with the life of a student. I used my vacation time to cover my absences, and the university provided me with a tuition waiver of 75% for my educational fees. I assimilated the course material quickly and I thoroughly enjoyed spending time doing homework and reviewing my class notes. It just felt right. I took this to be a positive sign that I had made the right decision about returning to school full-time. If I could actually enjoy statistics, imagine how much fun I could have in my theory and foundation classes!

When the fall semester rolled around a few months ago, I decided to take the next statistics course in the research sequence, Quantitative Research Methods I. Carving out six to eight hours a week from my hectic fall programming schedule was tough. I was determined to stay on top of my statistics homework and reading, but the demands of working full-time made this quite a challenge. I cannot begin to imagine how my colleagues, who are pursuing their degrees part-time, find the time to balance two academic classes and their professional responsibilities.

My return to the classroom has had a profound impact on my professional practice. Thanks to my own classroom struggles and triumphs, I have a much greater sense of empathy for the undergraduate students with whom I interact on a daily basis. I no longer brush aside their comments about the cost of textbooks, and I can relate to their concerns about finding time to study between work and their co-curricular activities. I have been able to connect with students on a different level this semester and am truly enjoying the experience.

This year of transition has not been without a few significant bumps and roadblocks. My to do list keeps growing and there are just not enough hours in a day. Finding time to study for the GRE, research potential doctoral programs, and develop my application timelines have been nearly impossible. Not to mention that I still have a full-time job that demands a great deal of personal time and energy. The word overwhelmed quickly comes to mind as an accurate description of my current emotional state, but I just keep reminding myself that I have to get through this tough phase to get to the greener grass that lies ahead.

What has been most surprising this year is the tremendous amount of guilt I have experienced since publicly announcing my decision to shift my emphasis within higher education. Although I am certain this is the right decision for me, I have struggled with the implications and others' interpretations of my choice. There have been many days during the past few months where I have felt like a failure as a student affairs practitioner. I have assumed that my decision to leave the field in favor of a faculty position is a sign of weakness or incompetence. Perhaps Tom was right, I am too intellectual and lack the common sense and intuition it takes to succeed as a student affairs administrator. The well known saying, "Those who can, do; those who can't, teach" has been on my mind a lot in recent weeks. I have thought that my guilt over leaving the student affairs field has been intensified due to the fact that I am making the choice to become a member of the dark side, the faculty. In my professional experience, faculty and academic administrators are still viewed as members of an elitist class who rarely come down from their ivory tower to support the mission of student affairs. I just cannot shake the feeling that my decision to exit the profession is really an act of treason.

Another source of guilt during this transition phase has been my level of productivity at work. I have always prided myself on my strong work ethic and commitment to excellence and innovation in programming, but lately the drive and passion to excel has diminished. My priorities have shifted and I am no longer able or willing to place work at the top of the list. I seldom go into the office on the weekends to get a head start on the week. Instead, I spend that time researching graduate school programs. Rather than working until 8 or 9 p.m. every evening (the norm during my first two years as a student affairs professional), I try to leave by 6:00 p.m. so that I can go home and read statistics or study for the Graduate Record Exam. I am no longer the first one to raise my hand when the director asks for volunteers to work on a new initiative, and I have even started the process of turning over some of the projects that have timelines past the end of the academic year. This is unfamiliar territory for me; I am used to being a workaholic. I have made significant sacrifices in my personal life to achieve excellence in my professional life. After all, is that not what it takes to be a great student affairs practitioner, to put the needs of the students and the campus above my own? Unfortunately, it has taken me three and a half years to realize how unhealthy and destructive that mindset can be. Given that I have been mistakenly operating under the assumption that my identity as a coordinator of leadership is more important that my personal identity, my recent battles with guilt should come as no surprise. For the first time in a long time, I have made a conscious decision to put myself first. I do not regret this choice but it has certainly not been easy.

Searching for Greener Pastures

There are many who might characterize my decision to enter and exit the field of student affairs as a never-ending search for greener pastures. To a certain extent they may be right. I pursued a career in student affairs based on fond adolescent memories of my father's college campus and a desire to steer clear of the 9-5 corporate world my mother inhabited. Unfortunately, the practice of student affairs was not as lush a pasture as I had hoped. I was passionate about the discipline of leadership education but was frequently frustrated by the lack of intellectual rigor and institutional respect that characterized my first job experience. Now I am jumping the fence once again, this time to the faculty pasture, in search of finding my true vocational home, a work environment and professional lifestyle that matches the ideal picture I have been painting in my mind for so many years. Although I will be the first to admit that the grass will likely not be as green as I hope, I truly believe I am making the right choice. It is a decision grounded in my core values (knowledge, autonomy, intellectual curiosity) and professional experience. Although it has been challenging at times, I have enjoyed my time in the field of student affairs and will treasure the memories forever. Even more importantly, I will use the knowledge and experience I gained during my short time as a student affairs practitioner to enhance my effectiveness as a faculty member and continue the work of building powerful partnerships between academic and student affairs.

13

PREPARING THE NEXT GENERATION OF STUDENT AFFAIRS PROFESSIONALS

Peter M. Magolda & Jill Ellen Carnaghi

> Good practice in student affairs uses high-quality information about students, their learning, their needs, and campus environments to design programs, activities, policies, and systematic change strategies to achieve stated learning goals. (ACPA/NASPA, 1997, p. 38)

Introduction

This quotation applies as well to new professionals in student affairs. Contributors to this book have provided quality information regarding new professionals' learning, needs and optimal work environments; they have offered specific strategies necessary to engage in good practice for the four intended audiences of this book — student affairs preparation program faculty, graduate students, new professionals, and the new professionals' supervisors.

Sandeen (1984) argued that "The successful student affairs professional is one who understands the difficulties facing higher education, knows the history of the profession, is able to adapt to changing issues and problems, and can organize people and resources around these matters to address the problems effectively" (p. 8). A primary goal of this chapter is to apply Sandeen's advice within the context of new professionals in student affairs. Thus, we summarize some of the difficulties new professionals encounter on a daily basis (based on the narrative and analysis chapters) with the hope this synthesis will lead to organizational change.

To accomplish this goal, we use Rozana Carducci's essay (Chapter

12): In Search of Greener Pastures to synthesize ideas of book contributors. Six themes in Rozana's narrative are evident in the other eight narratives. New professionals: [1] seek greener pastures; [2] recognize how their life histories and identities influence their career paths; [3]; struggle to integrate theory and practice; [4] strive to balance idealistic with realistic expectations; [5] express mixed emotions of strength and fragility; and [6] engage in in-depth and on-going reflection about their first job in student affairs. Later in this chapter we discuss how tending to these six themes can make learning and struggles explicit for graduate students, preparation program faculty, new professionals, and supervisors.

Experiences Shared by New Professionals
Looking Ahead: Seeking Greener Pastures

Although Rozana focused on the transition from job one back to graduate school (and the other new professionals discussed their transitions from graduate school to job one), searching for greener pastures, moving on, and starting over were common experiences for the new professionals. They sought greener pastures that, among other things, metaphorically would allow them to graze and nourish themselves personally and professionally. As the new professionals searched for these greener pastures, they encountered numerous crossroads, similar to the ones Kevin described in Chapter 1.

> Starting over involves saying goodbye to established relationships and being open to saying hello to new ones. The crossroads involves leaving a community and a job with which I am comfortable and adjusting to new environments, cultures, and people. ... The crossroads includes the doubt about whether or not I am doing the right thing and making the right decision.

Arriving at these crossroads necessitated contemplative decision-making. Making the right decision weighed heavy on Rozana's mind, as she relinquished her job and said goodbye to colleagues. Rozana's particular crossroads provided her with two viable yet distinctively different routes to professional fulfillment: pursue a mid-level administrative post or return to graduate school as a stepping-stone to a career in academia. For Rozana, this deliberate process created much angst, despite her certainty that the faculty route would lead to the greener pasture for her dreams and aspirations.

An examination of the other new professionals' crossroads provides insights into student affairs pastures that appeal to many new professionals. Each of Christana's (Chapter 2) on-campus interviews presented her with crossroads of sorts. In the end, St. Olaf College — a setting that affirmed her African American identity and allowed her to support students who have historically been marginalized in higher education — was the greenest pasture.

Craig and Kathleen's (Chapter 3) job search crossroads were particularly complicated since at each juncture, reaching consensus was necessary. Ultimately, the pasture needed to be large and nutritious enough to support this dual career couple's distinctively different professional aspirations (i.e., psychologist and residence hall staff member).

The new professionals encountered numerous viable options at every crossroads (en route to greener pastures). Inevitably, selecting particular paths necessitated the new professionals say goodbye and start over (which temporarily dulled the sheen on this greener grass). Despite Rozana's passion for pursuing her dream to become a college professor, saying goodbye to her colleagues and to her life as a student affairs practitioner was taxing. So, too, was the looming prospect of starting over, once again, as a graduate student. Diana (Chapter 7) and Molly (Chapter 5) also struggled to say goodbye to their graduate school learning communities, which supported their professional and personal needs.

Looking ahead and seeking greener pastures was both exciting and uncertain, which made the start of these job one journeys upsetting — temporarily making new pastures appear anything but green. Yet, as the case studies suggest, with patience and thoughtfulness the new professionals' pastures were, in fact, greener and worth pursuing.

Looking Back: History and Identity Matter

Not only did the new professionals continually look ahead, frequently and systematically they reflected on the past. In doing so, the new professionals recognized that their life histories and identities played a vital role in the greener pastures they sought (Carper & Becker, 1958). Goodman's (1984) research on the socialization of student affairs graduate students concluded, "students will construct personalized definitions of the field of student personnel work based on prior academic interests, personal interests, life histories, and self-confidence" (p. 377). This finding is particularly relevant to the new professionals' narratives.

New professionals' family backgrounds, educational histories, personal identities, and interests influenced how they conceptualized the profession, their job search processes, and satisfaction levels once they began their full-time work in student affairs. Family members' passion for education influenced Rozana's decision to attend college, pursue a master's degree in student affairs, accept a position in student leadership, and finally to pursue a doctorate. Kevin's (Chapter 1) Catholic University undergraduate experience coupled with his commitment to Catholic education, contributed to his decision to become an academic advisor at Notre Dame University. Deborah's (Chapter 9) cerebral palsy influenced not only the jobs for which she applied, but also regions of the country where she would work (e.g., snow-free environments). The opening line of William's story (Chapter 10) —"I am gay. I am also white, Southern Baptist-raised, Appalachian born and bred, from an impoverished area, and am one of thousands of people living with depression" — reminds readers that new professionals' life histories and personal identities matter and influence professional aspirations and career paths. Stephanie (Chapter 6) affirmed this assertion.

> I did know that social issues concerned me deeply. I had been heavily influenced by my undergraduate years at Occidental College in Los Angeles, where I enrolled in such courses as "Cross-Cultural Issues in American Society," where I sat under curfew during the Los Angeles riots following the Rodney King verdict, where whites were the minority among students of color, and where cross-cultural dialogue and interaction was a major institutional priority.

Like Kevin, Deborah, and William, Stephanie's past influenced how she viewed her work in student affairs as well as her career interests and job search process. This is congruent with one of Rich and Anna's assertions (Chapter 11): "They [new professionals] not only managed the demands of choosing a position aligned with their professional goals, they considered how the unique aspects of their identities related to those positions."

When graduate students are asked about the jobs they intend to pursue, frequently they fixate on the job market (i.e., available jobs), making that the most important consideration. Kirby (1984) wrote, "Because the atmosphere surrounding a job search can be filled with a great deal of tension, candidates can quickly lose sight of their own personal needs and values" (p. 25). The importance of one's family background, personal identity, educational history, and interests cannot be overstated. Reflecting on the past, as one looks to the future, is sage advice these new professionals offer to the profession.

Balancing Theory and Practice

"Practitioners who emerge from a strong, theory-based program often experience dissonance between theory and actual practice in their first practitioner setting. ... What is learned in the classroom at times may not seem relevant or even valued in the new professional setting" (Barr, 1990, p. 20). Several of the new professionals encountered the dissonance Barr described as they began their full-time work in student affairs. Strange and King articulated the origins of this dissonance between theory and practice and the importance of seeking a more harmonious relationship.

> Lewin (1936) asserted there is nothing so practical as a good theory, and Cross (1981) contended that, although theory without practice is empty, practice without theory is blind. Yet, linking theory and practice, and incorporating a theory and research base in the professional preparation of student affairs practitioners, is problematic for several reasons. The problems with the linkages are hypothesized to be: (a) the inherently imperfect correspondence between theory and reality; (b) the difficulties of translating theory to practice; (c) the nature of applied fields; and (d) the nature of individuals attracted to people-oriented, applied fields. (1990, p. 17)

The appropriate role of theory in a leadership seminar was a major source of conflict between Rozana and her first supervisor.

> I wanted to strengthen the theoretical foundations and academic integrity of the class by introducing new readings and reformatting the class project to reflect a stronger connection to the principles of service-learning. Rather than assigning hypothetical case studies and presentations, I envisioned utilizing community service projects linked to selected readings and structured reflection activities as the means for enhancing the students' understanding and application of the course material (collaborative leadership, civic engagement, goal set-

> ting, etc.). Tom favored facilitating an informal class structure, dedicating the majority of time to a discussion of current campus events and student concerns.

This ideological divide illuminates a question posed by several of the new professionals: What role should theory play in our lives as new professionals?

Kevin (Chapter 1) began his graduate studies unaware that theory would play any role in his education:

> I decided to pursue graduate education with few academic expectations in mind. Originally, I viewed my time in graduate school as a rite of passage that one needed to go through to enter the field, a necessary evil. I believed that if I wanted to work in student affairs, I had to get a Master's degree. I was more excited about my assistantship than I was about the academic curriculum. The classes were almost secondary. Sure, I was expecting to learn *how* to be a student affairs professional and figured that I would learn how to run a successful student affairs office. What I found after arriving was my program was going to be more than a student affairs boot camp. In fact, academic expectations were very high and the coursework rigorous. This was not a mere rite of passage, but an important component to becoming an effective professional.

After completing his graduate degree, Kevin was ready to apply theory to practice.

> Besides, I was confident my graduate education had prepared me well. I knew my Chickering vectors and could *layer* my developmental theories when applying them to practice. There were D'Augelli, Kegan, and a number of other theorists whom I could draw upon in my work to help students.

Would Kevin actually make use of these theories in his day-to-day practice? Would his supervisors be theory savvy? Would applying theory to practice make a difference in the lives of students? These questions were on the minds of many of the new professionals, an issue Susan and Michael (Chapter 4) explicitly discussed.

Many graduate students may retrospectively describe their

graduate school days as steeped in the study of theoretical perspectives on student development and higher education administration. Further, they may find the hard work of applying theory to practice begins in earnest with their first professional position after completion of a Master's degree.

Traditionally, student affairs practitioners view theory as something apart from, and applied to, practice. In this view, theory is about knowledge (i.e., the domain of the faculty), and practice is about action (i.e., the domain of the practitioners). Strange and King (1990) clarified the student affairs profession's estrangement from theory.

> Success in an applied field tends to be gauged in terms of what an individual has done. Accomplishments accumulated over time lead to a successful *track record*, which, in turn, becomes the mark of an experienced and "seasoned practitioner." Individuals must *pay their dues* as an apprentice, learning from those who have "been there." Advancement is contingent upon a succession of responsibilities and assignments. Basic knowledge, such as theory, that is acquired through traditional schooling is both a source of mistrust and perhaps even a threat to those already practicing in the field. It may be a source of distrust for several reasons. Claims of expertise, grounded in *what you know* rather than *what you have done*, will predictably be met with suspicion in an applied field. This is especially true of a field like student affairs where interaction with people is paramount. Nothing substitutes for experience and maturity in terms of learning about and responding to the complexities of human behaviors. Consequently, a status claim based on what you know (e.g., knowledge of current theory) rather than *what you have done* is understandably threatening because it tends to undercut the experiential foundation of the field. (pp. 18-19)

The dynamics of what you know versus what you have done are evident in many of the new professionals' stories. Molly (Chapter 5) was the only new professional in her office with a graduate degree in higher education. She wondered: Was her graduate degree necessary? Would her supervisors value her theoretically-oriented academic preparation? Would there be opportunities to make use of the leadership theories she learned in her graduate studies? Often implicit, an issue in this theory-practice divide is whether graduate school preparation is necessary to function as an effective full-time student affairs professional.

Stephanie's (Chapter 6) satisfaction with her job was, in part, because her supervisor recognized the value of a graduate degree in student affairs and encouraged Stephanie to blend student development theories (among others) with service-learning and women's studies perspectives acquired during graduate school into her daily work. Simply stated, Stephanie's supervisor wanted her to think and do; utilizing theory enhanced Stephanie's ability to implement and institutionalize what she knew.

Schön (1983, 1995) described higher education's view of the relationship between thinking and doing—or its epistemology of practice— as technical rationality, which sees sound professional practice as solving instrumental problems through the application of scientific theory and technique. Schön wrote:

> As one would expect from the hierarchical model of professional knowledge, research is institutionally separate from practice, connected to it by carefully defined relationships of exchange. Researchers are supposed to provide the basic and applied science from which to derive techniques for diagnosing and solving the problems of practice. Practitioners are supposed to furnish researchers with problems for study and with tests of the utility of research results. The researcher's role is distinct from, and usually considered superior to, the role of the practitioner. (1983, p. 26)

Susan and Michael (Chapter 4) rejected this separate and unequal world-view when writing their chapter; they valued both thinking and doing. They wanted theory to inform practice and vice-versa, because they view both roles as essential for effective student affairs practice. Kevin offered specifics about how he bridged this ideological divide and structured his everyday practice so he was not simply doing, but thinking and doing.

> Although the Chickering vectors may not be discussed in staff meetings, the knowledge of student development theory is so ingrained in my psyche that it does inform my practice. I reviewed the syllabus I use in the undergraduate course I teach

and see theory informing how I structure my class. I look at the peer-tutoring program I helped coordinate and I see theories there. I also see it most importantly in my advising and daily interaction with students. Whether it is working with a student who has not developed purpose or working with a student who is still struggling with his or her sexual identity, the theories I learned are always being referenced. Although I may no longer cite the theorists and scholars, it is impossible for me to go a day without using them to inform my work with students. Undoubtedly, the knowledge and use of theory make me more effective in being a student advocate.

Molly also revealed how her theory with practice (and vice-versa) strategies helped her make sense of her work environment.

Coming from a student affairs graduate preparation program in which I had frequently analyzed different work environments from a variety of organizational perspectives, I could not help but analyze my current work environment using different organizational models and theories. I found similarities between my work environment and quite a few of the organizational metaphors outlined in Gareth Morgan's (1998) book, *Images of Organization*. In my frustration at being underutilized, I would frequently return to Morgan's view of organizations as machines. Since my work responsibilities included planning and executing travel assignments, representing the university at college fairs and high school visits, meeting with prospective students and families who were visiting campus, and reviewing applications, I did not do anything that could not have easily been done by my colleagues. I felt as though I was little more than a cog in the machine — someone who could easily be replaced.

The kinds of professional practice the new professional contributors advocated (i.e., understand, generate, use, and teach others to value theory in practice) necessitated that they resist the dichotomy Schön described and embrace what Strange and King (1990) referred to as blending what one has done with what one knows. Finding ways to resist the dichotomization of theory and practice should be a priority for graduate preparation faculty, graduate students, new professionals, and supervisors.

Balancing Mixed Expectations:Idealism and Realism

Amey (1998) wrote: "No matter how carefully we prepare for a job interview, how thoroughly we question those employed at the institution, how confidently we assume the responsibilities of a new job, inevitably, once the newness begins to wear off (and sometimes even sooner), we realize that our expectations do not match the job realities" (pp. 6-7).

A fourth theme implicit in Rozana's narrative and evident in other book contributors' stories is the constant vacillation between idealistic and realistic job expectations. Several new professionals pursued the perfect job that they believed was attainable. Over time, their idealism collided with their real-life experiences. Abandoning neither, the new professionals engaged in a reflective process that ultimately strengthened their effectiveness and satisfaction.

Idealism oozed from Rozana as she projected how life will be as an academic. Much of Rozana's idealism about faculty life was a reaction to the realism she encountered as a student affairs practitioner. In the concluding section of her chapter, she acknowledged this idealism, but did not abandon it.

> There are many who might characterize my decision to enter and exit the field of student affairs as a never-ending search for greener pastures. To a certain extent they may be right. I pursued a career in student affairs based on fond adolescent memories of my father's college campus and a desire to steer clear of the 9-5 corporate world my mother inhabited. Unfortunately, the practice of student affairs was not as lush a pasture as I had hoped. I was passionate about the discipline of leadership education but was frequently frustrated by the lack of intellectual rigor and institutional respect that characterized my first job experience. Now I am jumping the fence once again, this time to the faculty pasture, in search of finding my true vocational home, a work environment and professional lifestyle that matches the ideal picture I have been painting in my mind for so many years. Although I will be the first to admit that the grass will likely not be as green as I hope, I truly believe I am making the right choice.

Rozana's idealism strengthened her ability to reflect continually upon her idealism as it collided with her lived-experiences. Christana

(Chapter 2) expressed a sense of idealism about the job search process as she wondered if the color of her skin would be a factor while finding her first job. She modified these views after she visited campuses and consulted with mentors, lessening the idealism-realism gap. Deborah's (Chapter 9) idealism about the job search also evolved.

> I wanted to be hired for my competencies and my commitment to the field. I did not want to be a champion of disability issues or even an educator on the topic (I would later grow into my role as an educator).

Learning his supervisors were gay reinforced William's (Chapter 10) idealism about higher education, in particular its support for lesbian, gay, bisexual, and transgender students and staff. Barnard's responses to several LGBT incidents challenged and tempered this idealism:

> There have been several instances where my faith in the college has faltered, such as when the basketball coach called another team's player a faggot, and on National Coming Out Day, when our facilities department washed away hours worth of students' campus chalking because of words that were perceived as obscenities – dyke, bitch and fag among them. There was little to no response from the college and surrounding Columbia University administration and even the queer community.

Reflecting upon their real job experiences, the new professionals developed a more complex understanding of higher education, recognizing that idealism strengthened practice and vice-versa. They articulated their ideals, pursued these values, and responded to organizational realities, which contributed to their many successes. Kevin (Chapter 1) reminded readers, "Over the past couple of years as I have delved deeper into my career at Notre Dame, my graduate school-inspired idealism has met the harsh realities of professional life and I barely have had time to notice." It is important for new professionals to step back from their hectic daily work routines to notice.

Too often in higher education, seasoned professionals dismiss new professionals' ideas or suggestions on the grounds that they are idealistic and do not understand the *real world* of student affairs. Often, new professionals respond by charging that senior professionals are closed-minded or petrified in their view and are simply sustainers of the status quo. There are some kernels of truth embedded in both these perspectives. Yet these different perspectives must come together now and again, or each will prove limiting and debilitating to the organization and its members. It is critical for seasoned colleagues to spend time with new professionals and get beyond discussing specific job responsibilities and the tasks at hand and to explicitly acknowledge and process the mixed and more conceptual expectations of new professionals.

Expressing Mixed Emotions: Strength and Fragility on the Job
In Chapter 4, Susan and Michael wrote:

> All three case studies pulse with the emotions associated with transitions: to graduate school, to a new job, new city, new colleagues, or a new institutional culture. Kevin refers to this as moving from "comfortable familiarity" to "the unknown." Although certainly not without anxiety and stress, Kevin, Christana, Kathleen and Craig utilized resources available to them and coped well with their transitions.

These mixed emotions that new professionals simultaneously experience and express reflect the fifth theme explicitly discussed by Rozana and permeate other narratives. In particular, several case study authors concurrently expressed feeling of strength /certainty and fragility/uncertainty. The new professionals did not unilaterally dismiss their strengths, nor did they repress their fragility. Instead, they used trusted peers and mentors to better understand and respond to these wide-ranging feelings. Rozana's dispute with her supervisor about the role of theory in her teaching practices illuminates this point.

> Tom made a keen and prophetic observation, one that I will never forget. "Rozana, I think many of the challenges you are experiencing this year stem from the fact that you are too intellectual in your work." I felt like the wind had been knocked out of me. Too intellectual? What did that mean? I was too stunned to interject a question or defend myself, so I let him continue. ... I ended the meeting as quickly as possible so I could exit before I started to cry. It is hard for me to express just how devastating and de-motivating I found this conversation.

Rozana exhibited an inner strength and certainty when designing and teaching her theoretically-grounded leadership seminar; yet, her supervisor's opinion stunned her. This strength-fragility tension reappeared later when Rozana expressed unswerving commitment to her proposed career change, but a sense of fragility (e.g., guilty feelings) permeated her self-analysis.

William (Chapter 10) and Deborah (Chapter 9) engaged in the never-ending coming out process with colleagues, William about his sexual orientation and Deborah about her disability. Both gained strength from these vulnerable encounters. Implicit in these and many other new professional tales (e.g., Stephanie's description of feeling like a fraud) were simultaneous feelings of strength and fragility, certainty and tentativeness, power and helplessness. Acknowledging these mixed emotions and processing them with others benefited new professionals.

New professionals' perceptions surrounding their low power status often exacerbated these dichotomous emotions. They perceived supervisors as the epicenters of power who deemed what was important and wielded power to advance their own agenda. These power differentials temporarily debilitated new professionals, contributing to their reluctance to act on their keen instincts. Molly (Chapter 5) and Diana (Chapter 7) intuitively knew something was not right about their jobs, but waited for long periods of time before confronting their supervisors. When describing her involvement in a committee charged with building a new residence hall, Deborah (Chapter 9) initially did not act on her intuition about what was right because she was the new kid on the block.

> Finally, toward the end of the semester, I vocalized the question I had been thinking for months: "Why would we build a new building that would, by its very design, exclude any individual with even minor mobility issues?" I attempted to present the likelihood that each of us would be – if we were not already – touched by a disability, and I suggested that we had the opportunity to remove rather than add to potential barriers.

Several of the new professionals shared the sense of powerlessness evident in Deborah's comment. Susan and Michael (Chapter 4) too discussed this power issue in their essay.

Determining how much of one's identity, racial or otherwise, a person is willing to compromise in an environment where it feels like the employer holds all the power, is a complex decision that requires the ability to author one's own life rather than be authored by the perceptions, biases, and expectations of others.

Fortunately, mentors and peers played an invaluable role in helping new professionals cope with the mixed emotions rooted in power-related issues. Rozana's father served as a mentor while navigating the challenges of her job as well as graduate school pursuits. Christana (Chapter 2) relied heavily on graduate school mentors to guide her through the many job search landmines she encountered.

My mentors reminded me of something important: I have never been one to change myself simply to be more acceptable to others. A long time ago I learned to accept and to be proud of myself and my race in the educational arena.

Helpful peers and mentors created a community of learners for new professionals, engaged in critical dialogue, encouraged doing-centered and integrative learning (i.e., connecting theory with practice), and endorsed cooperative learning opportunities. New professionals did not unilaterally dismiss their strengths, nor did they repress their fragility. Instead, they assimilated the power structure of their campuses and used peers and mentors to support them.

The reluctance of the new professionals to confront those in power reminds readers that higher education in general and student affairs in particular are not as egalitarian as we may want to believe. Explicitly examining power relationships and dynamics is a good starting point to better understand the vacillating emotions expressed by new professionals.

Taking Time for Reflection

The new professionals were not simply competent doers; on a daily basis, they thought about the issues they encountered. Rozana thought long and hard about her many interactions with her supervisor and other colleagues. A distinguishing characteristic of Stephanie (Chapter 6) was her keen ability to reflect on all of her experiences, especially the positive ones (which is the exception rather than the rule).

Diana (Chapter 7) looked inward and carefully examined her not-so-positive supervisor-supervisee relationship and learned from it (instead of automatically blaming her supervisor). Kevin (Chapter 1) continually reflected on the utility of his formal education as it related to his career preparedness. Molly (Chapter 5) processed her feelings of under-utilization before she acted. Craig and Kathleen's job search (Chapter 3) was more than a mechanical application process; it involved constant reflection and reassessment of individual and collective goals and possibilities. Christana (Chapter 2) reflected on issues related to racial identity at every stage of the job search process. William (Chapter 10) and Deborah (Chapter 9), too, on a daily basis reflected on identity-related issues as they began their full-time careers in student affairs.

Susan and Michael (Chapter 4) framed their analysis around the idea of reflective expedition. It is imperative for a new professional to "know oneself" through self-reflection (Brookfield, 1995; Brunner, 1994). Engaging in a self-reflective process reveals the ideological assumptions deeply embedded in one's self. Self-reflection in student affairs is fashionable, a practice with which few would take exception. Yet, self-reflection may be the most difficult task student affairs professionals undertake.

Often the busy lives of new professionals lure them into action and perpetual motion at the expense of mindfulness or self-reflection. This autopilot mode often leads new professionals to pay little attention to how their values shape their practices. Serious and constant self-reflection helped the new professionals interpret the frustrations, disappointments, surprises, and challenges they encountered in their first full-time positions. It is crucial for new professionals to develop habits of identifying and critically analyzing the values, beliefs, and assumptions underlying their work.

Implications for Practice

Although the six aforementioned themes are not exhaustive, they represent critical issues that warrant the attention of graduate preparation faculty, graduate students, new professionals, and supervisors. Case study authors and respondents raised numerous critical questions: How can professional associations support new professionals as they seek greener pastures compatible with their life histories? How can accepted professional standards bridge the gaps between theory and practice? How can supervisors support new professionals as they express mixed emotions and reconcile differences between their idealized views of work and realities of work? How can the power relationships between supervisors and supervisees be optimized to benefit new professionals and the organizations and students they serve? What is the relationship between one's personal and professional identity? How does personal identity affect new professionals' experiences in their quests for professional growth and development, achievement, and job satisfaction? For each of these four stakeholder groups (i.e., graduate students, new professionals, supervisors, and graduate preparation faculty), we pose and propose possible answers to these questions with the hope of enhancing the experiences of new professionals, the organizations of which they are a part and, most importantly, the students they serve.

Student Affairs Preparation Program Faculty: Considerations

Miller and Carpenter (1981) argue that the quality of professional preparation influences professional credibility and excellence of practice. Case study authors and respondents reinforced the importance of preparation programs in the development of new professionals, yet raised important questions for faculty to consider: Are curricula of graduate preparation programs pertinent? Does vital knowledge exist that is not being transmitted? Do new professionals utilize the knowledge they learn during graduate school? How can preparation program curricula be altered to better serve new professionals, their organizations, and the students they serve?

Scott (2000) identified several personal, professional, and career needs of new professionals that should be woven into the fabric of student affairs preparation program curricula.

> Understanding student development theory; learning to apply theory to practice; career development; learning how to network; developing a sense of professionalism; learning how to effectively work with students including student leaders and student groups; skill development (writing memos, serving on committees); using technology; developing professional ethics; professional association involvement; relating to peers, colleagues, and supervisors; balancing work and personal life (time management, stress management) (pp. 485-486).

The new professionals, in their discussions about their graduate preparation programs, conveyed that their academic programs provided them opportunities to hone many of Scott's personal, professional, and career-related qualities. They identified several curricular assets of their graduate preparation programs: [1] a continuous, cumulative, and integrative curricula that stressed life-long learning; [2] on-going opportunities to reflect on their in-class and out-of-class experiences, which crystallized their own beliefs and values; [3] seminars that explored and enriched understanding about issues of identity; [4] collaborative, rather than competitive, learning environments; [5] diverse practicum/assistantship opportunities; and [6] mentoring relationships with faculty. These curricular innovations assisted graduate students to a better understanding of themselves and the students they serve.

Although the new professionals' retrospective sense-making of their graduate experiences was overwhelmingly positive, an overarching shortcoming was the lack of formal opportunities to explicitly examine, critique, and understand their professional socialization process. They recognized that a major outcome of their graduate experience was to become acquainted with and socialized into the student affairs profession, but few fully understood this process.

Two overarching aims of student affairs preparation programs are to *socialize* and *professionalize* graduate students to prepare them for careers in higher education. Socialization is a complex and multifaceted series of human interactions, which leads to definitions, choices, actions, and enhanced self-consciousness. Merton, Reader, & Kendall (1957) define socialization as the:

> process by which people selectively acquire the values and attitudes, the interests, the skills and knowledge — in short the culture — of current groups of which they are, or seek to become, a member. It refers to the learning of social roles. ... Socialization takes place primarily through social interactions with people who are significant for the individual. (p. 287)

Simpson (1967) argued that being socialized into a role involves learning its cultural content (e.g., expectations, knowledge, rituals, traditions) and self-identification with that role (i.e., the internalization of its goals and values).

Professionalization is a process by which graduate students learn the skills, values, and norms of the profession. This process augments socialization, which centers on adopting the values, norms, and social roles. Both socialization and professionalization are on-going and social learning processes, involving observation, imitation, feedback, modification, and internalization (Goodman, 1984). In the case studies, examples of circumstances and events that socialize and professionalize graduate students and new professionals are abundant (although case study authors did not use these terms to describe their experiences).

Young and Elfrink (1991) identified eight essential values of student affairs work: [1] altruism (i.e., concern for the welfare of others), [2] equality (i.e., having the same rights or privileges, [3] aesthetics (e.g., creativity, imagination, sensitivity), [4] freedom (i.e., capacity to exercise choice), [5] human dignity (i.e., inherent worth and uniqueness of an individual), [6] justice (i.e., upholding moral and legal principles), [7] truth (i.e., faithfulness to fact or reality), and [8] community (e.g., cooperation, participation, collaboration). Graduate preparation program faculty and graduate student supervisors overtly and subtly socialize students to embrace these core values of the student affairs profession.

These values are evident in the new professionals' stories. Christana (Chapter 2) embraced the value of altruism as she sought a work setting that would allow her to express her genuine commitment and compassion to historically under-represented students in higher education. Stephanie's (Chapter 6) interest in women's issues supported the profession's commitment to educating students about the importance of and respect for gender equity. Molly's (Chapter 5) work in admissions integrated the profession's aesthetic value as she presented a positive image of higher education in general and her institution in particular when she recruits new students to her college. Kathleen and Craig's (Chapter 10) work in residence life and psychological services were connected in the profession's value of freedom; in their daily work with students, they encouraged the open discussion of controversial issues.

Deborah's (Chapter 9) autobiographical story embraced the profession's commitment to human dignity as she conveyed to students and colleagues that treating other with respect was non-negotiable, regardless of their backgrounds or limitations. William's work with LGBT students modeled the profession's commitment to justice — acting as a student advocate, especially for the less powerful students. Kevin (Chapter 1) incorporated the profession's value of truth as he documented and recorded students' academic progress accurately and honestly during his academic advising interactions. Diana's (Chapter 7) work in orientation exemplified the profession's value of community — assembling a team of orientation leaders who modeled for new students community values such as cooperation, commitment, participation, and collaboration.

Socialization to a profession begins with an anticipatory learning period when prospective members begin to assume the values, beliefs, norms, expectations and attitudes of the group they wish to join (Van Maanen, 1976). During this anticipatory learning period, the apprentices gradually assimilate the group's values and learn to become part of the group, thus ultimately altering one's self-image. New professionals quickly assimilated and immediately began to subconsciously promote the core values of the profession, without fully recognizing or understanding the implications of their choices. Graduate school curricula are well suited to bring to the forefront of students' consciousness these socialization and professionalization processes as well as the foundational core values supporting these processes.

Goodman (1984), summarizing the work of Olesen and Whittaker (1968), identified three central tasks in the socialization process that could be a useful guide for faculty as they provide leadership in this arena.

> First, students must become aware of what is required in the professional role. Second, they must recognize themselves as being in that role. Finally, the socialization process must foster their capacity to properly communicate about themselves as professionals... these three tasks lead students to see that they are separate from laymen [sic] by virtue of being aware of special knowledge, skills, and insights particular to their profession. Secondly, these students can communicate that special recognition to themselves and others. (p. 31)

Deborah's (Chapter 9) description of her climbing wall incident illuminates how one new professional assimilated these three socialization tasks into professional practice.

> As part of August training my second year, our department sponsored an off-campus retreat for hall directors. En route, I learned that one of the activities was a vertical climbing wall. The activity was billed as optional, but we were expected to cheer for our colleagues. I felt torn. I needed to support my colleagues; I wanted to be part of my work community; and I knew that attempting to climb the wall would make me vulnerable. Even more, climbing the wall would be physically difficult. Because of cerebral palsy, I have minimal leg strength and my muscles are unusually tight.

First, Deborah was aware of what was required in her role as a residence hall director (e.g., actively participate in team activities). Second, she viewed herself a hall director. Third, climbing the wall would properly communicate to others her allegiance to her colleagues, but her cerebral palsy was a potential barrier. Enhancing new professionals' awareness of and the implications of the socialization process will enhance the quality of their job experiences.

Austin's (2002) recommendations to aspiring faculty could easily be modified to support aspiring student affairs professionals. She recommended providing graduate students opportunities to: [1] observe, listen and interact with peers, [2] engage in systematic exploration of socialization ideas; [3] receive sustained feedback and mentoring; and [4] engage in guided reflection.

The works of Goodman (1984) and Austin (2002) provide conceptual roadmaps to assist faculty and aspiring new professionals in answering the question: "What does it mean to be a student affairs professional?"

Graduate Students: A Consideration

Clifford Geertz (1995), when reflecting on his graduate experience at Harvard University in the 1950s, wrote:

> Finding one's way through this maze of grand possibilities, only loosely related, and some even in fairly serious tension with one another, was however exciting (and it was enormously exciting), a perilous business. With so many ways to turn, so few tracks laid, and so little experience of one's own to go by, even small decisions…seemed enormously consequential — a reverseless commitment to something immense, portentous, splendid, and unclear. (p. 101)

Aspiring student affairs professionals encounter a labyrinth of opportunities and perils during their graduate studies. Attempting to understand, assess, and address these opportunities is a formidable task. The case studies reveal that as graduate students, new professionals created dichotomous categories and compartmentalized their work experiences to bring order to and simplify their in-class and out-of-class experiences.

In this context, new professionals treated theory and practice as discrete and opposing concepts. They juxtaposed their ideal world of work with the realities of work. They even expressed their emotions dichotomously (e.g., strong and fragile). Rich and Anna (Chapter 11) noted this compartmentalization when responding to Deborah's case study.

One negative outcome of this compartmentalization and dichotomization is cultural separatism (Tierney, 1993). Cultural separatism subscribes to the idea that different groups have distinct identities and the differences are so great that one group has little, if anything, in common with another. Cultural separatists often conclude that since they cannot understand the other's reality, they are absolved from further action. Using the theory-practice dichotomy as an example, the role of generating theory is assigned to academicians, while practice becomes the responsibility of student affairs practitioners. These roles are so dissimilar and so dichotomized that opportunities for genuine collaboration are greatly diminished.

Rozana's discussion of her current work life and her projected work life as a faculty member exemplifies this cultural separatism notion. She lumped all faculty into a category of those who write, think, and embrace theory. She relegated student affairs administrators into a discrete grouping who do rather than think. Within higher education these pure dichotomous categories do not exist. Such conceptualizations, which bring some order to the messiness of student affairs, diminish the likelihood that faculty and student affairs professionals will collaborate, which in turn, diminish the effectiveness of both cultures and the students they serve.

It is important for graduate students to resist urges to compartmentalize and dichotomize, and instead to embrace notions of integration and synthesis. Susan and Michael's case response (Chapter 4) is a model of this integration and synthesis. Both authors have distinct domains of expertise (i.e., Susan with theory and Michael with practice), yet the chapter synthesizes and integrates these domains of expertise.

It is important during graduate students' socialization processes that they address this propensity toward dichotomization and compartmentalization. A starting point in this quest is to reframe the discourse about these topics. The presentation of ideas and experiences as diametric opposites (e.g., residence life staff are generalists and career service staffs are specialists) encourages debates rather than genuine dialogues about these important topics.

Graduate school is a unique laboratory setting for aspiring professionals to experiment with ways to integrate and synthesize the many aspects of their professional identity, minimizing cultural separatism.

We invite graduate students to think and act holistically, recognizing that the whole is qualitatively different than the sum of the parts. To assist in this process, we invite new professionals to ponder the question, "Can I construct a view that integrates seemingly disparate ideas?"

Supervisors of New Professionals: A Consideration

Boyer's (1987a) research on the orientation of college students concluded that if college is to make a difference in a student's development, the first six to ten weeks are critical.

> The first weeks on campus are critically important. This is the time when friendships are formed and attitudes about collegiate life take shape. And yet we found during our study that new students have little sense of being inducted into a community whose structure, privileges, and responsibilities have been evolving for almost a millennium. (p. 43)

Boyer (1987b) criticized colleges for their casual approaches to introducing new students to the enterprise of learning: "We visited several orientation sessions and it sounded like the students were getting ready for summer camp or a weekend in Bermuda rather than launching a serious academic quest" (p. 1).

Boyer's observations, initially intended to optimize the undergraduate experience for students, could easily be applied to new professionals in student affairs. Like undergraduates, new professionals' first few weeks on the first job are critical. Unfortunately, as case study authors all too often conveyed, introductions to their new work settings were informal (at best), not comprehensive, and haphazard. Case study authors' experiences mirrored Winston and Creamer's (1997) research study findings.

> One of the most neglected aspects of the staffing process is the orientation to the new position and institution once a staff member has been selected and arrives for work. Of the staff who had been in their positions three years or less, only 61 percent had any kind of orientation to their new position. When queried further and asked if the orientation was formally structured, only 39 percent indicated it was. Thus, only 23 percent of the respondents who had taken a new job in the past three years had a formal orientation to their new positions. (p. 107)

The new professionals strongly advocated the need for a formal and comprehensive orientation program. Winston and Creamer (1997) identify essential components of an ideal orientation for new professionals: [1] explicating the educational philosophy and operating procedures of the institution; [2] introducing new professionals to the institutional and student affairs cultures; [3] articulating expectations for performance; and [4] introducing new staff to students, faculty and staff with whom they will interact. We recommend that orientation and supervision of new professionals be extremely high priorities for supervisors.

Supervision should be "a routine part of professional life" (Winston & Creamer, 1997, p. 210). Supervisors would be well advised to consult the two models: synergistic supervision model and the constructive developmental theory model advanced by Michael and Patricia (Chapter 8). These models provide a comprehensive and theoretically grounded approach to the supervision of new professionals. Michael and Patricia reminded readers that it is insufficient for supervisors to simply meet regularly with new staff. Supervisors must come to understand how new professionals internally understand or make sense of their job responsibilities and their experiences. The constructivist developmental theory, described in Chapter 8, is an excellent example of how supervisors can use developmental theory to achieve these important goals. "Employers of new student affairs professionals must recognize a responsibility to provide new staff with ongoing training and support to build expertise, develop professionalism, and provide opportunities to evaluate and improve performance" (Garland & Grace, 1993, p. 96). Knowledge of their employees' personal histories, identities and goals will allow supervisors to tailor their training and feedback to the unique needs of each professional.

During a workshop sponsored by contributors of this book, we asked attendees to jot down advice for supervisors of new professionals. Their recommendations are useful guidelines in assisting supervisors of new professionals when they rethink and redesign their orientation and supervision strategies.

> Provide constructive, meaningful and kind feedback...Create time for staff reflection... Listen and remain open to new ideas ...Mentor new professionals in the process of matching program goals with institutional culture... Carefully assess the fit between a new professional and the position... Listen... Don't

> assume new professionals have knowledge and do not assume they do not... Recognize that new professionals are unique individuals with unique supervision needs... Provide professional development opportunities... Provide clear expectations... Remember what it was like to be a new colleague. Be fair with candidates. Remember you are playing an essential role in the development of new professionals... Make time for regular sit-down meetings with new staff members... Think about how your comments regarding the age and/or appearance of staff members may be received by different audiences, especially if something could undermine the credibility of new staff members.

Effective training and development of new professionals takes into consideration the needs of the organization and the needs of the individuals. Embedded in the aforementioned list of recommendations for supervisors are many needs of new professionals that warrant the attention of supervisors.

New Professionals: A Consideration

In Chapter 8, Michael and Patricia argued, "Although supervisors clearly bear significant responsibility for the success or failure of new professionals, we acknowledge these staff members also must be responsible for their success in adjusting to a new job." Personal responsibility and self-authorship are cornerstones of the development of new professionals.

Barr (1990) suggests that new professionals take control of their professional destiny by forging mentoring relationships, balancing personal and professional responsibilities, maintaining friendships, maintaining a sense of humor, and being true to yourself. Cooper, Chernow, Kulic & Saunders (1999) solicited from past presidents of ACPA and NASPA four recommendations for new professionals:

> (a) seek personal development; (b) pursue opportunities for professional development; (c) understand the environment of higher education and the employing institution; and (d) develop strong leadership traits. (p. 398)

Trimble, Allen, and Vidoni (1991) identified characteristics to help motivate and sustain new professionals once they assume their first administrative position in student affairs. They recommend that new professionals: learn to function without unanimous support, develop political savvy, tolerate organizational ambiguity, endure delays of positive outcomes, and be receptive to negative feedback.

All of these recommendations demand developmental complexity. New professionals must possess complex ways of knowing in order to understand higher education, institutional environments, and tolerate ambiguity. New professionals must have an internal identity to balance personal and professional goals and expectations and to accept negative feedback. New professionals must also have a complex interpersonal development to function effectively without unanimous support and to accept negative feedback.

A key challenge noted in all three respondent chapters was the need for new professionals to strive for self-authorship (Baxter Magolda, 1999; Kegan, 1994). "Self-authorship is simultaneously a cognitive (how one makes meaning of knowledge), interpersonal (how one views oneself in relationship to others), and intrapersonal (how one perceives one's sense of identity) matter" (Baxter Magolda, 1999, p. 10). Case respondents invited new professionals to construct knowledge in a contextual world and construct an identity independent of external forces. Self-authorship is an ability to engage in relationships without losing one's internal identity. Simply stated, new professionals are encouraged to author their lives, not perform the life scripts dictated by others (e.g., supervisors). Striving for self-authorship, which is difficult to achieve, will assist new professionals as they make important career and life decisions and in navigating the transition inherent in crossing the bridge from graduate school to the world of student affairs work.

Susan and Michael (Chapter 4), citing the work of Schlossberg, Waters, and Goodman (1995), identified the nature of transitions and the potential resources from which new professionals may draw to manage these transitions toward self-authorship and personal responsibility. They include: [1] the situation (i.e., environmental and perceptual factors that vary by individual such as what triggers the transition, control over the transition, duration, accompanying role change and stress); [2] the self (i.e., personal and demographic characteristics as well as psychological resources upon which the individual may draw for support); [3] support (i.e., types and range of support available to the individual in the transition), and [4] strategies (i.e., behaviors used by individuals to respond to stressful situations). Tending to these four issues will help new professionals reflect on how they behaved upon entering their first full-time position and how they want to perform as an effective student affairs professional.

The case studies suggest that these new professionals are heeding Barr's, Cooper's et al., and Trimble's et al. advice. They are making optimal use of their mentors, seeking out professional development opportunities, maintaining a sense of humor while trying to function in ambiguous organizations that specialize in delayed gratification, and constantly soliciting feedback about their performance. In essence, they are en route to authoring their professional lives and taking responsibility for their own development.

Conclusion
Witherell and Noddings (1991) argue:

> … we live and grow in interpretive, or meaning-making, communities; that stories help us find our place in the world; and that caring, respectful dialogue among all engaged in educational settings — students, teachers, administrators — serves as the crucible for our coming to understand ourselves, others, and the possibilities life holds for us. (p. 10)

It is the desire of all contributors of this book that the stories of the new professionals will help graduate students, preparation program faculty, soon-to-be new professionals, and their supervisors find their place in the world of student affairs. Further, we hope the analysis chapters will spark caring and respectful dialogue among these stakeholders, which will lead to an enriched understanding of ourselves and others and the possibilities for change.

Deborah (Chapter 9) wrote:

> I wanted to make a difference in students' lives. I wanted to answer the question posed by the Wingspread Group (1993) on Higher Education, "What will we do today to ensure that next year's graduates are individuals of character more sensitive to the needs of community, more competent in their ability to contribute to society, and more civil in their habits of thought, speech and action?" (p. 9).

This is precisely the question we should modify to enhance the experiences of new student affairs professionals. What will we do today to ensure that future new professionals are individuals of character, more sensitive to the needs of community, more competent in their ability to contribute to society, and more civil in their habits of thought, speech, and action? No doubt the grass will be greener for graduate preparation faculty, graduate students, new professionals, and their supervisors if this question is thoughtfully discussed. These stories and interpretations introduce possibilities and conceptual building blocks for action. The difficult task of applying the knowledge contained herein rests with the readers.

REFERENCES

American College Personnel Association. Member Survey. (n. d.). Retrieved May 15, 2001, from http://www.acpa.nche.edu/corcouns/msi/serv03.htm.

American College Personnel Association. (2001). *Critical issues task force report.* Washington, D.C.: Author.

American College Personnel Association/The National Association of Student Personnel Administrators. (1997). *Defining principles of good practice for student affairs.* Washington, DC: Author.

Amey, M. (1998). Unwritten rules: Organizational and political realities of the job. In M. Amey & L. M. Reesor (Eds.), *Beginning your journey: A guide for new professionals in student affairs* (pp. 5-10). Washington, D.C.: National Association of Student Personnel Administrators.

Austin, A. E. (2002). Preparing the next generation of faculty: Graduate school as socialization to the academic career. *Journal of Higher Education,* 73(1), 94-122.

Barr, M. J. (1990). Making the transition to a professional role. In D. D. Coleman & J. E. Johnson (Eds.), *The new professional: A resource guide for new student affairs professionals and their supervisors* (pp. 17-29). Washington, D.C.: National Association of Student Personnel Administrators.

Baxter Magolda, M. B. (1992). *Knowing and reasoning in college: Gender-related patterns in students' intellectual development.* San Francisco, CA: Jossey-Bass.

230 References

Baxter Magolda, M. B. (1999). The evolution of epistemology: redefining contextual knowing at twenty something. *Journal of College Student Development*, 40, 333-344.

Baxter Magolda, M. B. (2001). *Making their own way: Narratives for transforming higher education to promote self-development.* Sterling, VA.: Stylus.

Bender, B. E. (1980). Job satisfaction in student affairs. *NASPA Journal*, 18(2), 2-9.

Boyer, E. L. (1987a). *College: The undergraduate experience in America.* New York: Harper and Row.

Boyer, E. L. (1987b). *The college as community.* Paper presented at the meeting of the Freshman Year Experience — West, University of California, Irvine, CA.

Brookfield, S. D. (1995). *Becoming a critically reflective teacher.* San Francisco, CA: Jossey-Bass.

Brunner, D. D. (1994). *Inquiry and reflection: Framing narrative practice in education.* Albany, NY: State University of New York Press.

Bryan, J. (1977). *A study of student affairs workers: An exploration in comparison of the demographic characteristics and background factors and perceptions of the field of student affairs workers and their perceptions of the degree of bureaucracy within their student affairs division.* Unpublished Doctoral Dissertation, Teachers College, Columbia University, New York.

Bryan, W. A., & Schwartz, R. A. (1998). *Strategies for staff development: Personal and professional education in the 21st century.* San Francisco, CA: Jossey-Bass.

Burns, M. A. (1982). Who leaves the field? *NASPA Journal*, 20(2), 9-12.

Carpenter, D. S. (1990). Developmental concerns in moving toward personal and professional competence. In D. D. Coleman & J. E.

Johnson (Eds.), *The new professional: A resource guide for new student affairs professionals and their supervisors* (pp. 56-72). Washington, D.C.: National Association of Student Personnel Administrators.

Carpenter, D. S. (1991). Student affairs profession: A developmental perspective. In T. K. Miller & R. B. Winston (Eds.), *Administration and leadership in student affairs: Actualizing student development in higher education* (pp. 147-165). Muncie, IN: Accelerated Development.

Carpenter, D. S., & Miller, T. K. (1981). An analysis of professional development in student affairs. *NASPA Journal*, 19(1), 2-11.

Carper, J. W., & Becker, H. S. (1957). Adjustments to conflicting expectations in development identification with an occupation. *Social Forces*, 36(1).

Cass, V. C. (1979). Homosexual identity formation: A theoretical model. *Journal of Homosexuality*, 4(3), 219-235.

Chickering, A. W., & Havighurst, R. J. (1981). The life cycle. In A. W. Chickering (Ed.), *The modern American College: Responding to the new realities of diverse students and changing society* (pp. 16-50). San Francisco, CA: Jossey-Bass.

Chickering, A. W., & Reisser, L. (1993). *Education and identity*. San Francisco: CA: Jossey-Bass.

Chronicle of Higher Education (2001). Almanac Issue, 47, August 31.

Clandinin, D. J. and F. M. Connelly (1994). Personal experience methods. In N.K. Denzin and Y.S. Lincoln (Eds), *Handbook of qualitative research (PP.* 413-427). Thousand Oaks, CA, Sage.

Coleman, D. D., & Johnson, J. E. (1990). *The new professional: A resource guide for new student affairs professionals and their supervisors*. Washington, D.C.: National Association of Student Personnel Administrators.

232 References

Cooper, D. L., Chernow, E., Miller, T. K., Kulic, K., & Saunders, S. A. (1999). Professional development advice from past presidents of ACPA and NASPA. *Journal of College Student Development,* 40(4), 396-404.

Cross, K. P. (1981). *Adults as learners.* San Francisco, CA: Jossey-Bass.

Cross, W. E. J. (1995). The psychology of Nigrescence: Revisiting the Cross model. In J. G. Ponterotto & J. M. Casas & L. A. Suzuki & C. M. Alexander (Eds.), *Handbook of multicultural counseling* (pp. 93-122). Thousand Oaks, CA: Sage.

D'Augelli, A. R. (1995). Identity development and sexual identity: Toward a model of lesbian, gay, and bisexual development. In E. J. Trickett (Ed.), *Human diversity: Perspectives on people and context.* San Francisco, CA: Jossey-Bass.

Ellis, C. and A. P. Bochner (2000). Autoethnography, personal narrative, reflexivity: Researcher as subject ordering. In N. K. Denzin and Y. S. Lincoln (Eds), *Handbook of qualitative research* (pp. 733-768). Thousand Oaks, CA: Sage.

Erikson, E. H. (1968). *Identity, youth, and crisis.* New York: W. W. Norton.

Evans, N. and H. Levine (1990). Perspectives on sexual orientation. In L. V. Moore (Ed), *Evolving theoretical perspectives on students (pp. 49-58).* San Francisco, CA: Jossey-Bass.

Forney, D. S. (1994). A profile of student affairs master's students: Characteristics, attitudes, and learning styles. *Journal of College Student Development,* 35(5), 337-345.

Geertz, C. (1995). *After the fact: Two countries, four decades, one anthropologist.* Cambridge, MA: Harvard University Press.

Goodman, A. P. (1984). *Professional choice, socialization, and career development of graduate school students in student personnel work.* Unpublished Doctoral Dissertation, The Ohio State University, Columbus, OH.

Hershey, P., & Blanchard, K. H. (1977). *Management of organizational behavior: Utilizing human resources.* Englewood Cliffs, N.J.: Prentice-Hall.

Holland, J. L. (1966). The psychology of vocational choice. *Journal of Counseling Psychology*, 6, 35-45.

Hunter, D. E. (1992). How student affairs professionals choose their careers. *NASPA Journal*, 29(3), 181-188.

Ignelzi, M. G. (1994). *A description of student affairs professional development in the supervisory context and an analysis of its relation to constructive development.* Unpublished Doctoral Dissertation, Harvard University, Cambridge, MA.

Kegan, R. (1982). *The evolving self: Problem and process in human development.* Cambridge, MA: Harvard University Press.

Kegan, R. (1994). *In over our heads: The mental demands of modern life.* Cambridge, MA.: Harvard University Press.

Kegan, R., Noam, G. G., & Rogers, L. (1982). The psychologic of emotion: A Neo-Piagetian view. In D. Chichetti & P. Pogge-Hesse (Eds.), *Emotional development.* San Francisco, CA: Jossey-Bass.

King, P. M., & Kitchener, K. S. (1994). *Developing reflective judgment: Understanding and promoting intellectual growth and critical thinking in adolescents and adults.* San Francisco, CA: Jossey-Bass.

Kirby, A. F. (1984). The new professional. In A. F. Kirby & D. Woodard (Eds.), *Career perspectives in student affairs.* Columbus, OH: National Association of Student Personnel Administrators.

Kirby, A.F. & Woodard, D (Eds.) (1984). *Career perspectives in student affairs.* Columbus,OH: National Association of Student Personnel Administrators.

Kohlberg, L. (1984). *The psychology of moral development: The nature and validity of moral stages* (1st ed.). San Francisco, CA: Harper & Row.

Kramp, M. K. (1995). *Dropping a line into a creek and pulling out a whale: A phenomenological study of six teachers' experiences of their students' stories of learning.* Unpublished doctoral dissertation, The University of Tennessee, Knoxville.

Levine, A., & Cureton, J. S. (1998). *When hope and fear collide: A portrait of today's college student.* San Francisco, CA: Jossey-Bass Publishers.

Levinson, D. J., & Levinson, J. D. (1996). *The seasons of a woman's life.* New York: Knopf.

Lewin, K., Heider, F., & Heider, G. M. (1936). *Principles of topological psychology.* New York: McGraw-Hill.

McEwan, H. and K. Egan (1995). *Narrative in teaching, learning, and research.* New York: Teachers College Press.

Merton, R. K., Reader, G. G., & Kendall, P. L. (1957). *The student-physician: Introductory studies in the sociology of medical education.* Cambridge, MA: Harvard University Press.

Morgan, G. (1998). *Images of organization.* Thousand Oaks, CA: Sage Publications.

Olesen, V. L., & Whittaker, E. W. (1968). *The silent dialogue; a study in the social psychology of professional socialization.* San Francisco, CA: Jossey-Bass.

Olkin, R. (1999). *What psychotherapists should know about disability.* New York: Guilford Press.

Perry, W. G. (1970). *Forms of intellectual and ethical development in the college years: A scheme.* Troy, MO: Holt, Rinehart, & Winston.

Piaget, J. (1967). *Six psychological studies*. New York: Random House.

Richardson, R. C. (1975). Staff development. *Journal of College Student Personnel, 46*, 303-311.

Ryan, K., & Canfield, J. (1970). *Don't smile until Christmas: Accounts of the first year of teaching*. Chicago: University of Chicago Press.

Sandeen, A. (1984). Careers in student affairs: An introduction. In A. F. Kirby & D. B. Woodard (Eds.), *Career perspectives in student affairs* (pp. 1-9). Columbus, OH: National Association of Student Personnel Administrators.

Saunders, S. A., Cooper, D. L., Winston, R. B., & Chernow, E. (2000). Supervising staff in student affairs: Exploration of the synergistic approach. *Journal of College Student Development, 41*, 181-192.

Schein, E. H. (1978). *Career dynamics: Matching individual and organizational needs*. Reading, MA: Addison-Wesley.

Schlossberg, N. K., Waters, E. B., & Goodman, J. (1995). *Counseling adults in transition: Linking practice with theory*. New York: Springer Publishing Company.

Schön, D. A. (1983). *The reflective practitioner: How professionals think in action*. New York: Basic Books.

Schön, D. A. (1995, November/December). Knowing-in-action: The new scholarship requires a new epistemology. *Change, 27*, 27-34.

Schwandt, T. A. (1997). *Qualitative inquiry: A dictionary of terms*. Thousand Oaks, CA, Sage.

Scott, J. E. (2000). Creating effective staff development programs. In M. J. Barr & M. K. Desler (Eds.), *The handbook of student affairs administration* (pp. 477-491). San Francisco, CA: Jossey-Bass.

Shapiro, J. P. (1993). *No pity: People with disabilities forging a new civil rights movement* (1st ed.). New York: Times Books.

Simpkins, W.D. (2001). *Queer leadership: GLBT leaders, leadership, and the movement.* Leadership Insights and Applications Series #8. College Park, MD: National Clearinghouse for Leadership Programs.

Simpson, I. H. (1967). Patterns of socialization into professions: The case of student nurses. *Sociological Inquiry*, 47(1), 47-54.

Sleeter, C. E. (2001). *Culture difference and power*. New York: Teachers College Press.

Strange, C. C., & King, P. A. (1990). The professional practice of student development. In D. G. Creamer (Ed.), *College student development: Theory and practice for the 1990s*. Alexandria, VA: American College Personnel Association.

Super, D. E. (1985). Validating a model and a method. *Contemporary Psychology*, 64, 264-268.

Tierney, W. G. (1993). *Building communities of difference: Higher education in the twenty-first century*. Westport, CT: Bergin & Garvey.

Toma, J. D., Clark, C., & Jacobs, B. (1998). Reconciling the professional and the personal for the new student affairs professional. In M. Amey & L. M. Reesor (Eds.), *Beginning your journey: A guide for new professionals in student affairs* (pp. 67-85). Washington, D.C.: National Association of Student Personnel Administrators.

Trimble, R., Allen, D. R., & Vidoni, D. O. (1991). Student personnel administration: Is it for you? *NASPA Journal*, 28(2), 156-162.

Van Maanen, J. (1976). Breaking in: Socialization to work. In R. Dublin (Ed.), *Handbook of work, organization, and society* (pp. 67-130). Chicago, IL: Rand-McNally College Publishing.

Weiner, F. (1986). *No apologies: A guide to living with a disability* (1st ed.). New York: St. Martin's Press.

Whyte, W. F. (1943). *Street corner society: The social structure of an Italian slum.* Chicago, IL: University of Chicago Press.

Wingspread Group on Higher Education & Johnson Foundation Inc. (1993). *An American imperative: Higher expectations for higher education.* Racine, WI: Johnson Foundation Inc.

Winston, R. B., & Creamer, D. G. (1997). *Improving staffing practices in student affairs.* San Francisco, CA: Jossey-Bass Publishers.

Witherell, C., & Noddings, N. (Eds.). (1991). *Stories lives tell: Narrative and dialogue in education.* New York: Teachers College Press.

Woodard, D. B., & Komives, S. (1990). Ensuring staff competence. In M. J. Barr & M. L. Upcraft (Eds.), *New futures for student affairs: Building a vision for professional leadership and practice* (pp. 217-238). San Francisco, CA: Jossey-Bass.

Yost, E. B., & Corbishley, M. A. (1987). *Career counseling: A psychological approach.* San Francisco, CA: Jossey-Bass.

Young, R. B. (1985). Impressions of the development of professional identity: From program to practice. *NASPA Journal, 23*(2), 50-60.

Young, R. B., & Elfrink, V. L. (1991). Essential values of student affairs work. *Journal of College Student Development, 32*(1), 47-55.